M000286440

The Buffalo Head

The Buffalo Head

R. M. PATTERSON

VICTORIA • VANCOUVER • CALGARY

Copyright © 2005 the estate of R. M. Patterson
Foreword copyright © 2005 Janet Blanchet

First TouchWood edition

All rights reserved. No part of this publication may be reproduced,
stored in a retrieval system or transmitted in any form or by any means—
electronic, mechanical, audio recording or otherwise—without the written
permission of the publisher or a photocopying licence from Access Copyright,
Toronto, Canada.

TouchWood Editions
#108 – 17665 66A Avenue
Surrey, BC V3S 2A7
www.touchwoodeditions.com

Library and Archives Canada Cataloguing in Publication
Patterson, R. M. (Raymond Murray), 1898–1984.
  The Buffalo Head / by R. M. Patterson. — 1st TouchWood ed.

Originally published: New York: Morrow, 1961.
ISBN 1-894898-16-8

  1. Patterson, R. M. (Raymond Murray), 1898–1984. 2. Ranch life—Alberta.
3. Rocky Mountains, Canadian (B.C. and Alta.)—Description and travel.
I. Title.

FC3670.R3P37 2005   917.123'3   C2005-903624-9

Book design by Frances Hunter.
Cover design by Fraser Seely.
All photos courtesy of the estate of R. M. Patterson.

NOTE TO READERS: In order to preserve the authenticity and the history of the
period in which R. M. Patterson wrote this book, we have chosen not to alter
the text to reflect modern-day attitudes.

Printed in Canada

TouchWood Editions acknowledges the financial support for its publishing
program from the Government of Canada through the Book Publishing
Industry Development Program (BPIDP), Canada Council for the Arts,
and the British Columbia Arts Council.

The Canada Council | Le Conseil des Arts
for the Arts | du Canada

BRITISH COLUMBIA
ARTS COUNCIL
We acknowledge the support of the Province of British Columbia
through the British Columbia Arts Council

This book has been printed on 100% post-consumer recycled paper,
processed chlorine free and printed with vegetable-based dyes.

To my friend

GEORGE W. POCATERRA

who taught me how to throw

the diamond hitch

Motto

How strange and wild a heart-stirring

was inspired by that vision

of far-off peaks, how much of beauty

and adventure was borne to me

on the blue wings of distance.

The Spirit of the Hill by F. S. Smythe, Hodder & Stoughton,
London, 1935

Contents

Foreword

My father once told me that when he was writing *The Buffalo Head*, he had initially concentrated solely on his time at the ranch in the Alberta foothills. He had then sent off his manuscript to his New York publisher, and it had been returned to him. "We need a bridge," he was told. "We need to know where you came from in England and how it was that you came to Canada and finally to a ranch southwest of Calgary." This explains the opening chapters of *The Buffalo Head*. Certainly one friend of mine thought them to be incongruous and wondered why they had been included; however, they do explain the circumstances that led RMP to his life as a rancher, dude wrangler and guide.

RMP himself explains that his need for freedom and for space was conditioned by confinement, by the nine months he spent in a German prison camp at the end of the 1914–1918 war in Europe, and by his three years as a probationer at the Bank of England in the City of London. His escape was complete. After he arrived in Canada he was never again confined by office hours, schedules and routines. RMP was one of those who had seen an exit from routine and taken it, with some measure of success. He was lucky: he always managed to keep his head above water. He was full of surprises; my mother said she never knew what he would do next.

The Buffalo Head Ranch is in a most beautiful part of the foothills country of Alberta. The Highwood River forms one boundary, and the eastern slopes of the Rockies are no more than 10 miles (16 kilometres) away. This is not prairie country; there are rolling hills with limber pines

growing along their rocky summits, groves of aspen poplars to provide
shelter for cattle, and small clear streams running through coulees treed
with cottonwoods and spruce. The Highwood is a beautiful, clear river
with rapids and deep emerald green pools. The water is frigid, but on a
hot summer day that fact is no deterrent to swimmers. RMP describes
his adventurous expeditions into the mountains, but he does not cover
some of the more mundane events of ranch life. As a child and a young
teenager, I spent many happy afternoons at a pool in the Highwood
that was close to the ranch buildings. We used to take a basket with
a thermos of tea and some sandwiches and cookies with us, and walk
across the river flats to our favourite place on the Highwood. First we
would swim, and then we would bask on a platform of smooth rock
that jutted into the river. The sun was hot, there was always a little
downstream breeze, and there were no mosquitoes. When the shadows
from the high banks fell across the river we would return to the ranch
house for supper; it was a wonderful way to spend an afternoon.

By the time I was 13 or 14, riding for the mail was one of the tasks that
I would undertake. I usually had a girlfriend staying with me during
the summer holidays from school, and this weekly expedition was one
of our great pleasures. The two of us would saddle our horses after
breakfast and set off. We crossed the Highwood at the shale ford that
was quite close to the Buffalo Head and then headed for our first stop,
the Schintzes' ranch, where we would pick up any mail that was to be
posted. We continued to the Runciman ranch, where we paused for the
same reason. We then went on to the Chinook Ranch, owned by the
Hansons, where we stayed for lunch. We timed our arrival carefully,
as we did not want to be late. Quite often we did not have to continue
to the nearby mailboxes, as someone would have already picked up
the mail and brought it to the Hansons' place. We then sorted mail
and started for home, making the same calls on our return journey to
deliver letters. The ride was 10 miles in each direction; we made the
journey last all day. Now, in these days of electronic communication,
it is difficult to imagine receiving mail just once a week. Back then, it
was simply the way it was in this remote area.

RMP describes his journeys with Marigold into the mountains,
expeditions that she remembered happily all her life. However, Marigold

was not only a cheerful companion on camping trips: she had an important role on the Buffalo Head. She was practical, capable, she had a sense of humour, and she was a good organizer. She planned the large vegetable garden and looked after the produce. She organized the household, and when there was no cook working, she took over the kitchen. Throughout all the ups and downs of ranch life she retained a balance, and she also retained the attitudes of an English lady who is involved in a life of adventure, but who must retain an air of civility at all times.

The years on the Buffalo Head Ranch were among the happiest years for my parents. Despite the responsibilities of building up, running and maintaining a functional cattle and dude ranch through difficult times, they were young enough and able enough to enjoy the country. And they had the energy, the initiative and the resources to do so. Their freedom was their great success.

Janet (Patterson) Blanchet

North Vancouver, British Columbia
January 2004

Introduction

Readers of an earlier book of mine have written to ask how it happened that I, with an Oxford degree and a probationer's training in the Bank of England, came to trap and hunt in the Northwest Territories of Canada and, later, to ranch cattle in Alberta. In this book I have tried to give the answer—which is, as I see it, that this progress was ordained for me by the various places in which it has been my fortune to live, work, play and be imprisoned. Putting it briefly, one place led to another and I just trotted along.

Some people maintain that heredity is almost completely responsible for the making of a man. I disagree with that: I am certain that environment has far more to do with it than is generally conceded. In my own case, and on the side of heredity, I have to admit that I was born with the disease of itching foot—and I came by that honestly enough. But—and now I am on the side of environment—the disease was aggravated for me by a nine months' spell in a German prison lager, followed soon by three years' hard in the Bank of England. Claustrophobia set in; and a break for the wide open spaces followed, as day follows night ... And so I have told my story by means of the places that have been the landmarks along my trail, and by recounting some of the events that took place on the way. Landmarks I have called them: they were more than that—they were signposts placed at turning points in the trail; and, one after another, they changed the course of my life until I, who might have been an official in the Bank of England, or a professor of history, or something in the Diplomatic Service, became a cattle rancher and mountain guide.

A queerly assorted lot these places are: the Southdown country of Kipling's Sussex, the Black Forest, a fortress town in Silesia, Oxford, a cluster of stone huts in the Swiss Alps, the Bank of England. And then Canada—a Peace River homestead, Deadmen's Valley in the Northwest Territories ... And the Buffalo Head Ranch in the Rockies of Alberta, a place that was home to me for more years than any home I have ever known. But this is not a book about ranching: it is a book of the hills—of all those hills, from Poland to the Rockies, that have been the background to my life. The one constant feature in a constantly changing scene.

In an age of wars, when almost every man of my generation has either taken part in a battle, or at least heard the crash of high explosive from close at hand, I have wondered whether I was justified in telling anything of my war days. But had these wartime events never taken place my story would have been a different one. If I had never gone back to get a forgotten revolver from a half-ruined dugout, then I should never have known the long, empty days of the prison lager. And without that memory as a spur to freedom I might never have seen the white sheep of the Nahanni River, or galloped with my wife full tilt after a fleeing grizzly in the Rockies. A whole wide world might have passed me by while I dutifully caught the 8:15 a.m. to the City, returning again to my suburban lair in the evenings by the 5:10 after drab, musty, meticulous days. And so I have included some of those war experiences, grave and gay. They left their mark, and so they have their place.

You will not find a chapter in this book that has not at least a hill in it. And when the Buffalo Head was my home the mountains themselves lay at my very door. The grazing lands of the ranch ran into the outer range of the Rockies, and west of the place there was no house or settlement until you came to the little village of Windermere in the East Kootenay. All the Rockies lay in between, crisscrossed with a spider's web of old Indian trails—an ideal safety valve for one who came to the foothills of Alberta straight from the empty countries of the north. It is of my escapes from ranch routine into this wild country, so close that in a few hours one could vanish into its green fastnesses, that I particularly wish to tell here. Later, in another book—that is, if fortune smiles on this one—I plan to write of my return to the rivers of the North, and so to complete the story. But here the mountains are the theme.

In the end I rode away and left those mountains of the Buffalo Head behind me, for it is in my nature to be moving on. But even now, as I write, I see them once again—blue-shadowed, outlined in gold against the setting sun, flaunting their tattered banners of glowing cloud . . .

They were my friends. Those earlier hills were but my pathway to them.

R. M. Patterson

Sidney, British Columbia
December 1960

PART ONE

Destination Unknown

I

Growing Pains

The Upland Road

The little outfit clattered up a steep, stony rise with Flat Creek down below, on the left. From the shadow of the hill, I saw the man ahead of me top the crest and ride straight on into the evening sun; for a moment he seemed to be outlined in fire: man and horse, big hat, fringed buckskin jacket and woolly chaps. Two packhorses swayed over the skyline close behind him, and then the full glare of the low sun hit me straight between the eyes. I turned in my saddle to see the last packhorse come into view, swiftly followed by the third man of the party whose cheerful countenance puckered into a screwed-up scowl as the light caught it—and the outfit was complete.

The man in the lead was George Pocaterra, owner and founder of the Buffalo Head Ranch over which we were riding. Before his time there was nothing there—only a Stoney Indian camping place sheltered by woods and hills, with good grazing for horses and a wonderful spring. It was a much used camping place; tepee poles were standing there, as they had always stood, waiting for the Stoneys to come again, ready to have the tepees rolled around them; Pocaterra and his cousin, Arturo Talin, picked them up and piled them out of the way—and so, with their going and with the whirr of the first mower, the long day of the Indian was over. For better or for worse the white man had come.

That was in 1905, and as time went on Pocaterra added grazing leases and more land, and so brought the Buffalo Head into being. There, for almost thirty years, he raised horses and cattle and hunted, trapped and prospected in the mountains that lay to the westward.

The ranch got its name from the horse brand—the small outline of a buffalo skull branded on the left thigh. It had started life as a bluebell in silhouette, but a casual remark from the local Justice of the Peace, to the effect that "he couldn't see any bluebell in it: it looked far more like an old buffalo skull," set Pocaterra off on a new track; he swung on to his horse and hit for home, to turn petals into buffalo horns and generally reorganize the design of his brand. He had plenty of models to work from. There were all kinds of old buffalo skulls whitening on the grass and one frequently dug them up in springs and peaty places. The brand, when Pocaterra had got it to his liking, was a good one—none better. The cattle brand that was allotted to the Buffalo Head was also good—X N on the right ribs: easy to read and not to be mistaken for any other brand in that district.

The trip on which we were now setting out was by no means the first that Pocaterra and I had made together into the mountains. So by this time we had come to know each other well—which was, in effect,

George Pocaterra at the Kananaskis Lakes

to know that at any moment anything might happen. Each one of us was (and possibly still is) utterly unpredictable. We each had enormous patience when it came to some long-enduring physical feat—and yet every shred of that patience could fly to the winds over some absurd trifle. Each one could rise to the crest of the wave and ride there, triumphant in the sunlight, only to pass with equal swiftness into the depths and the shadows. We usually managed to convince ourselves that we were completely practical. We were wrong: it was often the unacknowledged quest for romance that drove us on. The problems of history fascinated us; a map (especially if it had blank spaces on it) was an enthralling book to each one. Pocaterra spoke five languages and was liable to burst into song (or into anything else) in any one of them. I could be counted on to underline the absurd side of any situation, however grave, or to bring, often at the wrong moment, my gift of mimicry into play, with results that were sometimes devastating.

With us there rode a man of an entirely different stamp—the perfect foil. From behind I could hear, every now and then, Adolf's voice urging on the last packhorse, which seemed disinclined to leave home. It was some four years now since he had left his family farm in East Prussia and come to Canada. The hills had appealed to this man from the great plain of northern Europe, and for the last two years he had worked for Pocaterra, learning English from him and much of hunting and mountain travel. It was the desire to see new lands that had jarred Adolf loose from Aulowönen—that and the disorder of the Germany of that time. No man's life was safe, he told me, in those troublous years: stacks were fired, cattle and horses were stolen; it was all a man could do to guard his own.

Another reason for Adolf's leaving Germany was that he had had no wish to serve in the armed forces that were, even then, being rebuilt. He had seen enough of armies: in 1914, as a boy, he had hidden with his brother and watched the Cossacks—"big men on little horses" he told us—riding hell for leather after terrified, fleeing piglings, spearing them to roast over their fires. Boys, too? the young Baumgarts had wondered—but it was not so bad as all that. Full of roast suckling pig and bonhomie the Cossacks had not troubled themselves about small boys but had ridden up to "the lord's castle" to see what they could find there. It seems that the lord kept a well-filled cellar, for a terrific binge started up—and then, in the fullness of time, the Cossacks reappeared, driving before them the lord's pedigree dairy herd which they generously distributed amongst the farmers and villagers.

All this was told at the Buffalo Head at a bachelor Christmas dinner party in 1936; and at this point an old American cow-puncher, Art Baldwin, broke in. "Well, what the hell was wrong with that, Adolf?" he said. "Why kick about that?"

"We did not kick. It was wonderful. Yet there was something to spoil it: the Cossacks rode away to the west and left us with the lord's cows all right, but in a week or two they were back with the Germans after them, chasing them—and then we had to take all those good cows back up to the lord again! *What* a pity!"

He sounded so rueful about it, just as if it had all happened yesterday; and the table burst into an absolute roar of laughter.

And now here he was, riding behind me—active, capable and a good shot. We rode on into the shadow of the mountain. The autumn glory of Flat Creek faded into a blue, cold twilight. As darkness fell we made camp in the valley of the South Fork, at the foot of Mount Head, and there, later, we slept by the dying fire and the ice-rimmed stream—three men whom the chances of life had brought together in the Rockies from Lombardy, East Prussia and the north of England.

★ ★ ★ ★

Precisely what twists and turns of fortune had led Pocaterra and Adolf from their homelands to this camp below Mount Head must remain, for each one of them, his own affair. As for me, there is no secret about it at all—it was purely and simply the result of a long drawn-out love affair. Child, boy, and man, I had always adored the distant hills.

It was a natural thing, for my whole life has been passed within sight of hills. My first memory of them is of a sunny morning in a garden in Ireland. We were on a lawn and my father was holding me up so that I could see over a high hedge and across the waters of Killiney Bay to a couple of blue silhouettes on the southwestern horizon. "The Big Sugarloaf—and the Little Sugarloaf," he said, slowly and clearly in a rich Scots accent—and I repeated the words after him as well as I could. Those were the Wicklow Hills that we were looking at, around 2,000 feet and some eight or ten miles from home.

Another isolated memory of that period is of my first excursion into politics. The Boer War had broken out and Ireland was—as usual—split in twain. My father, a Scot from the valley of the Tweed, was editor of a strongly pro-English Dublin newspaper. The pro-Boer faction was violently active and my father was a marked man for he never let slip any opportunity of attacking his opponents—even to the point of priming and rehearsing me in his puckish fashion, so that I, charging across the lawn one summer afternoon, burst through the French windows into a sedate tea party at which my mother was entertaining a number of Irish friends—anti-Imperialist and pro-Boer, most of them—shouting "Damn Oom Paul! Damn Oom Paul!"[1] at the top of my voice. That performance won me no applause; and the speed at which I was seized, smacked and propelled through the drawing-room door into the clutches of a hastily summoned nanny was an eye-opener, even to one possessed of a young and agile mother.

Not long after that, the two of us were sitting together on a garden seat flanked at either end by big cypresses. My father was wearing some funny-looking clothes: khaki, he called them—a uniform, whatever that meant. He was going away to a place called South Africa, and he was getting a thorn out of my thumb and telling me to be sure and behave myself while he was gone. And then that picture fades like the rest of them and twenty-three years went by before I set eyes on my father again ...

The next few years were spent at my grandfather's in the north of England. I soon discovered that, from the upper windows of this tall, red-brick house, the blue outline of hills could be seen in the southwest, through the gaps in a row of pine trees. What hills were they? I wanted to know—and also, what lay behind them. The man who would have told me was in Africa. Here, in this large and cheerful house, people were busy and the days seemed always full: there were the family steel foundries, and tennis and garden parties with the most delectable strawberries and cream; and there were weddings, and comings and goings of men from all over the world—engineers, most of them, and not a few with strange-sounding foreign names. And somebody, sparing a moment in the midst of all this, said: "Those hills? Oh, I don't know. You can call them the Distant Hills—that's a good name"; and somebody else, paying no attention, said: "Behind them? The sea, of course. Ships and the sea." So I called them the Distant Hills for a time, till I noticed a smile going around. And I thought of the sea and built dream harbours beyond the hills and filled them with my ships, until, at an early age, I learnt the meaning of a map. Then I found that the sea lay in the opposite direction, to the eastward; and from that day I shut up, on that subject, like the proverbial clam, deciding that, where hills and maps were concerned, most grown-ups were not worth listening to—an opinion that time has done little to alter.

During these small-boy years a great-uncle and a great-aunt from Ottawa were often visitors at my grandfather's house. I think that even then they intended that I should make my home in Canada for they always brought me presents that would turn my thoughts in that direction—maple sugar, a real Indian war bonnet, small sugary candies with a tart red berry hidden at their centres—and books: *Mooswa*, *Murder Point*, Stewart Edward White's *Magic Forest*, and *A Child's History of Canada* which I absorbed up to the point at which it became parliamentary and therefore dull. Champlain and Frontenac, the Huron and the Iroquois were my constant companions. I read all the long story of raid and counter-raid, of armed men—Indians and coureurs de bois—"gliding on snowshoes through the frozen stillness of the forest." It all sounded wonderful, and in my mind's eye I saw them, a silent, hooded procession of ghosts, purposeful and relentless, "gliding" in some mysterious way down the frozen Hudson River towards unsuspecting Albany.

There came to the north of England a hard winter, and all through that January the tennis lawn lay under deep and thickly crusted snow. A small Canadian cousin was staying at the house. She didn't seem to know much about snowshoes but I noticed that she occasionally referred to them as raquettes, and that gave me an idea. Soon we were taking a couple of tennis racquets, the property of aunts or uncles, out of their presses; soon, with the racquets attached by a cat's cradle of string to my feet, I floundered forth on to the tennis lawn. Encouraged by the cheers and jeers of my cousin, I started to break trail up the

Richelieu River towards Lake Champlain. The thick crust made the going hard but, even so, there was something obviously wrong with the outfit—not even an Iroquois could have travelled far on things like these. Furthermore, these snowshoes were not standing up to the job, and soon I had put my foot through one and was wearing it round my knee. Baffled, we put the racquets carefully back in their presses and stowed them away. We told nobody and soon we had forgotten about the whole affair.

That particular storm broke over my head the following summer. With amazing discernment my elders pounced *straight* on to me; no other suspect was even considered, and I was assumed to be guilty unless I could prove my innocence—all of which is in direct contravention of British law and justice. I was very disgusted with the way things turned out—so much so that I gave Canada up for quite a time in favour of a coral island.

The years went by. In my playroom on the third story of this large house I secretly built a rope ladder. By means of a teetering chair, balanced on a chair that was set on a table, I could open a trap door that gave on to the roof and so fix my ladder to a ring-bolt set in the leaded trough of a valley. Once up there I could fling a rope round the base of a chimney and, by that means, scuffle up the steep slates to the sharp peak of a gable. It was a terrifying position, but it was also a delightful one because, from here, with the aid of field glasses, I could plainly see, over the pine trees, the distant line of the hills. Patches of dark woodland could be seen on the lower slopes, and up one spur climbed the thin white ribbon of a dusty road, making, before it vanished over the skyline, a dog-leg turn to the right. That road fascinated me. I knew by now exactly what sort of road it would be, for I had been up into that moorland country and seen the vale spread out below me like a map—crop and pasture; stream and woodland; shining, whitewashed farmhouses solidly built of stone. My road would be climbing upward between grey, dry stone walls with, here and there, a wind-twisted scrub oak or thorn. The summer scents of wild roses and sun-warmed dust would be on it, and through the heat of the day sheep would be lying in the shadow of the walls. And then there would come a gate and the walls would swing away on either side and the road

*A gable at the top of Patterson's grandfather's home provided
a dangerous perch for a view of the Distant Hills.*

would become a stony, rutted track running through a wild moorland
of heather and bog; of brown, purling streamlets and grey, lichened
stone. Where was it? Where did it go?

The Upland Road was what I privately called that crooked line of
white, perhaps twenty miles away but yet so sharp and clear. I hunted
for it on my bicycle. I knew just about where it would be but I had not
been taught, then, how to take a bearing on an object and so to work
out its position and visibility on a map. Nor, in any case, did I have the
pocket money for large-scale maps. I spent much time and energy in
that quest, but in all that hill country I never found that road of mine.
Which is, perhaps, as it should be, for it still has for me, today, all the
charm of the unknown, and it still leads, as it always did, to who knows
what hidden pleasance in what lost valley of the hills.

The time came when I went away to school—westward across
England, over the wide, purple moorland, through the great grass fells
of the country's backbone, down a brown, brawling river to the flats
of Lancashire and the school by the Irish Sea. There, for six years,

along with three or four hundred others, I was taught and drilled and toughened. Weather ceased to have any meaning for me: no matter what it was—bellowing west wind with rain driving in from the sea, or the thin, grey east wind from the frozen Pennine Hills with a powdering of snow in its icy breath—we were out in it. Games in that sort of weather and five- and six-mile runs across country, or down the hard-packed sands at low tide, kept us fit and hardy in the wintertime. The result was that one's private internal heating arrangements became most incredibly efficient. This came in handy in later years. Sometime during my first winter in Canada I went out with a friend, a Canadian born, on his trapline. The very first night we slept out in the bush it went down to 44° below zero. We had no stove-warmed tent with us; we just camped in the open, and all this was new to me. "How do we fix things?" I asked. "We pile up a good lasting fire against our back log," the answer came, "and then we just roll into our blankets and tough it out as long as we can. And the first man that's cold makes the fire up." As my friend spoke a happy smile flickered across his face at the thought of the comfortable sleep he was going to have while his greenhorn companion froze and stoked. But his smile was premature: he had to deal with one who had been at school at Rossall, and he not only made the fire up through the night but, to add insult to injury, had to call me for breakfast in the morning.

My study window at Rossall looked westward over the Irish Sea. Sometimes, on clear summer evenings as the sun sank below the northwestern horizon, jagged outlines would appear there, rising out of the sea. Those were the mountains of the Isle of Man, the island of Mananaan MacLear, king of the sea, the island raised by a magician out of the deep waters. Seventy miles away, those mountains were, straight down the golden pathway of the sunset. Soon they would fade once more into the summer dusk, and in the morning there would be no sign of them—only the blue, empty sea and the tragic island gone.

Twice in my six Rossall years, on days of crystal clearness, the faintest of shapes rose up against the sunset, a little to the left of Man. That was the Mountains of Mourne in northern Ireland, a hundred and thirty miles away across the sea. That would be Slieve Donard, I thought, after a careful study of the map—the mountain where the old Irish saint, Donard, lies buried beneath the heather with Ireland at his feet and the green and purple island of Man set like a jewel in the wine-dark sea. And so, even from that study window, the horizon was widening and the road, as always, pointed to the west ...

I celebrated my last year at Rossall with a go of double pneumonia and pleurisy and a temperature of over 106°. That was my own doing—a frolic in the sea on a bitter autumn day when the playing fields were frozen like iron and the sea water was freezing in the pools left by the tide. It very nearly finished me.

They sent for my mother from the other side of England and they even prayed for me, law-breaker though I was, in the school chapel. To everybody's surprise I came back to life—and it was then that my mother, coming every day to see me, brought me a book by Jack London. She ended by bringing me all of them; I had nothing else to do and I went on a sort of London debauch. They fascinated me, those stories of the North—and to this day I have met with no other writer capable of describing frost and intense cold as London did. Lying there, a feeble captive, in the Sanatorium at Rossall, I ranged at will (and, this time, on snowshoes that did not break down) over the wide Northland, from Skagway to the Klondike and east into the barren uplands beyond the heads of the Pelly. Those books were a signpost on the road: some day, I thought, I too would travel and hunt in those blank, empty spaces of the Yukon-Mackenzie Divide ... In twelve years' time I was there.

Walking delicately forth into normal school life once more, I put out of my mind the glittering sundogs of the Yukon trail, pulled my scattered wits together and went up to Oxford to sit in the hall of All Souls for a scholarship examination. It was with no great optimism that my tutors saw me go; however, I confounded the prophets—and astonished myself—by winning an exhibition in Modern History at St. John's College. That put Oxford within my reach and it also put the official seal of success on my school days. One more school term came and went, during which I gradually returned to physical fitness and to my normal state of conflict with the authorities. Then I followed all those of my time at Rossall, so many of whom had already been killed, straight from school into the wartime army.

The Higher Education

I arrived at my artillery cadet school on the first of April, 1917—All
Fools' Day, a most appropriate date. Next morning, around 6 a.m., I
found myself in stables and, for the first time in my life, grooming a
horse. Peering round the animal's rump at the man in the next stall to
see if I was doing it right I wondered what this new incarnation was
going to be like—perfect hell? or a pleasant change?

Army life was not entirely strange to me: for six years at Rossall I had
been marched, drilled and cursed in the Officers Training Corps. We
had thrown bombs, slept out in the open on high moorlands, drilled
companies of our fellow sufferers, been taught to shoot, dug trenches.
Rising the hard way I had become a sergeant. A sergeant under officers
who were also masters. A sergeant in a corps in which it was impossible
to prevent the likes and dislikes of house, classroom and playing field
from cropping up again on the parade ground. This was probably going
to be better—a breath of fresh air ...

"Damn it, you—what's your name? Patterson?—put some beef into
it, Mr. Patterson, and stop using that curry comb. Groom the horse,
man, don't just lean against him. Oh, God give me patience!" That was
Jessop, our squad officer, and that was his constant prayer.

With frantic energy I did my best to remove the hide from my
horse with the body brush ... The uproar passed on and soon I could
hear Jessop bellowing at some other would-be artilleryman, telling him
he'd have him hanged, drawn and quartered. Yes—on the whole this
promised well. It was going to be a pleasant change.

In a few days' time I more or less had my bearings. We were stationed
at Preston Barracks, just outside Brighton on the road to Lewes.
Supplemented by temporary wartime huts, the main buildings were
old—a Victorian-period cavalry barracks. Red brick and red-painted
ironwork and verandas, gravel squares, long lines of stables; bleak in
cold weather, red-hot in the summer heat, graceless, ugly—precisely
what one had expected. And nobody gave a damn. Nobody had any
time to do more than let fly a passing curse at the antiquated fixings of
this period piece, this survival from Kipling's "Soldiers Three." Those
in charge of us saw to that—farrier-sergeants, roughrider-sergeants,

sergeants and corporals beneath whose fingers the 18-pounder field gun and 4.5 inch howitzer breech and recoil mechanisms fell to pieces and reassembled themselves as if by magic. And Jessop ... One way and another it was daily impressed upon us that we were the worst squad ever to hit Preston Barracks—cretinous and leaden-footed to a man ...

Throughout these months I, a schoolboy pitchforked in amongst men, was being educated in things hitherto beyond my simple vision. I had had the good fortune to be placed in a squad of forty-odd in which only two others were boys like myself who had seen no active service. The rest were hardened soldiers, men singled out for their ability to lead. It happened that only a few in this squad were from the British Isles. Most were Australians and New Zealanders, with some South Africans and one lone Canadian. We were known as "the Colonial Squad" and no insult was intended—or felt. By the grace of God I made two strong friends: A. S. Mitchell, a South African who had fought with Smute and Van Deventer in German East Africa, and later in France; and E. P. Hill, an Australian who had made the Gallipoli campaign and had also served in France. As we moved through the barracks from month to month the three of us managed to keep our beds together. Even after I had been dropped out of the squad after being kicked by the horse ahead of me when a mob of us were galloping downhill, this friendship continued. Mitchell and Hill came to see me in hospital and I was their guest at the passing out dinner of the Colonial Squad, of which I was no longer a member. My mother was in Brighton, that week end, on a visit. They called on her, that evening of the dinner, to apologize for taking me away.

"You'll take care of him and see that he doesn't drink too much wine, Mr. Mitchell?"

I might have known it would be like that. To her, of course, I was still a child.

"We'll take great care of him," answered he of the flashing smile— and they certainly did. They said they were my legally appointed guardians for the evening. They wouldn't let me have unlimited sherry or burgundy or port. They said: "No you don't, young Patterson; we promised we'd try to keep you straight—and, by God, it's uphill work! No more port. But your mother didn't say anything about your not drinking a liqueur brandy ... " We pranced out of there in remarkably fine fettle, running smack into Jessop who was coming back for something he'd forgotten, and giving him in unison such a crashing salute that he burst out laughing as he returned it.

What I contributed to this friendship is hard to see—apart, that is, from a strong sense of the ridiculous and an ability to seize on mannerisms that could be mimicked and so turned into laughter. In return these men from overseas began the process of smoothing down and rounding off the rough edges and the prejudices and the awkwardnesses that came from long years spent in that almost monastic institution, the English public school. Here and now, for the first time in my life, I was living on equal terms with men and learning how not to tread on their toes. But best of all was when they forgot me and talked of home—of Africa and Australia. Then I would hear again words that I had heard from bronzed and quiet-spoken men at my grandfather's—words like veld and bush, outspan and outback and laager. They talked of camp fires and desert nights and the sounds of strange birds and beasts; and I, listening to them, knew that there was still room on the far side of the world.

Other things besides friendships came to me in this wilderness of brick and red-painted iron. The barracks lay in a valley of the Sussex Downs—the chalk hills that run along the south coast of England and on into the battlefields of France. Over the cropped turf of these treeless, unfenced downs we drove the guns, coming into action, sometimes clumsily but now and then successfully, amongst the earthworks and the burial mounds of a vanished race: a horsed battery, moving as artillery moved in Napoleon's day and little thinking that we and our way of handling guns would soon be as obsolete as the flint arrow heads of the old, bewildered ghosts whose sleep we had broken with the thundering beat of hoofs and the rumbling of the wheels.

The battery made a brave show, setting out in the freshness of the morning; watering and feeding, unhitched, round Falmer village pond at noonday; sweeping over the hills in line or column with the deep valley on the north, and on the south the grey waters of the Channel, splashed with silver from some trailing shaft of sun. Gunners on the limbers, chin-straps down and hanging on for dear life; six horses to a gun with lead, centre and wheel drivers mounted on the near horses; leg-irons strapped on to counter the crushing swing of the pole. "Swing those leaders over, Patterson, curse you—my leg's jammed. Oh, Christ, may I never drive a pair of mutton-headed, Roman-nosed pigs like these again!" "Drive on your marker, you bloody fool, or these wheels'll lock and we'll all go to hell together." "Look at Mitchell out there, doing battery commander with Jessop watching him. His horse is going to bolt and I bet you his brain's a blank and the right signal's gone clean out of his head. Nothing now'll stop this whole damned zoo from rushing violently down a steep place into the sea. Just like the Gadarene swine." "Speak for yourself, old man … " Suffer we might, but the normal uproar of a battery on the move more than covered the never-ending flow of light-hearted comment on men, horses and things in general.

Spring and its tribulations passed from us. Summer ripened into harvest time. Nominally, at least, we were becoming more intelligent, more like artillerymen. As if in recognition of this, "they" took to sending us, after months of theoretical work in the map reading school, to various high points on the downs from which we had the country at our feet. There we would spread ourselves, with our maps and field glasses, our notebooks and directors,[2] along the softly rounded, thyme-scented ramparts of some Stone Age fortress. From there we would identify our targets on some far-off sweep of open down or buried in the blue depths of distant woodland. Then various problems would be propounded: angles and lines of fire to an imaginary battery concealed in some fold of the hills; problems of visibility and problems of approach: how close to the target could you bring your battery of 18-pounders before the intervening ridge made fire impossible? How much closer to the ridge could you come with the 4.5 howitzer? "Surely, gentlemen, surely? Thank you, Mr. Mitchell, sir—that was the answer I wanted. You cannot come within range with the 4.5 how. and still remain under cover." Damn it, what an infantile question! Why had I let that one go by?

Because of the drowsy beauty of the afternoon, of course; and because I had been watching those men down below there in the valley stooking oats, instead of paying attention to the sergeant. Come to think of it—

did I really need to pay attention? Probably not, but it would be a sound idea to make some show of it: sergeants were sergeants, and why irritate the rest of the squad by a cocksure assumption of proficiency? For maps were an open book to me. They were not just flat sheets of paper, covered with hieroglyphics and backed with linen: when I looked at a map the bald hills rose up in relief and I could see the valleys twisting between them, deeply incised. All Kipling's Sussex lay there, plain to read: "Trackway and Camp and City," marsh and winding river valley. A map was a beautiful thing and it was wonderful what you could do with it. I could go back now and climb up on to the roof of my grandfather's house, and from there, with this new knowledge, I could pin-point in a few minutes that old upland road that had bothered me for so many years. But I knew already that I never would. The time for that had gone by ...

First out of the squad, as usual, I handed in my solution to the latest problem, drawing, also as usual, resentful stares from those who still grappled. The afternoon was drawing on and the shadow was stealing down the slope of the hill. The shadows thrown by the stooks, down below in the oat field, had grown longer. The harvesters were gathered in a little group on the shady side of a tall hedge. I picked up the field glass: yes, that was it—they were drinking great mugs of beer poured from a heavy crock which they handled with reverential care. It made me thirsty even to look at them.

A faint breeze came drifting from the eastward, heavy with the scent of sun-warmed grass. Borne on it was a muttering sound, rising and falling, sometimes almost dying away—but never stopping. That sound came from France. That was the guns firing. It was because of that sound that we were here.

To the east and west the line of the downs stretched away into the blue haze of summer. Rolling, close-cropped, bald-headed hills, their beauty lay in line and shadow, in their swelling curves and rounded, waterless valleys. All this was new to me and yet it was as if I had seen it somewhere before. A horse country. A grazing country, open and unfarmed. What queer byway of heredity would that be? And I wondered then, as I watched the shimmering headlands of the hills, what exotic nomad strain, hidden away in my Anglo-Scottish heredity and cropping out in me, could account for the instant friendliness of this bare, treeless grassland of the south, so unlike the purple moorlands of my northern dales ...

"You are to imagine, gentlemen, that an enemy battery is in position at Lower Standean Farm. What steps would you take?"

Other training schools took a hand in my education. There was precise and traditional Shoeburyness, down the Thames estuary, with its fogs and its frosts and a tall, mustachioed regular army major who lectured interminably on the calibration of guns and the behaviour of shells as they passed through different layers of air at varying altitudes and temperatures, covering, as he spoke, the blackboard with a maze of figures. This was over my head completely, and if these subjects ever cropped up in examination, ruin would be staring me in the face.

And finally, Larkhill with its miles of rolling grass country—tawny, wind-rippled, each seed head golden-tipped under the low November sun. Stonehenge with its black monoliths outlined in fire against the sunset. Driving drill above the Avon valley. Guns thudding from the artillery ranges ...

December came, and the shells that carried my fortunes tore through the upper air. At my bidding—though also, I now think, miraculously—they flew straight to their destination. A few weeks later I was decorating my uniform with single stars and ordering the most splendid boots and riding breeches that London could supply. Now, at last, I fancied that I was somebody. But I was mistaken, for the second lieutenant is less than the dust, and his numbers, in 1917, were as the sands of the sea.

Inside, Looking Out

The glory was short-lived, and the afternoon of March 21, 1918, found me sitting on a grassy slope in Picardy, a prisoner of war at a German field dressing station ...

It had been a busy day, starting officially at 4:30 a.m. Around four o'clock the fog, which had been lying since midnight in the wide, shallow valley, crept up the slope and swirled around the ruined farmhouse which was the observation post of our battery. I gave it plenty of time to clear. I took a stroll up the road to its highest point and still I could see nothing. Then I gave it up as a bad job, and went down into the cellar where my sergeant was reading by the light of a lantern and my two telephonists were snoring in unison.

"Got anything I can read, sergeant? There's a fog outside and I can't see a thing."

"Well there's a book here, sir. Don't know if you'd care much for it—it's by Charles Garvice and it's called *Just a Girl*."

He held it out and I stretched out my hand to take it. But I never got that book for at that moment the minute hand reached the half-hour. There was a tremendous "Woomp!" and the earth shook. The signallers sat up in their bunks as if jerked by hidden strings. The sergeant and I looked at each other. Something was happening outside—and far too much of it, judging by the row. I rushed upstairs again to find the air full of screaming metal ...

That was the start of the German spring offensive of 1918 which came so uncomfortably near success. For me the morning included a walk from the now useless observation post back to the battery position. I led the way on that promenade, holding on a compass bearing through the dense mist and through a barrage in which it was theoretically impossible for any living thing to survive. Yet no one was touched—though, at the last moment, we barely escaped mass destruction, for, with an accuracy so devastating that it would have been commended even at Shoeburyness, I had led my little party right on to our forward guns.

There followed hours of firing with those guns; a firing that sounded futile and squib-like against the overwhelming crash of German high explosive—though later in the day I had to revise my ideas about that when I saw the lines of enemy dead where our two guns had been traversing.

Around midday the mist broke into scattered patches of rolling vapour. Here and there the sun broke through. Suddenly the barrage lifted off and passed behind us. Rifle fire sounded from a short distance in front: Germans shooting at each other, presumably, for there was nobody else there. I sent word down to the captain who had orders, if attacked, to retire on our centre section of guns. Up he came and we sent the men off. Then we busied ourselves doing what damage we could to the guns. And then we ran.

But suddenly disaster reached out for me and caused me to remember—thereby changing the whole course of my life. "By God," I said, "my revolver's in the mess dugout. I'll get it and catch you up."

"Don't," I heard him say. "You haven't time."

But I was already on the way. I fell down the ruined stair, grabbed my Sam Browne with the revolver in its holster and climbed out into the sunlight again. Two Prussian infantrymen, waiting on the roof of the dugout, jumped down and collared me and I was a prisoner of war.

A sharp crack sounded in my right ear. It was very noticeable for the noise of the battle had rolled away over the ridge to the westward. I looked at the Prussian who was holding my right arm and he looked at me in a puzzled sort of way. But, whatever it was, it had gone by and there was no one to be seen—only a sunlit cloud of mist rolling slowly up the far side of the valley towards our second pair of guns. Inside the cloud, though I did not know it then, was the captain, running and re-loading his revolver ... He and I pieced the story together when we met, some years afterwards, in a midnight train northbound from London.

"Did I get that fellow who was holding your arm?" he asked. "I just fired at his head and ran."

"No," I said. "You just missed my ear."

☆ ☆ ☆ ☆

And now here we were, prisoners, and with the late afternoon sun shining on some most unpleasant things around us. Close by, a man in field grey lay face downwards, groaning steadily—and not without reason, for his backside had been shot off. Other and equally desperate casualties cluttered up the field dressing station and the doctor and his orderlies were busy. The row of prisoners, in various stages of exhaustion and dejection, sat listlessly on a grassy bank with a deep ditch immediately behind it. Here and there, amongst us, sat German walking wounded, silent and patient.

Like myself, many of the prisoners had been, by this time, thirty-six hours or so without sleep. Also like myself, many of them were

The author (bottom row, far right) with fellow prisoners of war in Schweidnitz, Silesia

variously bashed and bleeding. The fellow next to me—Cochran, he said his name was—was wounded in the hand. I had swallowed a certain amount of gas and my tin hat had a sizable dent in it where a German rifle butt had made contact. Few were untouched.

Away to the southward shells could be seen bursting around Fort Vendeuil, one of the outlying forts of La Fère. In the fort was an officer of the Royal Garrison Artillery who was to become a close friend of mine as a prisoner in Germany. His telephone line to his battery of 6-inch howitzers still held, though the Germans were close around him and between him and his guns. At any moment now, he thought, the guns would have to be abandoned before the oncoming tide.

"One last shot," he said to himself, and he looked around for a target. Far off on the northern slopes he could see a little gathering of men where nothing had been before. He didn't know what it was, but it was in German-held territory and that was good enough for him. He made a few rapid calculations and then gave an order to his battery.

Out of a blue and cloudless sky there suddenly came the sound of a large, well-aimed and steeply descending shell. The seriously wounded were too far gone to care. Doctor and orderlies hurled themselves flat. Animated by one common impulse, prisoners and German walking wounded alike executed a smart backwards somersault into the ditch. A swaggering, unpleasant little guard flung himself in on top of some poor wretch—rifle, bayonet and all complete.

The shell burst with a truly impressive crump. Somebody was killed and the man with no behind was put out of his misery. The Germans, excited, all began to yell and shout, and none more so than the guard, who was obviously of the bullying type. He leapt out of the ditch, trampling, as he did so, on a wounded fellow-countryman, brought his rifle to his shoulder and soon, with frightful pantomime and threats, had everybody out of the ditch and sitting on the grassy bank again. The German wounded came too. They seemed to be quite at home with that sort of treatment.

Up and down in front of us the guard marched, swaggering and threatening. He spat at one weary-looking officer prisoner, took a half-kick at another and was strutting past Cochran and me when a sound was heard in the air as of a tired and heavily laden bee. The droning of the bee came to an end with a quiet "Whup." The guard doubled up as if somebody had kicked him in the stomach. Then he sank on to his knees and then he laid his head gently on the ground. His slung rifle supported him in a kneeling position but he was quite dead, and, as Cochran truly said, that was just as well because the man was a pest and, anyway, "if it hadn't plugged him, Patterson, that bullet would probably have got you or me."

☆ ☆ ☆ ☆

Dusty, empty days of marching followed. Then there came a barren desert of time through which we clattered ever deeper into the German lands in a cattle truck—Namur, Liège, Aachen which was Charlemagne's city, Cologne. Black bread and an occasional bucket of the ersatz coffee—that was all we saw on that trip, and lucky to get it for Europe was a drab, hopeless, hungry place in those March and April days of '18. The roads were empty and on the railroads the rolling stock looked worn and dilapidated. The people we saw were colourless and shabby. Everything, it seemed, had gone into this last great effort of the Germans to snatch victory before American numbers could make themselves felt.

Eventually, after a Cook's tour of the Rhineland, our captors slung us into an old lager of the Russians on the flats of the Rhine south of Rastatt. For some reason they weighed us when they checked us in, and I found that, after fourteen days of captivity, I had lost twenty-eight pounds. Others were in similar shape, more or less, according to their build and stamina. Throughout the lager hunger was king.

After some weeks permission was given for a limited number of prisoners to cash cheques through Mees & Zoon, Dutch agents of Cox & Co., the army bankers. The odds were about five to one but I drew the king of clubs and so was amongst the lucky ones. A friend and I embarked on a mild debauch—oaten biscuits, dried fruit and Rhine wine—and that was the end of me. I have no recollection of going to hospital; only of waking there one evening in a clean bed and blessed quietness (except for a murmur of French voices) with a raving temperature that, according to my chart, was slowly coming down. And with, of all things, the mumps.

☆ ☆ ☆ ☆

The weeks went by and May drew towards its close. Early mornings were the quietest time in the hospital hut—but even then, even at sunrise, there would be sounds and stirrings ... Half awake, I turned so that I could see out of the low window. It was going to be hot again. The blue-green slopes of the Black Forest still lay in the morning shadow, but soon, I knew, the dark outline of the wooded hills would blur and soften in the shimmering heat-haze of the Rhineland summer. The French officers in the room next to ours were waking and talking. Soon they would be once more at their interminable game of bridge. All day you could hear them plainly through the thin partition: "Deux trèfles." "Deux carreaux." "Trois piques." "Oh, mon Dieu! Eh bien—c'est à vous, mon capitaine."

Across the corridor voices were rising in heated argument. That would be the Portuguese officers arranging the conditions and the wagers for the day's frog racing. Round and round the hut they would crawl in pairs, carrying, each man, a long stem of grass. Ahead of them would jump two desperate, heaving frogs. That would bring them, sooner or later, under the Frenchmen's windows; and invariably we would hear the disgusted mutter of the senior French officer from the bridge table: "Sacrés cochons de Portugais! Ils sont fous, ces gens-là—absolument fous! Faire des courses de grenouilles—pah!" One could almost feel the shrug that went with those contemptuous words.

My five companions in the mumps ward of the isolation hut were not waking or arguing or even thinking. Four Englishmen and one Welshman, they were leaving all that sort of thing, with true northern composure, to the Latin races. What they intended to do was to sleep as long as sleep was possible. It was clean and reasonably comfortable in the mumps zimmer.[3] Each man had a hospital cot to himself and there were no parades or appels to bother with. There was not much grub either, but at least one could stay in bed late and so conserve energy. The mumps, of course, had long since vanished but I had perfected a way of swelling out the neck muscles at will. We all made use of this, and either the young German army doctor was a kindly man or else he was very green, for it had been the same every morning now for weeks: "Guten Morgen, Herr Leutnant. Wie geht's?" Sitting up in bed I would bow and say good morning, presenting, at the same time, a horribly swollen neck for consideration. The doctor would feel it carefully. "Ach, ja," he would say. "Die Mumps." Then the sandy-moustached Feldwebel who accompanied the doctor would turn to the hospital orderly. "Die Mumps," he would repeat, sternly and with precision. "Die Mumps," the hospital orderly would murmur as he entered it in his book—and we were good for one more day. Without doubt this must have been the longest-lasting attack of mumps on record.

About this same time, when I was without books and longing for them, fragments of a poem of Kipling's kept milling around in my head. "His neighbours' smoke shall vex his eyes, their voices break his rest"—there was that line, and there was the start of another one: "He shall desire loneliness ... " How did it go on? Try as I would I could not, for the life of me, remember. But, by God, if I ever got out of this I would see to it that there was room around me for all the days of my life. And as for loneliness—after being penned in this zoo cheek by jowl with my fellow men I would greet loneliness forever afterwards with a smile ...

And now the sun was lighting up the western slopes of the Black Forest. Faint grunts and stirrings were coming from my four fellow Anglo-Saxons and our one tame Celt. Out in the compound the Portuguese were hunting frogs. The Frenchmen were flipping through their worn old pack of cards. The hot song of the cicadas heralded another empty day.

☆ ☆ ☆ ☆

It was June when we said goodbye to Rastatt. Glad of any change we entrained (not in cattle trucks this time) and wandered slowly across Germany. Our progress was like the wandering of a gypsy caravan—a happy-go-lucky sort of performance, as if they didn't quite know what to do with us.

We skirted the Harz Mountains and saw villages that had stepped straight out of Christmas cards, clean and beautiful. Then somebody must have had a bright idea and thought of a place to put us, because the train turned east and kept on heading east as if it had suddenly made up its mind—though it still stopped whenever it felt like doing so. In the crimson sunset of the last full day's travel we rolled slowly across a vast plain, out of which rose, at intervals, fantastic pinnacles of rock, each one crowned with a castle out of a fairy tale. That must have been in Saxony. Who holds those castles now?

The following afternoon we were decanted at the little fortress town of Schweidnitz in Silesia. Falling in with our bundles and our bits of things, we were marched through the cobbled streets and through a gateway in a high stone wall into a small courtyard garden. A tall building of whitewashed stone formed the northeast side of the courtyard. Standing—rashly, as it turned out—in the main entrance to this building, the German officer in charge spoke rapidly to a uniformed interpreter. The interpreter did his stuff, requesting "die Herren Offiziere" to enter the building "in good orderly way" and choose quarters for themselves. The parade was then dismissed.

As one man die Herren Offiziere surged forward. The German officer and the interpreter went down fighting gallantly. In the rear of the mob the startled guards shouted and threatened but refrained from shooting. Acting as a unit, the mumps zimmer (which had managed to stick together) fought its way upstairs and grabbed one of the best rooms in the lager—a high, vaulted room on the first floor with six beds, a long table and benches, and a huge, built-in, glazed-tile stove. The window looked out on to the guard house and the courtyard garden, and also over the wall into the little cobbled Fleischerstrasse— a quiet street of quiet houses and one small basketware shop under a Polish name. The number of the room was forty-eight—and so, from now on, we discarded the mumps prefix and referred to ourselves as "Zimmer achtundvierzig."

Schweidnitz

Life in the lager settled down to a steady routine, varied chiefly by escapes and recaptures, outbursts of temperament, and the arrival of mail and Red Cross parcels. To vary this, and also to do something constructive, I took on the job of co-librarian with a captain of infantry by the name of Pilley. Large boxes of books arrived, sent via Berne or Copenhagen. Pilley and I managed to get hold of a room off the great, stone-flagged hall of the place and Pilley got hold of a carpenter who built shelves to our directions against the stone walls while the two of us catalogued and arranged the books.

We were bombarded with demands for books that we hadn't got. We ceased to be surprised at any request, however mad. We simply made a list that ranged from architecture to zoology. I got this list into order and—having been thoroughly instructed, only two years before, in the history of eighteenth-century Europe—I added a request of my own for books on Frederick the Great's campaigns in Silesia. That should cover the surrounding district, I thought—and it did. The books came in August, and I retired to the solitude of the library to look at the maps. They were not detailed—I had not expected that—but they gave an excellent idea of distances and the lay of the Austrian frontier. And of Prague in Bohemia—for it was rumoured that if one could reach Prague and had the address of a certain Czech countess ...

"Ss-st!" A serpent-like hiss broke in on my calculations. It was my guard friend on duty again. He was out in the narrow, cobbled alleyway that ran between the library window and a high stone wall. His rifle was slung and he was fumbling hurriedly with his tunic buttons.

"Bitte, Herr Leutnant, bitte! Eine Karte!" he was saying anxiously, twisting his head this way and that, like a tennis championship spectator, in an agony of suspense. Quickly I took the map from him through the bars, giving him his promised chocolate and cigarettes in return. Off he clomped, his mind at ease, his shod boots ringing on the cobbles.

Today, evidently, was the day it rained maps. This latest arrival was an excellent road map of the Waldenburg Mountains—the wooded hills and mountains that began to rise close to Schweidnitz and which culminated in the Austrian frontier. I propped a chair under the library door handle and began to measure distances. The scale was about a kilometre to the inch. If one followed up the Weistritz (which was the little river of Schweidnitz) and then turned west up the Gold-Wasser stream, then a bare thirty kilometres, reckoned from the lager, would see one over the lonely frontier line and into Bohemia. After that anything might happen. It was said that Bohemia was a friendly land ...

I folded up the maps and took them along to the Senior British Officer's room to be placed with the Escape Committee, on loan for the use of all. That *Wegekarte vom Waldenburger Gebirge* was not the first map to enter the lager by the library window, nor would it be the last, for I had taken a lot of trouble with that guard. Being a librarian was definitely constructive.

The summer days marched by and I spent a number of them out in the garden in a deck chair (its ersatz seat was made of woven paper) under our few trees. My companion was a book that I had come across—an old, faded, Victorian-period book on sport and travel in the Himalaya. It had engraved covers and gilt edges and illustrations that belonged to the heroic, romantic period of Himalayan travel: mountain sheep on impossible crags and pinnacles which even a Rocky Mountain goat would fear to climb; sportsmen in Sherlock Holmes-type deerstalkers shooting from equally impossible crags and pinnacles, regardless of the intervening abyss into which the quarry would fall. They achieved their purpose, those old pictures, for they conveyed to the reader the spirit of the hills and the toil of the hunt in a way that is beyond the power of any photograph, however good. Penned in there in the courtyard garden at Schweidnitz, unable to move more than seventy yards in any direction, I could read that stirring book and then lie back in my deck chair and watch the shifting pattern of sunlight and blue sky through the rustling canopy of the leaves. That particular view is one that never varies. It is the same in a German prison lager as it is in an English garden. Under that roof of green and blue and gold even a prisoner of war is free to dream of the mountains that will be his future, of black canyons and wind-swept summits, of ibex with lordly horns ...

Towards suppertime the sun would go off the garden, sinking behind some high buildings. But supper was not my worry: I cooked breakfast for two every morning, in return for which my partner, the lieutenant of heavy artillery who had fired the six-inch shell at the field dressing station, produced both lunch and supper. All I had to do now was to take myself up to achtundvierzig and eat what was set before me.

But first one small observance, personal to me and shared with none. Most of us developed some small kink or other: this was mine. Upstairs I would go to the very top floor of this tall building and to a small window in the gable. From it, by hanging out and twisting around, I could get sight of the twin buttes of the Zobten Gebirge, the hills that bounded on the east the pleasant vale in which stood the clean, bright fortress town. There they lay, softened by the evening light, gently outlined against the pale blue eastern sky. One saw them beyond the girdle of small rivers and green meadows, beyond the treelined chaussees that seamed the ripening fields and linked quiet villages where ducks and geese beyond counting gabbled in the ponds. Their rounded shapes were friendly and unchanging.

Then to a dormer window that faced southwest, a window where one would sometimes find some fellow lover of the hills—solitary, absorbed, and in imagination free. There, all across the western sky and far into the south, lay the mountains that might hide a man as he started on the long road home. Nowhere did those mountains rise more than 3,000 feet above the level of the vale; but there, one knew, was a country of sweet-smelling pine forests, pleasant (though also dangerous) villages of forest folk, and clear streams. Over those green summits and into Bohemia soon my partner and I would be making our way. Those hills were indeed a heartening sight.

But it was our fate never to tread those forest paths. Others got out of the lager and, using various methods of travel, were eventually recaptured. Only one prisoner ever got clean away from Schweidnitz, which was the furthest lager but one from England and the sea. Accidents unforeseen and unpreventable upset our escape plans—and then came the allied victories in the west, and finally the armistice of November 11 with its perils of revolution and chaos.

The Allies came to Berlin. Soon an order came from there and the gate in the wall was opened and free men stepped out into the cobbled Fleischerstrasse. From early morning until curfew time Schweidnitz hummed. Wars and sieges had been the lot of this town throughout its history, and it was nothing new for the enemy to be in the streets. This time the enemy had money to spend and the inns and the wine shops did a roaring trade. Schweidnitz was a garrison town, and a man suddenly afflicted with a thirst had nowhere far to go. You could pick your fancy—it might be the Deutsches Haus or the Golden Lion, both of them in the Kupferschmiedestrasse; or there was the Crown and Sceptre in the Ring, the Two Lions in the Waldenburgerstrasse, the Sword in the Langstrasse. There was the Green Eagle—but one could go on forever: the place was as well furnished with pubs as an English cathedral city.

You could stick your head into any one of these Gasthofs in search of a friend—and you might find him; but more likely you would not, what with the crowd and the din, the laughter and the blue haze of tobacco smoke. And the maids laughing and shoving their way through the khaki-clad throng, carrying great fistfuls of foaming steins, dark or golden. Or, it might be, trays loaded with bottles of fragrant, ruby-coloured burgundy, or bright, winking noggins of liqueurs, green and red and amber. And the purple blackberry brandy of Posen in its squat, square bottles.

But if you wanted something quieter there was the old Rathauskeller where elder citizens sat amongst vast barrels and vats of beer and wine, quietly sipping and discoursing. The ceiling there was decorated with emblems and coats of arms, richly coloured; and on the walls were murals of old sieges and scenes from the town's troubled past. And, if that didn't suit you, there were Paul Winzig's Weinstuben in the Burgstrasse ...

Enough of that sort of thing was enough for the four younger and more active members of achtundvierzig. We headed out, one bright November day, into the country, to an inn we had noticed when out on parole walks—the Gasthof zur Merkelshöhe. The beer was good, the wine was good and the place was clean and warm. I was put on to bargain with the innkeeper.

How about a couple of roast geese for the following day at noon? Good. And also some of this excellent burgundy—five or six bottles, properly warmed? Splendid. And the rest we would leave to the lady of the house ... With the morrow thus provided for we returned by a different route to Schweidnitz, enlivening our march with song.

The following day we came again to Merkelshöhe to find a magnificent feast awaiting us. We demolished it and drank the burgundy in great comfort. Then we paid the bill, thanked the innkeeper's wife and asked the way to Burkersdorf. A footpath along the foot of the hills, they said—and they put us on our way, calling after us to come again. At Burkersdorf we found an inn and there we fixed up the same sort of thing for the morrow—only it was to be ducks this time, and not geese. Then we started back towards Schweidnitz with the sunset flinging our shadows ahead of us and the first faint stars showing in the eastern sky.

We got the thing down to a system, working right round Schweidnitz at a distance of six or seven kilometres. It took us about ten days and fifty bottles of burgundy to complete the circle, working through Pilzen and Giersdorf and villages whose names I have forgotten, round to Arnsdorf and so back once more to Merkelshöhe. Somewhere on the way there was a Gasthof von Moltke. Near to it we passed through the von Moltke estates and saw the tomb of the Field-Marshal of 1870—a lonely mausoleum on a little hillock amongst the pines. We went up to it and saw, through the steel bars and the doors of heavy glass, the sword and the cocked hat lying on the tomb.

A smiling welcome awaited us at Merkelshöhe and there, before embarking on the second round, we totted up the slain. Ten geese and fifteen ducks—and to eat these we had marched at least 140 kilometres. No wonder we were feeling well … A busy hour or two went by and then, well fed and wined, we thanked once more the innkeeper's wife, and took for the second time the footpath that led to Burkersdorf …

On a grey winter afternoon, with a hint of snow in the leaden clouds, we marched to the station. There a spirited rush gained for the three youngest members of achtundvierzig the tiny observation compartment at the tail end of the train. It held exactly three. There was no heat in it, but the seats faced to the rear and from them we would be able to see the world go by.

The whistle blew and we rolled out of Schweidnitz, bidding goodbye to the old Europe of 1914 which had been ours to play with for one hilarious month. No one will ever see it again, for in the two great convulsions of this century—which were, in effect, civil wars—it has torn itself to pieces for the benefit of the barbarians and the Tartar hordes …

A day later the wheels clicked slowly past a little station by the name of Königsblick and the forest closed in again. Never before had I seen anything on this scale. Steadily and without ceasing the evergreens marched by, clean and even and without underbrush. This was the empire of the trees—and in imagination I saw it stretching northward into Sweden, eastward into Russia, all across the northern world. It had something to say to me if only I could hear it. It was something that I had known once and long ago forgotten—like some tantalizing fragment of a dream.

Two days later the train came to a standstill in the middle of a level plain. A German soldier got off and started to walk towards the horizon. He never looked back. He just kept on walking towards the east with his own shadow going ahead to guide him over the rim of the world. I went out on to our little balcony and whistled to a guard.

"Where is that man going?" I asked.

"To his home," the guard answered—and I looked again towards the horizon. Good God—why it was like the homing of the birds and the bees and the salmon! There was the soldier, a small black figure in the flaring sunset light, marching confidently towards nothing at all under the great, empty bowl of the sky. He had room around him, that soldier, if ever a man did. For some vague reason I, brought up amongst trees and little fields, envied him. But there were other countries, lands of far distance and wide horizons—indeed the world was very big and one would have to hurry to see it all.

The soldier dwindled to a speck in the yellow immensity of the plain. Then the train creaked, shuddered and rolled on towards Danzig and the sea.

2

Outward Bound

Anzeindaz

England was full of homecomings in that winter of 1918–19, and to the very young the river of life appeared to be serene and sweetly flowing. No rapids ahead, the shadow lifted, not a cloud in the sky. All the same, the prisoner-of-war business rankled. Something ought to be done about it; and as for wartime army life, it could go on forever as far as I was concerned. Good companionship, new countries and strange people, no worries: there was nothing to beat it that I could see and one might even succeed in making it permanent. Why drop it all just to go back to school again? And so the first bright idea that occurred to me was that of going with Churchill's army to Archangel. Far pastures already looked green to me, and Archangel, just then, was about the farthest thing in sight. In the very name there was something of old Muscovy—a hint of walrus ivory and rich furs, a vision of Byzantine crowns and jewelled icons gleaming beneath pale northern fires …

My uncle, who was also my guardian, trampled rudely on that project. Soon, he said, these adventures would all be ending. Even now the cutting down of the armies had begun. England would be able to pick and choose whom she would retain: could I, one out of six million under arms, expect with any certainty to be among the chosen?

Finally he produced his best and most crushing argument—a financial one. That fixed it, and I went resentfully to Oxford, putting aside forever my chances of glory amidst the mud and the mosquitoes of Archangel.

The resentment soon faded. If there had been good companionship
in the army it was redoubled at St. John's. Never had I imagined that
there could be a life so pleasant as this that we led in this College
with its beautiful Canterbury quadrangle, its famous garden and its
atmosphere, at one and the same time, of country house and club.
There were friends on hand ready to share in every mood or to take
part in any enterprise, however insane. Few obstacles or restraints were
set in one's path: in fact, authority seemed to have made up its mind to
endure with patience where the war generation was concerned. As for
restraints, I spent a week of each Hilary term as the guest of a cousin
for Cheltenham races and the Cotswold hunt ball, and nobody seemed
to care or even to notice.

The Vice-President of the College may have noticed my absence
and may even have approved of it. His rooms were above mine—and at
times his sleep must have suffered ...

It was during my Oxford years that I first came to the high
mountains. Somebody suggested a couple of weeks in Switzerland
for the winter sports. The idea seemed to be a sound one and the
main body set off, followed, a day later, by myself and one other. The
railways of Europe were tired and worn out with years of fighting: the
train lumbered slowly across old battlefields and past ruined villages
where I had ridden with the Divisional Ammunition Column. Then
we were held up for hours by the floods of the Marne near Châlons
and it was not until after dark of the second day that we came to the
Lake of Thun. Our compartment was in darkness and I could plainly
see, in the light of a clouded moon, the black water of the lake and,
beyond, a mountainside sweeping up to the rimrock and streaked with
snow. And though we spent two sunlit weeks close under the giant
peaks of the Jungfrau, the Mönch and the Eiger, that is the picture
that remains—the lapping waters of Thun and the dark mass of the
mountain with the cloud shadows drifting over it and the moonlight
on the snow.

On the way home we stopped in Berne and saw from there the famous
view—the snow-clad peaks of the Oberland, rose-pink with the setting
of the winter sun. I saw those peaks again, the following summer, from
the high points of the Jura when I was staying with a French family at

the little château of Palente near Besançon. Nominally I was bringing my French up to the standard of the Diplomatic Service—for that was the vehicle I had decided to use in order to get out of England. A post in some remote and obscure capital was what I had in mind, some place with mountains in the background, preferably a horse country ...

Actually my attendances at the University of Besançon were becoming less frequent. Colloquial French was what I wanted, not old Professor Rouget droning on about the genealogy of the language. I was becoming more and more interested in the ancient city itself, the old Spanish fortress, the Vesontio of the Romans, the "Place of the Bisons" of ancient time. The citadel, the old heart of the fortress, perched on its rock and caught in the loop of the River Doubs, fascinated me. In the seventeenth century it had been one of Vauban's fortresses; it must have served, at least in part, as a model for Viollet-le-Duc's imaginary fortress of La Roche-Pont;[4] every stone, every yard of ground had a tale to tell if the listener possessed imagination and some knowledge of French history, sufficient so that he could understand. As for colloquial French, that could well be learned from a brown-eyed, smiling Hebe in a small café near the Porte Noire ...

There were days when I never came into Besançon at all, days when I took my lunch and walked for miles into the forest of Chailluz behind Palente, climbing to some high point from which could be seen, on clear days, the Ballon d'Alsace, the mountain at the southern end of the Vosges, and, in the northwest, the Plateau de Langres. Then three of us, two other "étudiants d'Oxford" and myself, made a hilarious tour of the Jura country in a large open touring car that was tastefully painted in flaming vermilion—thus suiting perfectly our mood of the moment—and from some summit that we came to, I saw once again, far away to the eastward, the jagged outline of the snows.

That was enough. To the crocodiles with the heat and the thunderstorms of the Jura, with the programme of lectures at the University, even with colloquial French as taught in the café by the Porte Noire—on my return I stuffed a few things into a small packsack and said goodbye to Palente.

The following day I lunched at Gryon in Canton Valais. The tables were set out under an awning, on a wooden terrace that was built out from the hotel into airy space, almost overhanging a mountain stream. Far below, the Avançon River tumbled down towards the Rhône. Up the far side of the valley climbed the dark curtain of the forest. Then came green alps and dark brown châlets, more forest, the last high alps and then the rock. The place was full of the sounds of falling water, and a cool breeze drifted beneath the awning, stirring the flowers on the tables, ruffling the golden hair of a girl who was sitting against the rail, caught in the full glory of the sun against the sombre background of the firs.

But my path was not here amongst the lotus eaters: my mind was sternly set on higher things. There was a place, they said, that was called Anzeindaz—a collection of stone huts, inhabited only by herdsmen and only in the summertime. It was a lonely place, high up and remote, but there I would find food and shelter, and a welcome, too, for the people of Anzeindaz did not see many strangers ... In that place, I thought, as I ate my omelette and drank my wine, I shall see for the first time the open country that lies above the trees and below the barren rock and the ice. I thought then that it was curiosity that drove me on—but, indeed, it was fate, for from Gryon I could so easily have gone on, not to the heights, but to Villars or Les Plans and so again to the Rhône valley. But that was not to be, and I took instead the mountain path to those alpine meadows which ever since have been my heart's desire. "The timberline country" I would learn to call it in the years to come—refuge, pleasance and hunting ground ...

☆ ☆ ☆ ☆

Afternoon was fading into evening and still the path zigzagged steeply upwards; cut in the slope of the mountain, it passed out of sight to the eastward between two spurs of rock. On the left hand the precipice towered against the northern sky; below, on the right, the torrent which was all that remained of the Avançon cascaded down the rocky slope into the meadows of Solalex.

It was hot and it was still. Resolve was not nearly so lofty or so stern as it had been at Gryon and a thirst of noble proportions loomed large in the scheme of things. I sat down to rest on an outcrop of rock, letting my pack fall beside me. The last trees lay below me now, ending on the slopes above Solalex; beyond, in the evening shadows, the valley of the Avançon plunged out of sight into blue, unfathomable depths. Far away in the southwest a mountain reared its head, caught and held in the V of the steep-sided valley as a foresight is in the hindsight of a rifle: that was the Dent du Midi, blue-shadowed against a copper-coloured sky. Long ago, at my first small school, I had, with tongue extruded in an agony of concentration, pencilled that mountain into its place on the map. An old friend—a name of romance and hot southern skies ...

A warm air, laden with the scent of the firs, came drifting up the valley. It brought with it the sound of cow bells to mingle with the harsh roar of the Avançon torrent. Together these two sounds made the song of the mountains. I would hear the same song (though that was hidden from me then) in the Rockies—the horse bells and the stream. For a while I sat on that rock on the path to Anzeindaz and listened ... and then I got up to go. The upland road, it would be, for me—though, of course, there was much, too, that could be said for the path of the lotus eaters down below in the dimness of the valley where, one could not forget, tomorrow's sun would gild again that head of shining hair ...

Another mile went by. The slope eased off, and ahead, in a basin of green meadows where four streams met, lay a cluster of stone châlets. That was Anzeindaz, a minute grey hamlet that might almost have been a group of rocks tumbled into the meadows from the Tête d'Enfer.

☆ ☆ ☆ ☆

Clothilde came out and stood, tall and, in the twilight, very fair, looking down at me. "If you are ready now?" she said, smiling.

I was. I set the empty stein on the bench and went in, stooping lest I should crack my head on the lintel, going down two or three steps into the low-ceilinged kitchen. On the table there was a great bowl of meat cooked in milk with onions and potatoes in it and a dish of croutons standing near. There was fresh home-made bread and a bottle of wine, and cheese of Anzeindaz that Clothilde had made. There was a jug of cream and a bowl of wild strawberries, and the scent of coffee pervaded the room. I sat down and gazed at all this as one who sees visions. Then I poured myself a glass of wine.

"You should eat first," Clothilde said severely. "You have come far— and then, just think of all that beer! You will make yourself sick."

"Never," I said firmly. "I am a student of Oxford." And, as if that explained all things, I raised my glass to her, receiving in return the quick sunshine of her smile ...

I woke the next morning to find a grey mist down on the valley. All that morning and most of the afternoon the cloud sat down on Anzeindaz, lifting now and then but always coming back again. "Stay here," my hosts said. "It may be thick on the Pas de Cheville and then you will lose the path, you will fall, you will break a leg. Do not go far away. Besides, today is Saturday."

Now why, in heaven's name, should one not go far on a Saturday? I wondered. Still, they were probably right about the Pas de Cheville— and I took some bread and cheese and went off into the grey-green world of the Diablerets. I found the little glacier of Paneyrossaz, and I played happily with it and bothered nobody until an empty feeling and an angry squall of protest from within proclaimed that it was suppertime.

There was a great scurry and bustle in the kitchen of the stone châlet. Clothilde was moving on winged feet, and in a corner sat the patron, her father, smoking a huge curved, carved and lidded pipe and occasionally letting fall some comment or suggestion in the odd-sounding French of the Diablerets Mountains. He got the same answer every time from Clothilde: "Oh-h—tais-toi, tu m'embêtes!" "Keep quiet, you're bothering me!" Plainly it was as much as a man's life was worth to get in that girl's way.

Impressed, I ate and got out. I went upstairs into my room, banging my head, as usual, on the lintel of the door, stooping beneath the low sloping ceiling. I read for a while by the little window whose sill was at most five feet above the level of the grassy slope. My bunk with its blankets and its sweet-smelling alpine hay was just beginning to look good to me when I heard the first of the strange voices in the kitchen.

I closed the book and looked down the valley. The clouds had gone and in the clear twilight, under the first of the stars, two giants could be seen striding up the steep path that came from Solalex. I was watching them when, suddenly, Clothilde appeared in the doorway of my room. "Every Saturday it is like this," she said with a smile. "It is a little fête—and now you will join us? Come."

I followed her. She went outside to greet the two from Solalex. Up they came, sweeping off their hats—enormous men, dressed in traditional Swiss-guide fashion, young and with long brown moustaches and deep voices. Cautiously they bowed their heads and went in. I could see two more of the sons of Anak swinging down from the Col de Cheville—and, good God, there was a third coming down by the stream from the glacier of Paneyrossaz! They climbed mountains, then, to get to this place—or was it not, rather, to this girl who drew them as a flower draws the bees?

I went in and the vast men rose to greet me, their bowed heads vanishing in the smoke and the shadows of the rafters. There was not a man in that room that was under six feet—and if anyone wants to know what that night was like, let him read Kipling's story, "The Lang Men o' Larut,"⁵ and change the tropical setting of it to one of grass and rock and ice ... The wine flowed and the giants sang happily, beating time with their hobnailed boots on the stone floor and with pipes and fists on the table ... Some inspired mountaineer had brought with him a liqueur of a glowing amber colour that tasted like liquid fire and made young men see visions and dream dreams ... Midnight came and went and, somewhere in the small hours, grasping firmly my second glass of this dynamic tipple, I rose to address the assembled company.

I spoke fluently and I allowed no barrier of language to spoil the even flow. Stuck for a word in French, I supplied it in German or in English. I spoke well—of that I am certain though, of course, God alone knows what I said. All I can remember of that speech is the end of it—a few apt words regarding the close ties that now would always exist between Oxford and this fount of learning and good fellowship—fontaine des humanités et de la bonhomie—Anzeindaz. These sentiments brought down the house in a roar of cheering and laughter, and about half an hour later a couple of amiable giants escorted me upstairs and laid me gently and reverently in the hay ...

Dawn was flooding in the east when I woke for the first time. The last two of Clothilde's suitors were still saying goodbye to one another outside the door, each unwilling to leave before his rival. They said it for a long time and then they went their separate ways. Then each one came back to make sure the other had gone and they said goodbye all over again, and when I fell asleep once more they were still saying it—and there seemed no good reason why they should ever stop, this side of eternity.

I slept a blessed sleep—and then my sleep was troubled by a dream. A river of ice was creeping down upon Oxford and all the bells of all the churches and all the college chapels were ringing the tocsin. Desperately they pealed, louder and louder, till I could stand it no more—and I woke to find the head of a cow looking in at my window, rubbing backwards and forwards on the sill and sounding its bell with every move. That finished it. Damn all cows! I thought, and I got up and went out into the sunrise and stuck my head into the ice-cold Avançon stream ...

Breakfast put new heart into the traveller and Clothilde and her father came out to start me on my way. Peace reigned once more over Anzeindaz. The giants were gone, vanished into the mountains, God knows where, for in all that day's march until evening I never set eyes on a man.

"Bon voyage et bonne chance!" Clothilde called after me. "And come again. That speech of yours ... ah, ah! Never shall I forget it ... ah, ah, ah! Come again, soon!"

"I will," I said—and I meant it then. And I turned and walked away towards the Pas de Cheville.

✬ ✬ ✬ ✬

Oxford in the autumn mists was haunted by memories of that mountain summer. With the thunder of the ice avalanches of the Matterhorn still sounding in my ears I found political science uphill work. Nevertheless, I gave the pundits a fair trial. I read them grimly, but there was no sparkle to them. From Aristotle onwards the philosophers all seemed, to my dim comprehension, to state and re-state the obvious and, having done so, to elaborate on it *ad nauseam*. I was not interested in the golden age or the city state or the perfect state; but I *was* intensely interested in this new world of the mountains that I had found—a world useless to man except as a gathering ground for the snows, yet orderly as the stars. There was nothing in it that had not a reason for its being, which was more than one could say for the involved ravings of the philosophers. Finally I consigned the whole pack of these venerable sages to the crocodiles and went and raided the Union library. I came away with Whymper's *Scrambles Amongst the Alps*, and before long I was, in spirit, back in Zermatt taking part in the first tragic ascent of the Matterhorn. And, as usual in research work, one thing led to another ...

My last summer term came and, with it, the grim prospect of Final Schools. Good God, I thought, how awful! And what have I done with my time? A confused vision answered me—bright memories of country cricket matches, golf, lunch parties; of quiet inns and the cool reaches of a small river. I saw arrows wildly flighting in the noonday sun across a sacred lawn; they flew always, let me add, under the influence of a very potent hock cup and no man in that garden could truly say that he was safe. I saw the float of the College barge slowly up-end and tip a full score of the fairest maidens, dressed in their flimsiest and rarest, solemnly into the river. Oh, the clinging hats and dresses, and oh, the red-faced, useless apologies!

And I saw green lawns and lovely, ancient buildings, and a whole treasure of beauty in this one old city for which England, and perhaps the world, has not the equal. That is what I brought away with me— those memories and an apprehension of that beauty. And, I hope, a small seed of scholarship, sown in ground that was not yet ready to receive it by men of enormous faith and patience ...

Faced now with Schools, I flew, as is my custom, to the opposite extreme. I worked—or, it might be more correct to say, crammed— with furious energy. Putting my trust in a very good short-term, photographic memory, I was fairly certain that I could get through the balance of three years' work in one frantic term. And so I went at it through the summer days, being dragged out from time to time by friends to play cricket, see the Derby run, attend an Archery Club luncheon, go on the river, drink beer and eat strawberries.

The immediate result of all this frenzied activity was most peculiar. Retiring to bed towards 1:00 a.m., thoroughly weary after a long day of work, cricket, and then more work, I would close my eyes—but not to sleep. This was where the photographic memory got its own back: pages of print, accurate to the last detail, would appear, floating in the blackness, and I would be forced to read them. Any subject was liable to turn up—it might be pages and deadly pages from Grant Robertson's *Constitutional Documents*; but most persistent of all was my special subject, Napoleon's Jena campaign of 1806. And so, through the hours of darkness, and unless I kept my eyes open, Berthier's despatches would parade before my restless brain, one after the other, full-worded and complete.

When the dawn came and a nearby cock began to crow the pages would fade and I would get some sleep.

The ultimate result was "a highly creditable second." In other words I had produced, without one original idea in my head, a most remarkable memory test, and had been rewarded precisely and exactly for that alone. It was said, in those days, that a third or a pass was the mark of a man who had quite honestly come up to Oxford for a good time and any old sort of a degree, no matter what—whereas a second showed that a man had tried for a first and failed, either because he was incapable of using his brain or because he had allowed the locust to consume his days. A sad epitaph and I drew no comfort from it.

In seven terms we, the war generation, had skimmed the cream off Oxford—or so we thought then. Friends were going down and the place would not be the same without them. Time was passing, too, and I now felt that I could not face the prospect of two or three more years working at German and French, at Oxford and abroad; it was time to be doing something.

It was suggested to me that, as a sound training for a possible business career, I should take the three probationary years in the Bank of England. A nomination was available.

After all, I thought, why not? Three years in London and then— "over the hills and far away!" And so I bought a book on the theory of money which I was able to follow with ease as far as the chapter on barter and cowrie shells; after which it might just as well have been written in Sanskrit for all it had to say to me.

On a sunny September morning I stood outside the Royal Exchange, looking across Threadneedle Street at the low walls of the old Bank of England. The building looked like a cross between an old-fashioned fortress and a county jail. I eyed it without enthusiasm, kicking myself for not having had the patience to carry on with my languages and follow out my original plan. Then I crossed Threadneedle Street and entered the Bank by the main gate, passing for the first time the top-hatted, pink-coated porters, who, if they fancied that in this novice they might be greeting a future Governor or a Secretary to be, were never more mistaken.

Desert of Stone

To the end of my years in that venerable institution, the action of a cheque in the Bank of England remained, in my dim understanding, absolutely without rhyme or reason. For an instant a cheque would pause in some office in which I happened to be—in the Bill Office, perhaps, or the Chief Accountant's Office. There it would be seized, punched, marked, or in some other way disfigured. Then it would be entered or slapped through an adding machine—and that would be the end of it. Where it came from, why it was there, where it went next—all that remained a mystery. I tried to find out. I questioned people, but they took refuge in floods of words. Either the whole process was so clear to them that they were incapable of explaining it to the yokel mind, or else—and this is what I now suspect—*nobody knew*. Cheques, I now think, do what they do in the Bank of England because it has been so ordained through the centuries. They follow certain well-defined flight routes as do the birds in their migrations; and, provided nobody tries to make any silly innovations, this admirable arrangement will continue until the bombs fall and we all go back to cowrie shells. So be it. But on no account ask questions of the inmates; it only embarrasses them.

For the rest, life there was full of interest, for the "Old Lady of Threadneedle Street" was not as other banks. One had a feeling there of being in the very heart of things. Going out to lunch or coffee at the Bank club I sometimes met a van rolling in at the Lothbury gate, drawn by the large, shining Bank horses. The load always seemed to be a heavy one—lumpy-looking sacks piled carelessly under the open tilt of the van. A couple of porters would swing open the gates into bullion yard where two or three of the Bank staff would check the load into the vaults, disturbing the dreams of the one unarmed London policeman who dozed contentedly on the sacks, embodying the Law. That was millions in gold coming home with the minimum of fuss—gold bars salvaged from the sea bottom off Malin Head where the German torpedo had sunk the armed merchant cruiser, H.M.S. *Laurentic*, in January, 1917. Where else in the world would that precious cargo have been treated like a load of hay?

Working late at night in the Bank and going from one office to another, one would run into armed men, tall and grey-coated, posted at strategic points. The bearskins and the rifles with bayonets fixed reminded one that the Bank guard had arrived—a small detachment from the Brigade of Guards under a junior officer, an Ensign. The custom of the Bank guard originated in 1780 at the time of the Gordon Riots. More than a hundred and forty years had gone by since Lord George Gordon's time but, in England, a thing once started is hard to stop. Nightly the guard was posted and nightly the Ensign dined with his two permitted guests in the sober splendour of the inner rooms where no sound penetrated and where footsteps were lost in the heavy pile of the carpets. Indeed there *was* no sound to break that quietness for, with the coming of the evening, the human herd departs and the City is silent and deserted, given over to a few night watchmen and to innumerable birds.

As time went by I began to be summoned to the inner rooms, there to sit at a small table while important matters were debated and settled round a vast, gleaming table in the centre of the council room. This, I was told, was a mark of favour and meant advancement. It was difficult for me to see how I had earned this promotion and, years later, I was completely flabbergasted when my wife told me that the director of the Bank who had nominated me had confided to her that I had "done very well at the Bank of England." There might, I suppose, have been a place for me in the Secretary's Office; but it was not to be, for I had found again the grass hills and the open country that I loved.

The South Downs were only fifty miles south of London. By two o'clock on a Saturday afternoon I could be on the crest of the escarpment, striding energetically westwards towards Steyning and Chanctonbury Ring, or eastwards towards Lewes. Sometimes I would break new ground further to the west; more often I would traverse again the country over which we had worked from Preston Barracks in the war days—past Lower Standean Farm and up to Ditchling Beacon of the map-reading afternoons—through Falmer and up on to Newmarket Hill where we had brought the battery into action among the humped tumuli of the stone age men. During the following week I would seek out Mitchell, who had adopted England as his country and was now working with a firm of wool-brokers in London. Together we would have lunch at the Doctor Butler's Head or at the George and Vulture; and I, red-faced from the sun and the sea wind, would speak to Mitchell of dewpond and tumulus, and of the down-land that we both had known. All around us would be the gossip of the City—but that would fade and we would hear again the bellowings of Jessop and the rumbling of the battery on the Lewes road. "God!" we would say to each other. "Those were the days!"

When funds were plentiful, two or three of us would go down to Lewes and take horses from a stable there. That blew the cobwebs out of one's brain—galloping in the sunset light over the close-cropped turf towards Mount Harry and Blackcap, with the blue dimness of evening settling on the wooded vale below and, far away in the southwest, the silver gleam of the Channel. The most memorable of all those rides was the time when, through a series of mischances, all the stable could let us have was a stallion, a mare and a gelding. Across thirty miles of grassland, under a brilliant summer sun, he who rode the mare fled in terror from the screaming stallion and its swearing, struggling rider, while the third member of the party, helpless with laughter, brought up the rear on the excited, pulling gelding. After that strenuous Sunday we said goodbye to horses for a while and took to the sea, buying for an infinitesimal sum a five-ton sloop which we kept in the estuary of an eastern river. We had no sex problems with her.

Fifty miles to the northwest of London lay Oxford. It was possible to leave the Bank of England at 4:00 p.m. and be on the river in a punt or canoe before six of a summer evening. By eight one would be changed and drinking sherry in somebody's rooms in College prior to a King Charles Club dinner. The small hours would find some of us still on the go: coffee and liqueurs by this time and a quiet game of blind hockey in some K.C.C. member's rooms—and I still have the silver-plated pint pots that I won from a Canadian Rhodes scholar on one of those visits. Then back to London with the milk train—and at 9:10 a.m. a dazed but outwardly respectable probationer would enter the front hall of the Bank and sign his name with about five seconds to spare before the book was removed by the porter on duty.

A close run thing; and precisely what value the Bank got out of me on those days of sorrow it is hard to say. About as much, probably, as it got after the dances and the parties of the London season—for it was not necessary to go as far as Oxford just in order to stay up all night. It was a Cinderella life that I led. But it was gay and it was interesting and in its way exciting, and for two and a half years I burnt, with great energy, the candle at both ends.

I came home one evening to find a letter waiting for me. I slit it open and read it with considerable interest. " ... in London for some time on mining business," it ran, "and I should very much like to meet you again. It must be twenty-three years now since I took a thorn out of your thumb on the day I left for the Boer War. There is much to tell you ... "

That letter was from my father. As may be imagined it gave me food for thought and I was absent-minded and preoccupied all that evening. I was still preoccupied next morning at breakfast time, and the friend with whom I was sharing a flat must have found me silent and strangely unsociable.

I met my father at the Cock Tavern in Fleet Street. We shook hands and took stock of each other. "Of all the places in London," he said, "to think that you should arrange a meeting here! Here in this street that meant so much to me when I was young!"

It was no accident, that choice of the Cock. I had felt that it would bring back memories of the days when he trod the royal road to success in journalism—of the days before the lure of Africa took and held him. I had hoped that the sight of the old, familiar rooms would break the ice.

It did. We became friends and there opened for me months when my real life began with the evenings and the days passed in a dream. I stepped back into that wide-open world that I had glimpsed as a small boy at my grandfather's—the world of blazing suns and far horizons out of which had come my grandfather's engineers, my golden-haired South African aunts, and Mitchell and Hill. Now, at nights, over coffee and Benedictine, I listened to my father's quiet Scots voice telling tales of Africa as only he could tell them. London became unreal: I saw instead my father's campfire winking beneath innumerable stars, crossed flooded rivers, heard in the dusk the ghostly trumpeter sound the charge on the old battlefield of Paardeberg, sought for lost mines. I heard the story of Christian Joubert and the wounded leopard in the Cave of the Golden Arch, and I saw the great ones of Africa go by—Tchaka, Moselikatze and Lobengula; Hendrik Potgieter, Kruger and Botha; Rhodes and Jameson, "those two great men who, for many years, held in their hands the destinies of Africa." The sentiment there is my father's, but the words are those of the famous American scout and Rhodesian pioneer, Frederick Russell Burnham.[1]

☆ ☆ ☆ ☆

On Saturdays we would go to the geological museum in Jermyn Street, and there I learned of the habits of gold and diamonds in South Africa, saw the conglomerate "banket" pebbles of the Main Reef of the Rand and the "yellow ground" of Kimberley, heard my father's views on the occurrence of diamonds in the "pans" of the Kalahari Desert—a land guarded by scorpions and yellow cobras, last refuge of the little Bushmen. Other names, famous in Africa, went hand in hand with the dusty cases of specimens in Jermyn Street—Rudd, Barney Barnato, Alfred Beit and the American mining engineer, John Hays Hammond.

I heard the Matabele give the last wild "Bayete" at Rhodes' funeral in the Matoppo Hills—the royal salute that had been given only to the Zulu and Matabele kings. I saw my father ride away when the ceremony was over, with old Gambo, Lobengula's war chief, trotting at his stirrup, talking of Ulodsi—who was Rhodes—and of Moselikatze, the founder of the Matabele nation.

My friends saw nothing of me in those days. They may have wondered what new thing had come into my life but I did not trouble to enlighten them. My Spanish teacher looked for me in vain. I had been thinking of going to Argentina, but under my father's rampant patriotism that idea died a violent death. "There's plenty of room in the Empire," he said. "Why help to build up a dago republic?" With those few, sweeping words he disposed of the sixteen sovereign states of South and Central America, and a few islands and scattered bits of real estate as well.

The teller of tales went back to Africa, bidding farewell without regret to the "grey desert of stone" that London now was to him. He knew and I knew that, for the sake of peace in the family, I could not go with him—nor, to my sorrow, could I follow him to Africa. For a time we corresponded. Then he went again into Portuguese East, searching once more for the Golden Arch. We lost touch—and the next news I had of him was years later in an article in *The Geographical Magazine* by Mrs. Etheldreda Lewis, the co-authoress of *Trader Horn*. She described, in that article, a man "tall and dignified" who was often at her house in Johannesburg, and she described him in such a way that I knew it was my father. I wrote to her and had a letter back to say that he had died recently in Johannesburg. He had always been a welcome guest at her house, Mrs. Lewis said, and she had particularly enjoyed the few occasions when he and old Zambesi Jack—who was Trader Horn—were there together. I look sometimes at old Horn's picture in his book and think of those two old-timers sitting on the stoep of that friendly house in Johannesburg, weaving for Mrs. Lewis a shining web of wondrous tales ...

With the going of that man I came up to the surface again and took a look at the workaday world of London. And by God, my father was right! It *was* grey and it *was* a desert of stone! It was high time I did some serious thinking about it; and so I took a week's holiday and went up north to my own hills for a breath of air, taking with me Stefansson's *Hunters of the Great North* to read in the train ...

I returned to town from the moorlands refreshed and mutinous. Clear in my head was the picture that Stefansson had drawn of the Athabasca and Mackenzie Rivers; and from the train windows I eyed the outskirts of London with distaste. A maze of drab, monotonous terraces and mean houses—there was something terrifying in the thought that this was the greatest city on earth, the supreme effort of civilized man. If you looked at it closely and thought about it at all, the whole swarming city was like a nightmare by H. G. Wells. It was a vast human ant heap through which the inmates scurried with set, expressionless faces, tied to some fixed routine. These people—though it was hard to believe it—were the descendants of men who, for untold millenniums, had been hunters, wanderers and dwellers in the sun. Yet it had taken them only two thousand years of city life, or rather less, · to reach this insect state; and now, God help them, they seemed to be content with it. It was Thomas Hobbes who wrote, three hundred years ago, that the life of primitive man was nasty, brutish and short. I could not see that things had vastly improved for civilized man. His dens looked extremely nasty on this summer's day; and as for the length of a man's life, that could not, it seemed to me, be measured by the number of his years but rather by what he had seen and done ...

The train from the north slid into the bay in King's Cross Station. Thinking these heretical thoughts I stood up, took my suitcase from the rack and joined in the mad scramble of my fellow ants.

The following week end I spent walking over the Sussex Downs. I headed west, and late in the afternoon I came over the top of Truleigh Hill. The day was perfect and the lovely countryside lay spread out at my feet in the heavy green and gold of harvest time. A small breeze came in waves and ripples from the eastward, bringing with it the scent of thyme and summer flowers. Somewhere a sheep bell was tinkling and, four or five hundred feet below, men were stocking oats on Truleigh Farm. I sat down on the sun-warmed turf and watched them for a while—and then the drowsy softness of the afternoon had its way with me and I fell asleep.

It was almost an hour later when I woke. The shadows thrown by the stooks, down below in the oatfield, had grown longer. The harvesters were gathered in a little group on the shady side of a tall hedge. I picked up the field glass with the mad feeling that I had seen all this before, but that something somewhere in the picture was missing ... And then I remembered: it was the sound of the guns. Exactly six years had gone by since I had watched those other harvesters, eastwards along these same grass hills and on just such an afternoon as this. Only then adventure lay ahead and life was dangerous and uncertain, whereas now a limpet on its rock was a wild sea rover compared with me.

A sudden terror seized me. Another six years and I would be over thirty and getting old. It was time to get out before life passed me by— time to get away from the ant heap before I succeeded there and before it held me through my active days. And as if mere movement would avail I scrambled hastily to my feet, slung my pack and marched on towards Steyning and the sun-rimmed outline of Chanctonbury Ring ...

A day or two later a secretary ushered me into a large, quiet room in London Wall. The door closed behind me and I walked forward over a mile or so of carpet towards a table at which sat, watching me, the director of the Bank who had given me his nomination. He was a Canadian, which, I felt, was the very best thing he could be at this particular moment.

"Well, Raymond?" he said.

"I've decided to go to Canada, sir," I said. "I thought you should know before I tell them at the Bank."

Hours passed and I just stood there, waiting for the storm to break. Suddenly the man raised his head and smiled. "I think," he said, "that it will be a great adventure."

Peace River

The following May found me—brown, blue-overalled and thousands of miles from the Chief Accountant's Office—working on a dairy farm in the lower Fraser Valley of British Columbia. The farm maintained, besides myself, one other hired man—Roy Scott, a Prince Edward Islander, short, stocky and quick-tempered. For the rest there was the boss—rosy and apple-cheeked, down-trodden relic of a good-looking man; and his wife, Mrs. Fletcher, a woman with a soul above cooking. Good food appeared rarely, and then only when guests came out from Vancouver; and while these pastures were undoubtedly far distant from London, and while they were also, at this season, green, yet somehow the atmosphere of romance was lacking—as, indeed, it so often is on dairy farms.

This job on Fletcher's Farm was my first job in Canada. I had found it through the Soldier Settlement Board, having some vague idea in my head of farming and being anxious to gain experience before committing my small capital. Fletcher's Farm proved to be indeed a memorable experience: in fact it cured me forever of any desire to have anything to do with farming. Yet it was a necessary agony, one last prod of conscience. From then on I fully acknowledged to myself that what I wanted to do was to get out of settled country—to the outskirts, and then beyond the outskirts to some place where boundaries were still unknown and where the horizon was the limit. There the only barriers would be natural things—mountains and fast rivers, swamp and forest, ice and snow. These could be overcome: persistence and endurance would be the keys to that far-off kingdom. There would be something that I could do in that far country, wherever it was—of that I was certain. People, I had now come to realize, liked living in communities, or, as I saw it, in herds. Those who could go far from their fellow men, and who could go alone, were so few that they could be sure of their reward.

With these still half-formed ideas in my head I had picked up somewhere a government booklet on the Peace River country. Scott and I had become interested in those northern prairies of Alberta, which were still remote and only sparsely settled, and which would be for me a step nearer to the unmapped Mackenzie Mountains, the Jack London country of my Rossall days. Scott and I had pored over these Peace River maps and pamphlets in the evenings in the bunkhouse at Fletcher's, and already we had decided where we would take up land: we would head for Battle River Prairie and then, if that failed to please, we would go on north, downstream to Fort Vermilion.

To tell the truth, there was no "if" about it as far as I was concerned: though Scott demurred, I was all for making it Fort Vermilion or bust. I am susceptible to names, and there was something in that flamboyant name that drew me—though God knows, now, what wild pictures I painted for myself of life in a place that was called Vermilion. Whatever those pictures may have been, for once reality was far ahead of my imaginings—and I see again a winter evening at the Battle River Crossing and the men of Fort Vermilion appearing suddenly, with sleighs and on snowshoes, headed by the mailman, Louis Bourassa, out of the twilight and out of the north. Their head-dresses were the

Patterson and Scott, 1924

capes of timber wolves with the ears and the upper jaws and teeth still on them; their mitts were of the paws of lynx and their parka hoods were lined with wolverine. They wore beautifully beaded moccasins, gay scarves and gaudy sashes; their rifle covers were fringed and beaded and so were their buckskin jackets. It went down to sixty-seven below zero that night and we gave a dance for the Fort Vermilion men. All night long the fiddles sawed and scraped and moccasined feet thudded to the wild yell of the square-dance caller—and such a roaring success was the party that nobody hitched up his horses to drive home till the sun was well risen and the morning had warmed up to zero. It was from one of those men, on that lively night, that I acquired my first pair of snowshoes, trading for the shoes an English knife with a handle that was fashioned in the shape of a thistle.

But all that still lay in the future and, indeed, might never have been seen by me; for I still hesitated to take the first step into wild country, knowing that I knew nothing of its ways. However, by a happy chance, everything fell neatly into my lap of its own accord. One late May morning Mrs. Fletcher—who had been, instead of getting breakfast, dilating on the beauty of a Japanese quince—suddenly realized what time it was and rushed off to the Tulip Festival at Bellingham, leaving us, as usual, only half-fed. I had, the evening before, in a fit of energy such as this feckless farm had rarely seen, combed the barn loft for hens' nests and brought into the house a huge basket of eggs—eggs, it dawned on me later, of all ages and stages. Old Fletcher now boiled a pot full of these and set them on the table.

Scott put one in an egg cup and hit it a crack with a spoon, obtaining, from this simple action, results beyond his wildest expectations. There was a tiny but clearly audible report and the egg blew up in his face with a puff of greenish powder and a highly coloured, completely devastating smell.

He flung his spoon down on the table. "Mr. Fletcher," he said, "this is just one thing too many. It's been nothing but boiled eggs for a whole week back, and now it's boiled rotten eggs for a change. I'm through. I've had enough Japanese quinces and tulip festivals to last me a lifetime. I'm going where there are no tulips or quinces and where, thank God, they'll never grow. I'm quitting and Pat's quitting with me and we're going to the Peace River and that's that!"

"Boys, boys, boys ... " the old man began—but it was no use. We stayed with him for ten days longer while he hunted around for another two men. Then we departed, northwards, beyond the Rockies, shaking the dust of British Columbia from our feet—and over a score of years went by before I returned. Truly that was an egg of destiny.

☆ ☆ ☆ ☆

There came an evening of midsummer and the long three-day trail from Peace River town lay behind us. The wagon of a pioneer settler of the Battle was banging and clattering down the stony slope of the hills and Scott and I followed on foot, rhythmically swatting at the mosquitoes with willow branches; our axes and bedrolls were loaded on the wagon. The slope was easing off, and soon the little outfit rolled out from under the last of the trees; from here on there were no more stones and the wagon wheels turned softly and silently in the black dust of a prairie trail.

Ahead of us, to the north, stretched a lake of green, broken only by two trees and by the small homesteads of the Scandinavians. We moved on into this green lake of grass and oats and wheat, and the sunset light threw the long, distorted shadows of men and horses and tarped-up wagon far over its level surface. Our guide and host, perched high on the load and urging on his horses, was shouting back to us that no man had ever found a stone on this old lake bottom, that the black soil went down as much as ten and eleven feet ... And that was my first sight of the Little Prairie of Battle River.

Some six miles further on, and on the far side of Little Prairie, we came to a log house by a stream. There we unhitched and unloaded, and there we stayed while we rode and walked over the country that ran north towards the Battle, looking it over. It was a fine country that we saw, and to me, fresh from England, there was a fine feeling of spaciousness about it: now, thirty-odd years later, one can no longer ride over a country as good as that, picking today 320 acres[7] of open parkland, only to discard that tomorrow for some other 320 acres somewhere else, something entirely different: Land traversed by a beaver stream, it might be, and with spruce-ringed meadows of tall grass on it, harbouring perhaps a family of moose ... To my sorrow one thing quickly became clear: so good was this land here on the Battle that I could find no valid argument for going on to Fort Vermilion.

Scott picked for himself land by Bear Creek. My own fancy was a stretch of prairie and parkland with a small creek meandering through it just inside the northern boundary and, in the southern portion, a slight rise or eminence—you could hardly call it a hill. On that rise, I said, I would build my cabin and dig my well. What I did not say, not wishing to appear impractical, was that the view from this spot had an irresistible appeal for me. To the south and southwest I could see Little Prairie and the smoke curling up from the Scandinavian homesteads. Beyond that lay the low, blue line of the hills down which we had come from Peace River town. To the west there was nobody and nothing— only the line of the Peace River-Fort Vermilion trail about a couple of miles away, and then, far beyond that again, the outline of distant hills. Sometimes from the trail a cloud of sunlit dust would rise as wagons or perhaps a string of packhorses went by—but that was all. To the east again there was no settlement, only the bush and a dim line of far-off hills. Sometimes, at sunrise, banks of mist would hang some miles away in that direction, curiously beautiful and, as time went by, I found out that those silvery clouds marked the line of the Peace River itself, the old highway of the fur-traders, the river road to my mountains of the Yukon Divide. And to the north there was my own land; and then open parkland and fireweed prairie till you came to the Battle River. An empty land—and today it is the centre of a well-settled district in which a crop failure is almost unknown.

I borrowed a horse and rode in to Peace River. At the Land Office there I paid my five-dollar filing fee on my land, describing it by its position on the survey. Then I got together a miscellaneous load of tools, grub, nails and lumber, and somehow got that hauled out by wagon to the Battle, through bogholes and over beaver dams and on a trail that was practically non-existent. And then, in the summer heat with its mosquitoes and flying ants and thunderstorms, Scott and I began to build on the ridge a sixteen- by thirty-two-foot log cabin that would do for the two of us. And by the second half of August we were broke—and ahead of us lay winter. So we slung everything inside the cabin, boarded up the place and hit for Peace River, intending to go "outside," to the southern prairies, harvesting.

Fate, however, ordained otherwise. We reached town, and there, while drinking a much-needed pint of beer in Macnamara's Hotel, we fell into conversation with a stranger—a kind-hearted man who seemed anxious to stand us more beer—and then more and more. Our benefactor proved to be George Macrae, the owner of a nearby lumber camp. Macrae was short of men and, by the time Macnamara had lost patience and chucked us all out of his tavern, we simply hadn't the heart to see him stuck: in effect we were shanghaied, and that very evening found us on the train to Driftpile on Lesser Slave Lake.

Three months went by in Macrae's Camp: three months at good pay under rough conditions, and with grub that varied from terrible— which was terminated by the one-man rebellion of old Mr. Waggoner who danced in his heavy boots the full length of one of the long tables, kicking stews, cakes and pies to the four points of the compass—to excellent with the inauguration of an Australian, Harry Bettany, as cook.

We worked ten-hour days. Breakfast was at six-thirty and the whistle blew at seven. We knocked off at noon for dinner and then we carried right on through from a quarter to one till old Oscar pulled the whistle cord at a quarter to six. Supper was at six and we were ready for it.

After narrowly missing getting killed on two occasions through my own carelessness or ignorance, I woke up to the hazards of the place and kept my eyes open. Skilled men helped me in the ways of the bush with advice and instruction—indeed, I met with much kindness, and it was not long before I was asked to join the little circle that met every night in George Macrae's office. They said that it was time I was instructed in the rudiments of poker.

They did their best to teach me, but I have no head for cards and the things I did with them went beyond all reason. And furthermore, beginner's luck was with me. Micky Macrae reached over once, after I had bluffed them all out, and picked up my hand. "Fellows," he said, "it's hopeless. If we see him he's got four kings, and if we don't see him—well, hell, just take a look at this! Not a damn thing in his hand—just a backhouse flush! I'm through. Come along to the cook-shack and Harry here'll give us all some coffee."

Scott stayed on with the lumbering but I went back to my homestead on the Battle. There I spent the winter finishing off the cabin, cutting and pointing tamarack fence posts, learning a bit about the trapline and finding out how to make a winter camp in the bush. I went everywhere on foot—to the store on Big Prairie, to the little settlement at the Battle River crossing, to my friends the Swedes and Norwegians on Little

Prairie. If I needed anything special I would go to Peace River on foot, taking two and a half days over the trip and making stages of thirty, thirty and twenty miles. On the way in I would stay the first night at the Clear Hills Post, and the second at Steve Gjerstäd's farm in the Bear Lake country. On the way out I would load my purchases on to somebody's sleigh, paying in return the horses' feed bill. Happy days…

That winter was a cold one with temperatures down to fifty and sixty below zero. I travelled regardless of temperature, and on a certain cold evening I got benighted on the trail. I was in the twenty-five-mile stretch of howling wilderness that lay between Little Prairie and the trading post at the Clear Hills where I had meant to pass the night. Darkness had fallen, and the trail—which was drifted—faded into a uniform whiteness that was hard to see and too slow to travel. Away to the left, across a stretch of open snow, I could just make out the dark mass of a belt of spruce. I was fed up with blundering on in the dark, and the spruce began to look like home. I headed for them.

I had no axe and no tarpaulin, but I did have a hunting knife, and I was carrying a packsack that contained one light blanket and a book, a teapail and some raisins, bannock and cheese. I got a fire going and then, with the hunting knife, I soon made a bed and shelter of spruce boughs. The empty packsack I made into a small reflector at my back. To assemble a stack of heavy firewood I climbed up on to dead leaning muskeg spruce and swung on them till they collapsed, crashing into the snow. Then I dragged the dead trees up to the fire. Very soon I had the place all snug; the tea was made and I was stretched out on the spruce mat, warm and comfortable, reading by the firelight and downing a frugal supper. I was content: I had triumphed over my hostile surroundings; and the distant howling of coyotes—which, in my innocence, I thought were wolves—proclaimed that the Bank of England and the grey desert of stone, though less than a year away in time, were already things of another world.

So comfortable did I make myself that I slept too long and it was the dawn that woke me. Hastily I breakfasted and then hit the trail. I was swinging along at a tremendous pace, warm and carrying my fur hat and mitts in my hand, when, in the distance, I spotted a moving sleigh. Slowly it crawled towards me, pulling heavily in the dry, powder snow—and as it drew near I recognized the horses of a Norwegian friend, Andrew Clauson. Every hair on their hides was picked out in hoarfrost; their breath floated heavily behind them in the sunlight; long yellow icicles drooped downwards from their bits: it was evidently colder than I had thought. As for Andrew, all that was visible of him as he sat hunched on the driver's seat was his eyes and a small portion of his nose.

"By golly, Petersen," he called out, "wherever have you sprung from?"

"Those spruce, Andrew," I said, pointing.

"You mean, you spent the night there?" His tone was one of utter amazement.

"Yes, Andrew."

"I tell you, Petersen, you will surely freeze to death one of these days! Do you know how cold it was last night at the Clear Hills?" He was shouting now in his excitement.

"No, Andrew," I said. "Somewhere round about zero?"

"I am telling you it was *thirty-three below*," he bellowed, "and, by Yesus, you do not even notice it! And here you are, bareheaded and barehanded—you will kill yourself … "

But I never killed myself—neither in that camp nor in all the frozen camps that were to come. And, for that, once more to Rossall let me make my bow.

Even that winter came to an end, and the first crocus stuck its head up through the yellow grass and the wildfowl came back to the little creek by my northern boundary. Then spring, too, went on its way and flaming summer rode across the northern prairies of Alberta. And it was intimated to me that the correct thing to do was to give a housewarming dance in the cabin on the ridge.

Loup Garou

Midnight had come and gone and the short July twilight was already fading towards the dawn. Around the cabin was a disarray of wagons and democrats,[8] their poles on the ground, the teams that drew them hitched to the wheels and sleeping. Saddled horses were tied amongst the willows by the slough. Broken oat sheaves lay tumbled in the wagon boxes or littered on the ground by the trees.

Out on the prairie, from its stovepipe which was wired to a lone poplar tree, my cookstove belched forth sparks and a quivering tongue of flame: somebody had left the draught full on and the pipe was red-hot and glowing dangerously. A regiment of coffee pots was dancing a Highland fling on top of the stove and erupting in a cloud of steam. I went over and made things safe again, feeding more wood into the stove and rescuing the coffee.

The cabin was royally lit: lamps and candles shone and flickered and, from doors and windows, shafts of yellow light streamed out over the dark prairie. Inside I could see the dim figures moving in a haze of tobacco smoke, and from them came a din of voices and laughter—the fiesta was at its height. They were taking their partners for the last square dance before supper, and it was amazing how much giggling and shoving it always took to get that settled. Suddenly the scraping of the fiddles sounded, and the rhythmical beat of the fiddlers' feet on the floor. George Robertson from the Battle River Crossing was calling the square dances and I heard him ask: "Everybody set?" Cheers and shouts of "Lets go, George!" answered him, and he raised his voice and let fly with the opening call: "A-all jump up and they never come down!" A joyous whoop as the dancers leapt into the air, and a crash as they hit the floor again—and then: "Alaman right and the ladies go left, and a grand right and a left!" The dance whirled on through its maze of figures …

"And a-all swing out!" They swung like mad—girls with their feet off the floor, crowing with delight, firmly clasped. "Swing 'em around again, you did it so well the time before! Now swing your own, leave mine alone … "

A hand grabbed me and slung me into the arms of a beautiful half-breed girl—"Take her for God's sake, Pat, and let me get a drink. I can't keep this up any longer without one!"—and the dance became a whirl of faces, brown, plum-coloured and white; Cree, half-breed, Norwegian, Swede, Scottish, English, Canadian born …

"Alaman a bootjack!" the caller sang, "and a promenade a horse-back!" It would be a drink that I'd be needing, myself, if George didn't saw it off short pretty soon …

Supper was served to us as we sat on boxes and benches round the dance floor—and then the fiddlers struck into the Red River Jig. Three couples had taken the floor, but the one I was interested in was Baptiste Savoy and Louise Desrochers. They were neither of them light weights and they were dancing right on my cellar trap door. I watched it and them, fascinated. Baptiste was really going to town, prancing his damnedest, while Louise went to and fro before him in the quieter movements of the woman. Now and then the cellar door sagged a little under Baptiste's more frantic efforts, but still it held. I heard Andrew Clauson's voice at my ear: "Yesus, Petersen," he was saying, "you surely made a good solid yob of that trap door. Yust look at what it is holding up!"

The tune changed and a youth appeared at the north door with a broom over his shoulder. With a sudden movement he flung back a mop of raven hair; his dark eyes glittered; his Mongol features shone. A few stilted steps and jerky head movements—and then his soul went into his feet and he danced the broom dance like a man inspired. "Saka-pa-chow!"[9] they yelled at him. "Bravo! Bravo! Saka-pa-chow!" The tune changed again and he passed into the chicken dance, which is the courting dance of the prairie chicken; it seemed as though he had a dozen feet and each one flying a different way ...

The sun climbed over the world's northeastern edge. Soon its first glittering shaft struck through the trees where the horses stood. It was an unwelcome guest but George Robertson knew how to deal with it. "Shut that north door," he ordered. "And hang blankets over the windows. Keep those lamps going. Keep everything going. Now then—take your partners for a square dance and step lively; the night's still young!"

The sun was far above the tree tops when those who had helped me with the supper sorted out their plates and cups and packed them in their wagons. Then they helped me in with the stove and the heavier things. It was towards six when the last wagon rolled away down the slope to the north, with the last riders a little way in the lead. I watched them out of sight and then I walked away to catch my mare and water her.

The party was over. My house had been warmed for me by the whole of Battle River—and how! Now it even had a name: it would be known to them all as Patterson's Place. Almost it seemed that I was in danger of striking roots on this little ridge with its far horizons.

✩ ✩ ✩ ✩

Two eventful years slipped by; and then a May evening saw a party
of us from the Battle camped down by the Peace River at Brown's
Landing. The Peace flowed north at that point, confined between five-
hundred-foot banks that were densely wooded with spruce and poplar.
From shore to shore the river was well over half a mile wide; it swung
into sight from the south around a left-hand bend and swept past
our encampment to divide, a mile downstream, on an island thickly
forested with tall old spruce. Some distance below the island it faded
from view round a bend into the northeast. There were no riffles and
the brown, swirling flood moved without a sound.

We were waiting for the first boat of the season, the Hudson's
Bay Company's sternwheeler, *D. A. Thomas*, from Peace River town.
Sometime soon—we hoped—the *Thomas* would appear, thrashing
round the bend, waking the echoes with her whistle, bringing for
us a mixed load of mail and everything that an isolated settlement
might need. But you never knew for certain: she might come today or
it might be tomorrow, or she might even now be hopelessly stuck on a
sandbar somewhere upstream, waiting for a rise in the river. Anything
was possible. In the meantime, we waited with the quiet patience of
the north—Harry Murdoch, Bill Asmussen and myself, homesteaders
all three of us; the storekeeper from Big Prairie and four half-breeds.
Supper was over and the day was fading. Dusk was softening the
outlines of the valley and the fire leapt more vividly against the dark
background of the trees.

Time passed ... a light frost came down from the first glimmering
stars ... the small murmurings of spring were stilled.

Darkness fell—and suddenly a fearful wailing filled the valley. It
struck several of us as not having the same note as the whistle of the
Thomas, but two of the breeds, Jerome and Gaston Marie, furiously
disagreed with that and so we all went to the water's edge. But there
was no sign of anything on the river and soon the wailing began again.
Then we knew it was timber wolves on the far bank watching our
fire, and I, thinking of the old Canadian legend of the werewolf, said
carelessly: "Maybe the loup garou."

The breeds laughed, a shade too heartily, and Jerome hit for the fire and got very close to it, his eyes peering anxiously this way and that, into the bush. Precisely at that moment the pilot of the *Thomas*—which was still hidden from us by the upstream bend—pulled the whistle cord in the pilot house. A most blood-curdling howl echoed up and down the hills. The wolves went clean out of business and Jerome, certain that the loup garou had come for him at last, backed closer to the fire and singed his breeches. Gaston Marie, Boniface Weazelhouse and Napoleon Laboucanne, all fled for the safety of the firelight, falling over bedrolls and wagon poles in their panic and fear. That left the four of us on the bank: the storekeeper and I shaking with silent laughter, and Murdoch and Bill Asmussen trying to find out what it was that I had said to scare the breeds.

A beam of light shot out from round the bend. It flickered up and down the wooded hills, picking up its landmarks. The beam became stronger—and then the *Thomas* hove in sight. Holding the landing in the beam of the searchlight she churned towards us, a noble sight, engine throbbing, sternwheel lashing the water to foam, brightly lit and conveying the impression of a church surging down river. She swung and nosed gently upstream to the landing, sliding her scow on to the muddy shore. Deckhands leapt for the bank and snubbed her to the trees. Planks were run out and the work of unloading began.

It was after midnight when the *Thomas* splashed away down the Peace. The others went back and rolled into their blankets by the fire, but I waited to see the last of the boat. Her lights dwindled till they became one single glow; the thrash of the sternwheel and the beat of the engine faded. The bright finger of the searchlight still crawled along the shores and the captain, one could be certain, would still be talking to that red-headed beauty on the bridge ... And then the *Thomas* swung behind the island and vanished round the northern bend. She was on her way to Fort Vermilion.

I stayed by the river. The first paleness of the dawn was showing, and in that ghostly light every boil and every swirl on the surface of the Peace was plainly visible, hurrying silently on into the north, changing always but never stopping. The impression was one of permanence and power: this was a force that had existed before the time of man, even before the earth's crust wrinkled and upheaved the Rockies in the river's path: it would continue when men were gone and the Rockies were nothing but grains of sand carried hither and yon by its waters.

The homesteading years had been good ones—but did I want to stay and farm that land? Or was it not rather the adventure of finding and building up the place that had appealed to me? No—one farm in my life had been enough, and now the signposts pointed north: somebody else could work those acres on the ridge. There was nothing to keep me there—though I did have one tie, and that was the best little saddle mare in the country. She was a strawberry roan; she could do her sixty miles in a day without turning a hair, and once I had ridden her in one day from Peace River town to my place on the Battle, a distance of over eighty miles. "The Urchin" was about as tough as they made them and I would not be the first homesteader to prove up on a saddle horse—nor the last. Besides the cabin there was a barn on the homestead now, and the place was fenced and partly broken: in a little over a year's time I would win my bet with the government on the home quarter—a hundred and sixty acres to five dollars that I couldn't stay the course and get my title to the land. Well, that was almost done—and now, what next?

I looked again at the river, and in my mind's eye I saw the water flowing on—over Vermilion Chutes, down the Slave Rapids, through Great Slave Lake to the Mackenzie River. Into the Mackenzie from the west would come the Liard, the river of many names. From men who ventured further north to trap I had heard a few things about the mysterious Liard: I had sat up all one summer's night in a cabin on Big Prairie, drinking, together with Bob Henderson and Albert Gray, a home brew that was fit to poison a rattlesnake. And all night long the two of them had argued about the Liard: "Gold up there, Albert. All kinds of it. And springs of oil, and a tropical valley where there's never a fleck of snow comes and everything grows like hell. That's where I'm heading ... "

And then from Albert: "Don't touch it, Bob. You'll never come back. She's a bad river—rapids, they tell me, and whirlpools that'll draw you straight under. Better stick to trapping on the Fontas, Bob ...

Why, here's a queer thing—the glasses are all empty! We'd all better have another drink and try and forget about the Goddam Liard ... "

The oldest whiteman name for that far-off river was "the River of the Mountain." Somewhere in its upper reaches, far into the northwest, rose the unmapped ranges of the Mackenzie Mountains, where, they said, there were mountain sheep that were white the year round, winter and summer—if you could believe a yarn like that and if it was not just a traveller's tale. There, too, were the old, forgotten trails of the Klondikers that led to the heads of the Pelly. And all that one had to do to reach the Liard was to throw a canoe into the Peace and run downstream. Not, of course, that I knew anything about canoes, but that would come. I knew the essential thing—which was how to handle myself in the bush—and, as for cold weather, I could tough out the worst of that with anybody. In fact a legend arose (it was purely a legend) that the colder the weather got the more I enjoyed it. So firmly fixed was this belief that ten years later, riding into the mountains in November with my ranch foreman, Adolf Baumgart, I heard the forest ranger shout after us: "You're with a dangerous man, Adolf. Mind and don't let him freeze you to death!"

Curling wraiths of mist were rising from the Peace. They thickened and the river vanished in the pearl-grey magic of the dawn. I picked my way through crates and kegs and boxes, back to the ashes of the fire. There they lay, the seven sleepers, humped up, muttering and snoring, each with his dreams. I raked the embers together and laid a log on the fire. Then I rolled into my blankets with a mind at rest. This year I would finish with the prairie and prove up the homestead. Then I would follow the great rivers down into the north ... to the Liard ... to the nameless mountains of the sunset where the sheep were always white ...

A nightmare yell roused me for the last time. That was Jerome. The loup garou was after him again. It was gaining on him and he twitched and scuffled with his feet, whimpering like a puppy with bad dreams. Then he quietened down and silence fell again and the camp slept.

Venture to the North

Plans, in this imperfect world, have a habit of breaking down. But those that I made on that night of the werewolf fulfilled themselves so completely and so marvellously that even I, with my love of far places, could ask for nothing more.

It so happened that, about this time, the North American economy was warming up for the boom that preceded the crash of 1929 and the depression of the thirties. From the odd paper that reached me I could see that the prices of stocks and grain were rising. It seemed a pity not to be in on a good thing and so, on my annual trip to Edmonton or when I rode in to Peace River town, I began to do a little buying and selling. I did this without knowledge or discrimination—but that didn't matter a bit, everything I touched turned to gold. I watched this at first with goggle-eyed incredulity. Then I came to accept it as the natural order of things: after all I was in a new country and things were just going ahead and opening up as one would expect them to do in a new country—what of it? It never once dawned on me that this was one of those golden times when any fool could make money on the stockmarket—mainly because every other fool in the Americas was trying to do likewise.

The good time went on and I never got my fingers burned. With money one's horizon broadens, and I debated with myself whether to go, the winter of 1926-27, to Australia and work on a sheep station there, bringing back some Australian horses to the Battle, or whether to take a trip to England. On account of my mother I plumped for England—and it was when I was there that winter that I picked up Michael Mason's book *The Arctic Forests*.

I absorbed it, every word. This was exactly what I wanted. Mason had skirted on three sides the unknown country of the Mackenzie Mountains, and the stirring names of the northern rivers rose from his pages like the names of old battles—Pelly, Porcupine, Mackenzie, Liard. I got my tonsils carved out that winter and I took the book into hospital with me—there was one river mentioned there that came down to the Liard from the north, and I, captured as usual by the music of a name, wanted to know more about the South Nahanni.

But Mason knew nothing, he had never seen that river; and when the carver of tonsils bade me depart from his nursing home and said: "But I *strongly* advise you to do no heavy work on your Canadian farm, at least for several months," I, knowing that the work was all done and the homestead secure, replied to him: "No. As a matter of fact, I had rather thought of taking a canoe trip."

"Splendid!" he answered. "Gliding along, day after day, over the placid surface of one of your great rivers. The gentle splash of the paddle, the song of the wilderness in your ears. Peace—rest—the very thing! *How* I envy you!"

"Yes," I said weakly, trying in vain to imagine this London surgeon, in morning coat and sponge-bag trousers, busy around his campfire on some lonely shore.

☆ ☆ ☆ ☆

Spring came and I returned to Canada. And then, in June of the rains and the floodwaters, I threw my canoe into the Clearwater River at Waterways in Alberta, the end of steel. Denis France, English and known to me since childhood, was coming as far as Fort Simpson, he knew even less about rivers than I did and our combined knowledge of canoes had been gained on the little rivers of England—and yet we gave no thought to our lack of skill or to the hazards that might lie ahead but, with the full confidence of ignorance, carefully overloaded the canoe and shoved out into the river.

Down into the north we went, down the Athabasca River, hunted by the mosquitoes whenever we touched shore. Through the mazes of the delta we somehow found our way, and then we came out into the open sweep of Lake Athabasca. There a storm caught us—and only by sheer strength and fitness did we manage to paddle the canoe against the wind and into a sheltered cove on a rocky islet. There we made camp and there the storm held us for three days.

Then onwards—past Fort Chipewyan, past the mouth of the Peace, down the Slave to the Slave Rapids and the portage road into the Northwest Territories. Below the portage we loaded the canoe and outfit on to the scows of a mining company which had business in the north. Then through the endless days (for by now there was no darkness) we would lie flat out on the nose of the forward scow, listening to the rush of the water beneath us, watching the glittering, mile-wide river unfold its sunlit vistas into the pale blue distance. The same horizon retreated endlessly before us—the low forest of the distant shores, and the river moving without haste towards its end a thousand miles away in the Frozen Ocean.

We threaded a vaster delta and came in the evening light to Fort Resolution on Great Slave Lake. We slept through that calm evening when we should have been travelling, and the next day a storm caught us on that lake which is greater than many a sea. With half the crew seasick, the boat lurching dangerously and the scows pounding and threatening to break apart we made, in the nick of time, the safe harbour of Hay River. And from there, having learnt our lesson, we fled in the evening calm, travelling in the light of a blood-red midnight sunset, hurrying over a lake that lay still and silent as a sheet of glass until the furrows of our passing broke it into a sea of liquid fire.

Steering by small landmarks, we found the outlet where the Grande Rivière en Bas, the River of Disappointment, Mackenzie's River, flows clear and green out of its inland sea. There were those who cursed the monotony of these blazing days and this endless river. But I was not among them: to me this was the highway of romance. The pilot, old Pierre la Hache, pointed out the landmarks to me: that spot, he said, was Tête à la Ligne—and now we were in the Line itself, the confined, fast stretch of the upper Mackenzie ... And that was the Rabbitskin

Portaging the Muriel *at Fort Smith,* 1927

River—and there, far over by the northern shore, light on the water as floating leaves, were sprucebark canoes, each with an Indian in it, but so far away that all the naked eye could see at first glance was the flashing of the paddles. I watched them through the glass; sometimes an Indian would turn to look at us, but it was never his head that he turned: a flick of the paddle would bring the fragile canoe into line so that its occupant could see us and still be balanced and looking forward ...

Green Island passed by and old Pierre caught my arm and pointed. Twelve miles away down a wide reach of river a collection of white objects was dancing a lunatic fandango in the mirage. Sometimes these capering fantasies looked like grain elevators or tall, four-masted sailing ships, sometimes castles and palaces—but according to Pierre they were the whitewashed log buildings of the Hudson's Bay Company on the point of Fort Simpson Island. As we drew near they sobered down—but I had no longer any eyes for them, for the left bank had ended in Gros Gap and into the Mackenzie from the south there came a river.

This was no ordinary river: it was so big that it was a fit mate for the Mackenzie and it drove into the clear green of our own river, a yellow, rolling flood, carrying with it forest trees and all the debris of the far-off mountains. This was the West Branch, the Courant Fort, the Rivière aux Liards of the old voyageurs, the River of the Mountain. And its biggest tributary was the South Nahanni.

The green water and the yellow ran side by side without mixing. The boat and the scows passed from the green into the yellow and headed for Simpson Island. Others might be uncoiling ropes, making ready to jump ashore; I just stood there by Pierre la Hache, observing with awe the Liard flood, wondering what it was that I had run my head against this time and whether I could cope with it.

★ ★ ★ ★

One hundred and ten river miles up the Liard from Fort Simpson a mountain rises abruptly from the level plain. Seen from the east, from the Long Reach, the mountain appears to be rounded and bell-shaped; it forms the end of a range which runs like a wall away into the north, sinking gradually from view beneath the horizon. The name of the bell-shaped mountain is Nahanni Butte and there, in its shadow, is the mouth of the South Nahanni River.

There, too, in the shadow of the Butte, stood, in 1927, the Indian village and a couple of traders' cabins. These were the last of the habitations of men, for beyond them, in the Nahanni country, there was nothing—an old rotting cabin or two at the Hot Springs with the bush waiting to take back its own again, but nothing more—no white men, no Indians even. The Nahanni it seemed, was a river shunned. Men told strange tales of it ...

The trader was away from home on this evening of late July. But I was not alone in his cabin. I sat at supper there with Albert Faille, trapper, prospector and canoeman. We had met in the last few miles of the Liard; and now, ahead of us, lay this new river, the South Nahanni.

As we sat at table we pieced together the scraps of information we had gathered: it seemed there were canyons to be passed with dangerous water in them, and somewhere beyond there was a place that was known as Deadmen's Valley—a valley of the mountains where, a long time ago, a party of men had been found murdered, their skeletons tied to trees, their heads missing. Undoubtedly they had been murdered for the gold which they had found—gold which we, of course, expected to find, too. Who had murdered them? And was there really some wild tribe of Indians hidden away in these blank spaces of the map? A tribe that remained aloof and had no traffic with any trading post? One thing was certain: no man had ventured alone up this river for seven years. It might well be that Faille and I would provide, for the denizens of the Liard country, the answer to these interesting questions.

Nothing of this had been known to me when I read Mason's book in that London nursing home. Yet here was my good fortune—that of all the rivers in the north it should be the South Nahanni that had attracted my attention. And that was not all. Here was I, at the mouth of this dangerous river[10] and lacking the skill and experience to cope with it. True, the lower Liard lay behind me, but there luck had helped me—and luck in the end runs out. So, at this juncture, who should turn up but Faille—and there by the Butte we camped, stormbound, for a day and two nights during which time I bombarded this patient man with questions and learned from him the tricks by which a man may defeat the current of a river. By the time the sun broke through on the second morning and we loaded up and left the Butte, I knew at least how to arrange the balance of a canoe and how to track it. As for poling, without which one cannot ascend a mountain river, I had mastered that at Oxford, punting on summer Sundays upstream to Islip in search of beer and strawberries and cream. With the pole I could lay the nose of the canoe exactly where I wanted it—which proves, beyond any shadow of doubt, that a B.A. Oxon. is of value even on the South Nahanni.

Travelling independently of each other, Faille and I disappeared from human ken into the Nahanni country. Sometimes we met and camped together; more often we travelled and camped alone. Wonders awaited us on the way. We saw them and passed by: canyons whose walls towered four thousand feet above the river; the wild white sheep low down on the ledges, drinking by the water's edge; wild water where the canoe spun madly, caught in the whirlpools; bears and moose swimming; hot springs with a tropical growth around them and humming birds flashing like pinpoints of fire across the sulphurous pools; grey-green uplands, windswept and austere, carpeted with alpine flowers, and the ptarmigan moving quietly amongst the stones. Meeting on the Flat River and combining our forces, Faille and I took his big canoe up through the broken water and the low, red-walled canyons to the great Falls of the Nahanni—and I took the first photograph of them ever to reach the outside world.

But summer wore on and the little poplars of the river bars began to turn to gold. There came a day when I said goodbye to Faille at the Twisted Mountain and slipped away down the wonderful river. I passed the Indian village at the Butte in the silence of the morning mists; no man saw me go and I turned upstream on the Liard, poling and tracking my way for two hundred and fifty miles to Fort Nelson in northern British Columbia. And by the time I got there I was beginning to know something about rivers!

From Fort Nelson I made my way south with a light heart and with various adventure, on foot and with packhorses, over the two hundred miles of trail that led to the banks of the Peace. And from there a chance-met riverboat, the last of the season, ran me downstream the

Falls of the Nahanni, 1927

last two hundred and fifty miles, from Hudson's Hope to Peace River town ... That was the trip of trips. No poor beggarly millionaire could buy himself a time like that because such things are not for sale. They are in the gift of the gods; and if a man is lucky, then perhaps once in a lifetime—and once only ...

It was in this mood that I went in search of my friend, Gordon Matthews. Gordon had come to Canada from England after the Kaiser's war; the colour and romance of the north had called to him, and it was not long before he was driving a hand-picked team of huskies and managing a string of fur-trading posts between Norway House at the northern tip of Lake Winnipeg and the shores of Hudson's Bay. We had met by the purest chance at the Calgary Stampede—and now, I knew, Gordon was in Edmonton, a northerner exiled from the north and longing, at heart, to return to it. I told him the tale—and, as I had expected, he agreed that we would hit the trail together, northwards in the spring. I then took ship to England.

There was a girl in it. We had met a year or two previously—rather an unfortunate meeting in a way, for it took place at the opera at Covent Garden. I found myself, on that occasion, faced with *Tristan und Isolde*. In the second act the main trouble was a certain Kurvenal, a devoted but tedious retainer of Tristan's. This man was obviously worried about the non-arrival of a ship. In a blue and unnatural twilight he scanned the sea from the castle window. "Das Schiff," he sang, and then, alternatively, "Kein Schiff." And he went on and on about it for hours, thereby advancing his wounded master's cause not one inch—for obviously either the ship would come or else it wouldn't, and any normal man would have awaited the event with patience and made less noise about it. I lost interest and fell asleep— right beside this girl with the golden hair. The legend, of course, has it that I snored, but I hardly think we need put too much faith in that. And anyway, even if I did, our friendship survived this outrage. It grew and ripened.

So it was on a mission that I crossed the Atlantic. The mission was crowned with success; not, as might be imagined, in the hectic atmosphere of a hunt ball, but (and here is courage for you) in the frozen January woods, in cold blood, by a deserted swimming pool that was drained and empty except for a carpeting of dead leaves. Then I returned to Canada, and through the month of February Gordon and I got together the canoes and outfit and completed the training of the dog team on the ice of the North Saskatchewan River at Edmonton in Alberta.

Gordon and I built our cabin for the winter of 1928–29 in Deadmen's Valley, right in the heart of the Nahanni country. From it we trapped and hunted; to it we would return thankfully after days on the trail, nights of camping in the frozen bush. Sitting there in the evenings, downing by candlelight a supper of moose or blue grouse, we would recount to each other the small events of the day. After supper there would be marten or weasel to be skinned—and then I would be busy with the carpenter's square, carefully measuring the weasel which, in a politer world, are known as ermine. A hundred and twenty of the biggest and finest of them I set aside for Marigold. Into these, I thought as I did so, she will disappear almost completely, wrapped up like a queen in a mantle of white, adorned with black-tipped tails, faintly stained with pale gold. "This," I would say, "shall be my atonement for snoring at the opera. Though mind you, Gordon, I take no blame for it. Not in that twilight and with that Kurvenal fellow raving on about his canoe. I do think—"

"All right, old man, all right. No need to get worked up over it. You're quite safe here."

It was a happy place, that cabin. I came to that spot again, twenty-four years later. The cabin was gone; burnt—perhaps by the Indians. It was hard even to see where it had been: there was just a faint hollow in the moss with sizable spruce already growing in it. The only thing that remained was the stout lid of our four-ringed, collapsible cookstove. Rusty souvenir of many a good meal, it lay there in the moss, speaking to me alone of days that were long since gone by.

✫ ✫ ✫ ✫

Among the many good things that the Nahanni River brought me I would include the performance of a stock that we might call Trans-Canada Copper. Before taking off the second time into the wilderness

I was strongly advised to buy all I could of this stock. The advice was from a good source and I took it, sweeping up everything I possessed for that purpose and departing for the north with a good outfit, all paid for, and eighteen dollars in my pocket to last me the next fifteen months. All the eggs were in one basket this time—and just to make the venture more interesting Marigold and I had arranged to be married the following year. It was essential that T-C.C. should do its stuff.

In May of 1929 Gordon and I came down from Deadmen's Valley to Fort Simpson on the Mackenzie. I found an old newspaper there that had come in with the Christmas mail—and to my horror, while everything else had gone up, T-C.C. was standing almost exactly where I had left it over a year ago—somewhere around $41. This was frightful, and for the next three weeks, while waiting for the Mackenzie ice to break, I nearly went raving mad whenever I thought of the mess I was in. In the meantime we got a very good price for our fur.

It was not till I got to Edmonton that I found out what had happened. By that time T-C.C. was standing at $43 (a peak which it never reached again) and, it now transpired, the shares had been split the preceding summer, three for one. Dazed, but already on the road to recovery, Patterson of the Golden Touch rushed frenziedly to his brokers and sold the lot—and fortunately rested there, having tripled the original

Buckspring, near Cochrane, 1929

capital and had the fright of a lifetime. Marigold and I got married on
the winnings and had a honeymoon that began in London, transferred
itself to the north of Scotland and ended at Jasper Park, Alberta ...

Everything that one does on the way through life leaves its mark.
During the Nahanni years I had lived in a splendid mountain country
and had the free run of thousands of square and very empty miles.
That sort of thing gives one a liking for elbow room, and it also makes
one intolerant of authority and the restrictions that are imposed by the
presence of men.

And now, here I was back in Canada with two incompatible
possessions—a brand new wife, and a love of wandering and the
wilderness. This was indeed a problem. Narrowing things down, I sold
the homestead. Mistakenly, I now think, I ruled out the Northwest
Territories. That left one bit of country that I knew and thoroughly
approved of—the foothills and mountains of southwestern Alberta.
There, I thought, I could have the best of both worlds; there I could eat
my cake and have it.

We bought a place in the foothills, in the Bow Valley, and I embarked
on a sheep venture. That was short, though by no means sweet; the
sheep hit the catastrophic fall in prices that came with the early thirties
and I just unloaded them by the skin of my teeth and at some loss. That
left me at a loose end for a time, and Marigold and I began to make our
first ventures into the mountains with packhorses. We came sometimes
to the Buffalo Head Ranch in the valley of the Highwood River, and
many happy days were spent there by us as guests of the owner, George
Pocaterra, with whom we became friends.

Our few horses soon became as much at home on the Buffalo
Head as they were at Buckspring on the Bow River. Then, on several
occasions, it happened that I went with Pocaterra into the mountains,
hunting. And so it came about that I first set eyes on the deep valleys
of the East Kootenay, and on the blue peaks, the furrowed glaciers,
the golden autumn meadows of the high Rockies. It was to this that
the winding trail of my life had brought me—the trail that started, I
suppose, with my first sight of the Wicklow Hills, and which now had
led me to this autumn camp with Pocaterra and Adolf in the valley of
the South Fork.

PART TWO

The Rocky Mountains

3

The Old Days

To the Heart of the Mountains

Always a light sleeper in camp and therefore a nuisance to those who travel with me, I sat up in my eiderdown and considered the frozen darkness surrounding the valley of the South Fork. One could just see the outline of the mountain against the stars—that was all. I reached out of bed and poked the fire with a stick. A few embers still glowed; I raked them together and threw on some dead pine needles and then some twigs. There was a sudden crackle of flame, and Adolf sat up as if impelled by some hidden spring. He blinked at the fire for a minute; then he dressed and disappeared without a word into the darkness to see to the horses. Wriggling around, still in my eiderdown, I drew the logs of last night's fire together; soon there was a blaze and I stood the teapail, which was frozen, in the heat to thaw out a bit. And when these various things were done I rolled out of bed and dressed by the fire.

Soon the tea water was boiling and porridge was made. I got out some eggs and then set to work slicing bacon. Adolf came back and sat by the fire. Between us we upset some plates or something and Pocaterra's voice came from a humped-up sleeping bag, wanting to know what the devil we thought we were doing, getting up in the middle of the night like this. But the smell of coffee simmering and the sizzling of a frying pan fetched him out, still muttering things about midnight and so forth, but becoming more human every minute.

I offered Pocaterra some porridge—just to see what would happen—but, as usual, he pushed it from him, turning away his head with a gesture of disgust. "No, no, Patterson! You know I *loathe* the beastly stuff!"

I knew, perfectly well; he couldn't bear the sight of it. So now, in the darkness, under Mount Head, Adolf and I cleaned up the porridge while Pocaterra fried the bacon and eggs. Then, breakfast over, we packed up camp, saddled and packed the horses in the first feeble light of day and rode on towards the Grass Pass.

For Pocaterra this trip was, in a sense, a pilgrimage. As a very young man he had hunted with the Stoney Indians in the country to which we were going; and while it might now be known to a few as the West Fork of the Elk, to Pocaterra it was still the hidden valley, the valley of youth. He called it always by its Stoney name, Nyahé-ya-'nibi, the "Go-up-into-the-mountains-country"; and I can see now the name translated, in an article that he wrote for the *Italian Alpine Club Journal*, as "Il paese nel cuor delle montagne"—"The country in the heart of the mountains." No better name could be found for that great, silent meadow, six thousand feet above the sea, ringed around by glaciers and by mountains that rose to 11,000 feet, shut off from the world by passes that were no better than goat trails, by drowning rivers, a wild torrent and a tangle of huge, fallen trees ...

I had formed a picture in my mind of this valley and I pondered it as we rode, at an easy pace and mostly in silence, up to the Highwood River. The forest ranger station was deserted, which was all to the good as we did not wish to advertise our going, and we rode all that day without meeting a soul. We followed the Highwood until it forked into Storm and Misty Creeks and there we made camp below the first spurs of the Misty Range.

At noon the next day we crossed the Highwood Pass, dropping on to the head of Pocaterra Creek, which was the south fork of the Kananaskis River. There we turned our horses loose to graze and made our noonday fire.

What we planned to do now was to pass unseen through the Kananaskis country by taking an old and almost abandoned Indian trail to the Elk Pass—a trail that was forgotten except by the Stoney Indians, and by Pocaterra who had travelled and hunted with them. This would take us over the Divide into British Columbia; and the first rain would wash out our tracks on this stony ground, leaving no trace of our going.

Rex and Mollie in Misty Basin

The others saw to the fire and I went a little distance away to get a picture of the outfit and the valley. In a day or two's time it would be October. Of all seasons in the mountains this was the loveliest: bronze-coloured slopes of short grass and dwarf willow, slashed by the dark green of spruce and fir; larches at timberline spearheading the dark evergreens with points of shining gold. Away in the distance two mountains barred the view: they would be Mount George and Mount Paul, so named after George Pocaterra and his blood brother, Paul Amos, the Stoney, the old hunter. Between these blue-grey limestone peaks ran a gentler, more rounded ridge of sandstone and coal—the grazing ground of the Bighorn sheep.

In the foreground were the scattered horses and, closer still, the two men busy around the fire from which a blue wisp of smoke was drifting up the valley towards the pass. All seemed peaceful and serene—until I saw the horseman approaching.

Pocaterra had seen him, too, and his very attitude expressed acute annoyance that this man had come blundering into his plans. Now, he was thinking, we should have to ride all the way down to the ranger station on the main trail, and from there double back to the Elk Pass. Catch him showing old Indian trails to any stranger ...

The rider proved to be McKenzie, an Australian, recently appointed forest ranger of the Kananaskis country—and he very decidedly got off on the wrong foot with Pocaterra. Instead of dismounting and passing the time of day in the manner of the hills, he sat on his horse and opened fire far too abruptly. "Are you the guide of this party?" he asked.

Pocaterra stared at him with all the anger of an old-timer who is questioned by a newcomer. "Guide?" he said. "I don't know about that, but I am George Pocaterra. Those are my coal claims down there— that ridge between the two mountains—and this creek was named after me by the survey. And this is a private party." And, with that, he took a savage bite out of a ham sandwich, thus rendering himself speechless for a while ...

Down went lunch in record time, followed by mugs of steaming tea. Then the horses were brought in. Things were slapped together and tied on to the saddles; rifles were replaced in their scabbards, from which they were always removed during a long halt lest the horses should roll on them. At this point McKenzie remarked that he would ride with us as far as the ranger station—whereat Pocaterra, in a gust of fury, leapt on his horse and set off at a lope across the open meadows of the pass. The outfit followed him down into the green timber. The trail worsened and we crashed and slid at a fast, racketing trot down the screes and the rockslides, over the debris of avalanches. In this fashion we dropped a thousand feet to the junction with the Elbow River trail; from there on the trail improved but the pace increased. I rarely saw Pocaterra owing to the winding of the trail. After him came two packhorses, then Adolf, then one packhorse, myself and McKenzie.

On a straight stretch of trail through green timber, I saw Adolf
hurriedly whipping his lines round the saddle horn. I wondered why—
when, suddenly, he leaned out from his saddle and made a terrific swipe
at a spruce branch with a willow switch that he held in his right hand.
A puff of feathers flew and a fluttering bird appeared. Adolf swung still
further out from his saddle, and caught the "fool hen" with his left hand
before it could fall to the ground. In one easy, gliding motion he swung
back into the saddle, wrung the bird's neck and stuffed it inside his
jacket. Then he picked up his lines again and pursued his packhorses.
All this was done without the slightest hesitation at this fast, raking
trot of Pocaterra's that could keep pace with the average man's lope
or canter.

A few feathers floated on the air. I rode through them and turned in
my saddle to see if McKenzie had observed anything—but he was only
then coming into sight round the last bend. "Does he always travel at
this rate?" he shouted.

"Always," I called to him—and I fetched the packhorse ahead of me
a crack with my lines ...

McKenzie had had enough by the time we reached the Kananaskis
Lakes ranger station. A brief farewell—and then we rode away south-
wards, across the meadows and into the timber, climbing steadily
upwards, headed for the Continental Divide. The pace slackened as
Pocaterra's equanimity became restored—though still, from time to
time, some blistering comment on greenhorn forest rangers would
come floating back to us from the head of the pack train. And then, as
the sun touched with its dying fire the wall of the Elk Mountains, we
crossed the flat meadows of the Elk Pass and came to the brink of a new
valley—almost of a new world, for now the water drained to the Pacific.

Pocaterra checked his horse and sat there looking down the blue,
shadowy valley of the Elk. It faded away out of sight into the dim haze
of the evening, and there was a feeling of mystery to it that cannot be
caught and set down in words.

The sight of it moved Pocaterra to speech. "It is beautiful, is it not?"
he said. "There is a softness to it that Alberta does not have; it is almost
as if one could feel the breath of the Pacific. There is something about
this that draws a man—or is it just that I hunted and was happy here

when I was young?" We rode on in silence down into the trees and down the rough, steep trail that led to the Elk Lakes. Halfway down we stopped at a narrow place between great rocks and plugged the gap with fallen timber. This would serve as a drift fence in case the horses strayed back on the homeward trail during the night. Towards the end of the job there was only room for one man to work so I mounted and rode on, leaving Adolf to it.

Pocaterra had already gone on with the packhorses. From far down below his voice floated up to me on the stillness of the evening ... but this time it was raised in song.

Nyahé-ya-'nibi

As we sat around the fire that night Pocaterra remarked that we were a bit behindhand in our programme. "There should have been trout for supper tonight," he said, "but owing to our running into that ranger we arrived here too late in the day. However, I'll get up early in the morning and we'll have all the trout we can eat for breakfast." He went on to outline the trip, planning for the number of days we had to spend and, amongst other things, I noticed that we would shoot a goat on the third day from now, in the morning.

This was so unusually precise that I couldn't help asking him if he had the fish and game of this country in his pocket that he could promise all these things.

"You will see, Patterson—you will see!"

In the morning, as I was lighting the fire, I heard the thud of hoofs on the frozen ground and in came Pocaterra leading his saddle horse. On went blanket and saddle and then he came over to the fire to warm the bit of his bridle. "Good morning, Patterson," he said. "I am going to get the trout I promised you and it will take me about an hour—perhaps less. You and Adolf go ahead. Have your coffee and eat that frightful mess that you call porridge—and have plenty of bacon cut." And he rode away just as the even line of the Elk Mountains was becoming visible against the dawn.

Adolf and I proceeded with breakfast in leisurely fashion, speculating more in hope than in certainty on the arrival of trout. But in about an hour a song was heard in the distance. It came nearer; it resolved itself into "The Road to the Isles" and the singer's voice was triumphant. "By God's truth, he's got them," I said. "Rake out some coals and I'll put the big frying pan on ... "

We spent that day making a circuit of the Upper Elk Lake on foot—a trip which involved some difficult scrambling on mountainsides which in places plunged down sheer into deep, icy water. The day was grey and a haze of forest-fire smoke had crept into the country on a north wind. At the head of the flats the glaciers towered above us in a vast semicircle. They were shadowy and indistinct; they seemed almost to overhang—but we were not interested in them nearly so much as in the long files of goat that we could see moving high up under the rimrock, on their well-trodden trails. Truly this was a country of game, for the sand bars at the head of the lake were covered with tracks. Black bear, grizzly, goat, elk and moose—all were there. So, too, were the fish when we came in the evening, at the appointed time, to the fishing place, and in camp that night there was feasting.

It was at this camp that I made an annoying discovery. Coming from Alberta, but carrying prospectors' licenses for British Columbia, we had thought that we were entitled to shoot game in the sister province, and were accordingly travelling light. Poring over the B.C. game regulations by the light of the fire, I now discovered that this provision for prospectors did not apply to the southern part of the province: in other words the shooting of game, and even the possession of rifles, was illegal. We were, in effect, outlaws in a strange land. This, we agreed, was unfortunate; however, we had gone too far to turn back. We would go on: the odds were that we would meet nobody.

By noon the next day we were away down the valley. We had come to the ford by which the trail to Nyahé-ya-'nibi crossed the Elk, and there, in some meadows on the main trail, we stopped to let the horses graze. The next four or five miles into the big meadow were all in the tall timber; there would be no more horse feed and the trail would probably be so badly fallen-in that it would take us the rest of the day to get over it.

Each man picked up a packhorse by its lead rope and we rode towards the river. To avoid making tracks we crossed, not by the ford, but well away from the trail which, itself, was faint and barely visible.

This was not at all easy to do owing to the close growth of trees, but somehow we wallowed across in deep water and somehow clawed our way up the far bank. Then Pocaterra rode back into the river with an improvised broom of spruce with which he did his best to wipe out the tracks, backing his horse in the water as he did so. But as we rode away into the timber, I looked back. We had made a gallant effort to cover our tracks but I feared it was a vain one, for if any British Columbian, nosing around, ever got a proper sight of that far bank where six horses had cascaded into the river, we would indeed be lost men: it looked as if Hannibal had passed that way with all his elephants.

All that afternoon we fought our way towards Nyahé-ya-'nibi through the giant trees. The trail skirted the mountain slope; then it dipped and swung into the west. Soon the roar of a torrent floated up to us from below, and we found ourselves in a wild gorge, heavily forested with magnificent spruce. Some of these enormous trees must have been up to one hundred and sixty feet in height, and many of them had fallen. They were too large for the Indians to cut, and the trail twisted and turned to avoid them, so much so that the head and the tail of the outfit were frequently in a position to reach over and shake hands from opposite sides of some huge log. However, by winding around, and by jumping everything we could possibly get over, we only had to cut in a couple of places. I was riding a horse of Pocaterra's, Socks, that jumped beautifully—but a little black packhorse of mine, Brainless, was too small for this sort of thing. A number of times he tried to leap some big log, only to land with his belly on it and all his four legs off the ground. Then, if he couldn't kick and struggle himself over, we would come to his help and somehow shove and haul him across his tree and down to earth again. But it was Brainless who proved to be the best at finding a way round the various obstacles—so much so that we wondered if he hadn't been named in too great a hurry. No man or horse was hurt in this dangerous passage and towards evening the trees became smaller and thinned out, and we rode down a gentle slope into the meadow of Nyahé-ya-'nibi.

The evening was grey and cold and still, with a threat of snow in it. Nothing was stirring and there was no sound—not even from the stream, which here wound swiftly and quite silently through the level flats of this old lake basin. It was as if the stillness of death lay on the place. The mist crept along the walls of the valley like grey, formless, frozen ghosts, and the mountains were hidden from us by a low canopy of leaden cloud.

No one had camped in this spot for many years. There was a place on the knoll on which we off-saddled where a fire had been made—but the sign was old: grass and the dry seed heads of dead flowers were poking through the ashes; moss covered the blackness of the charred logs. A set of tepee poles were piled against a nearby rock but it was long since the

Pocaterra, Patterson and Adolf

poles had been used and they were all old and rotten. So much the better: the valley, it seemed, was little travelled. We unpacked and unsaddled the horses quickly and quietly; what we needed now was the snug warmth of a firelit tepee; this deathly hush seemed weird and uncanny after the windswept uplands of Alberta, and we spoke in low voices.

Not wishing to disturb the wild creatures of Nyahé-ya-'nibi we put no large bells on the horses; we simply turned them loose with two of them trailing their picket ropes and belled with small but clear-sounding bells—a sheep bell and a little silver Mexican bell. These

two horses would be picketed later on, but now we pushed the bunch upstream. Then each man set about his own jobs: Pocaterra went off to cut new tepee poles; Adolf disappeared into the bush to cut firewood, and I coiled the pack ropes and the cinches, stacked and covered the saddles and saw to the outfit.

The tinkling of the bells faded away up the valley. From the bush came the sharp click of axes and out of the east came a thin, cold breeze. It rustled the yellow grass and the dead willow leaves—and a fleck of snow came eddying down. And then another ...

Fluttering down from heaven, along with the snowflakes, came a bright idea. Casting around for a convenient empty space it made a beeline for my head and found a ready welcome there. It was this: a tepee, when erected, is entered by a low, triangular doorway. Carrying a camp outfit through this low entrance is a bit of a chore—in fact, the best way to handle the stuff is for a man outside to pass it through to somebody waiting inside who then stacks it where it is needed. Owing to the lack of sound poles our tepee was not yet even in sight and this snow was getting heavier. It would be foolish to make two jobs out of stacking and covering the outfit where one would do; I would pile the stuff exactly where Pocaterra wanted to put the tepee and cover it there with the pack covers. Then we could set the poles up around the outfit and spread the canvas over the poles—and there would be the tepee erected with everything already inside it, and dry ground instead of wet on which to light our fire and sleep. Excellent—and so I went ahead and did that, being careful to draw the pile well in so as to leave lots of room for the poles.

Pocaterra came out of the bush with a load of tepee poles, singing. He was so happy at returning to this valley after the lapse of so many years that it did one good to hear him. But this happiness was fleeting: the song broke off short and he said, in a tone of dismay, "My God, Patterson, you've stacked all the stuff just where we decided to put the tepee!"

"I know. But you'll find I've left plenty of room to set the poles up around the outfit."

It occurred to me later that he probably hadn't caught what I said, for we were speaking very quietly: we had not yet got used to the silence of the place. I didn't think of that at the time and, when Pocaterra said in reply, "But all that stuff is right in my way. We'll have to move every bit of it," I began to feel annoyed. However, I made one more effort: I said, "I think you'll find it's all right. We can set up the poles and —"

"But damn it, we can't stand here arguing all night. I want to get that tepee up before this snow gets heavy."

"You mean you don't want that stuff there? You want it shifted?"

"That's exactly what I've been trying to tell you for the last five minutes."

"Of course you have," I said. "Well, there's nothing easier." With that I whipped the tarpaulins off the pile. Right on top, in the place of honour, was Pocaterra's bedroll. I picked that up and sent it flying into the wild, wet willows. I got both hands to work: away sailed a pannier from my right hand—and another from my left ...

Pocaterra dropped the tepee poles with a crash. He picked up my bedroll and it took wings and flew. Between us, in less than ten seconds, we had that tepee site completely free of all encumbrances ...

Just as the last bundle was taking off Adolf appeared, all smiles, carrying a load of dry wood cut into tepee lengths. He stared for a moment or two in utter bewilderment at the two energetic lunatics who were making the outfit fly so briskly through the air. The smiles vanished, the wood fell clattering from his hands. In his travels he had seen much that was new and strange. And now this—what could this portend? One thing was certain—it was not the way they did things back in East Prussia. It would probably be best to keep out of it—and he turned on his heel and hit for the safety of the bush.

Pocaterra and I took our axes and followed him, and for a while a furious cutting was heard. I was kicking myself. Here was this man, my friend, back after almost thirty years in a valley that his youth had made sacred to him—and what did I have to go and do? Invent a bright new way of making camp and then lose my temper because it was not instantly understood. Fool! Idiot! Probably I had wrecked the trip. Even then I knew exactly how Pocaterra was feeling. Years later I was to experience the same sort of thing myself when, in a far-off valley to which I had returned after the passing of twenty years, I had to sit where once there had been nothing but laughter and listen to a silly wrangling quarrel.

Meditating, I walked back to camp with a load of wood. I found Pocaterra struggling with the first three poles of the tepee frame—the tripod. I went over and helped him. Without a word we laid on the remaining poles, completing the circle. With a long pole the canvas was hoisted into place; we whipped it round the frame of poles, fastening it down the front with pegs of peeled willow. Then we pushed two long, light poles into the slots at the tips of the two canvas wings which formed the smoke cowl; this was then adjusted to the direction of the wind. At this point Adolf appeared with more wood. "I can no longer hear the horses," he said. "I am worried about the two who are trailing ropes ... " And he vanished into the gloom, heading up the valley.

In silence we pegged down the bottom of the tepee canvas. Then we rounded up the outfit from the four points of the compass and I handed each piece through the tepee door, *in the orthodox manner*, to Pocaterra who arranged them inside. We cut spruce boughs for three beds and laid them in place; a fire was started and candles lighted; we laid out things for supper. Outside the wind was rising and a fine snow was driving in from the east.

Pocaterra went to the door and looked out. Snow whirled out of the darkness into the shaft of light thrown by the fire; it danced there for a moment and then was gone. You could see nothing and the only sound was that of the wind. Pocaterra spoke: "I am worried about Adolf," he said. "Those horses can go for miles in that direction and this creek is so silent and winding. A man can easily get into a mess in this darkness ... "

So it was peace ... We listened there together for what seemed hours ... A faint shout came to us—and then another, closer. Shadowy forms of horses appeared, and then Adolf riding one of the belled horses bareback; he had fixed up a rough hackamore bridle out of the picket rope. We grabbed several horses, including Brainless who had led the bunch up the valley, and picketed them. Then we piled into the tepee for supper and shut the door on the darkness and the driving snow.

The Indian knew what he was about when he invented the tepee. You only carry one piece of canvas and yet, from it, you get the comfort of a tent together with the warmth and cheer of an open fire—and, somehow or other, the glow of the embers and the flicker of the flames do more to promote good fellowship than does the soulless heat of the camp stove, however blessed that may seem in moments of stress.

On this occasion the fire received a helping hand. Into a simmering pot of coffee I poured the contents of a half bottle of brandy that I had brought with me. It was all we had, but now seemed the time to use it. More wood was piled on the fire and we lay around it, relaxed and warm. The coffee royals worked their magic: tongues were loosened and tales were told. And then Pocaterra was moved to song. He sang us a song in Stoney—and then one in German that he had learnt at the University of Berne. "The Road to the Isles" was followed by a selection from Italian opera. I cannot recollect anything in French, but I do remember very clearly (and it is the last thing that I can recall for, by that time, I was rolled up in my eiderdown and my eyes were closing) a voice that was lifted in Spanish. It began:

"Yo tengo un buen ranchito,
Más asombrado de flores ... "

Goat in the Sky

The mists were parting and the sunrise was breaking through. The flats were still in deep shadow but the sun's rays were striking the cliffs of a low mountain that seemed to surge forward into the meadows as a ship ploughs through the waters of the sea. We came to call this low mountain The Warship; it was really an 8,000-foot spur of Mount Abruzzi which could be seen in the background, emerging from the clouds. These mountains were named, though not accurately mapped, about 1915 in the course of the Alberta-British Columbia boundary survey. Our valley was walled in by Mount Aosta, the three giant peaks of Mount Cadorna, the Abruzzi massif and a nameless range to the northeast. The stream that flowed so quietly through the meadows from Cadorna Lake—the wild torrent of yesterday's trail—was known to the Stoney hunters as Nyahé-ya-'nibi Waptán. On the map it is Cadorna Creek.

Breakfast was over and done with. Pocaterra was mending his saddle by the fire. I took the glass and a tarpaulin and strolled out. There was about an inch of snow over everything but it would soon be gone. I shook the snow off the saddle pile and sat down with my back to it to see what I could see. This was the morning appointed by Pocaterra for the shooting of the goat, but Adolf and I had had sense enough not to bring that up at breakfast time—it is unwise to be too witty in the hour before the dawn.

I focussed the Zeiss and swept it along the cliffs of The Warship. The wind had swung into the west and the snow had already melted up there. This enabled me to spot a creamy white object that seemed to be different from the surrounding rocks. I watched it for a few seconds. It moved slightly.

"Pocaterra."

"Yes?"

"There's a goat about a mile and a half away."

"That is the one we will be shooting. You remember, it was planned for this morning? Tell Adolf to get the saddle horses and keep the goat in view. I'll be out as soon as I've finished mending this saddle of mine ... "

What a man! This goat, of course, was the one that had been foretold three days ago at the Elk Lakes and his number was up now, poor fellow, whatever he did. It was written in the book of fate ... Pocaterra came out of the tepee. He took the glass—and in about ten seconds his plan of campaign was formed: "You will shoot the goat, Patterson. We will ride straight across the flats towards that mountain. That will not worry the goat; he will feel secure up there. When we are out of his sight we will tie the horses in the trees. Then you and I can climb up that rock slide—that will take us quickly and easily above timberline. Then we swing to the left under the rimrock, round the prow of The Warship, and come upon the goat at short range—and he is ours! Adolf can go up the valley of that side stream that comes in below the goat and then climb up through the timber. If you wound him he will go that way and Adolf will get him ... "

Things went with machine-like precision. Adolf disappeared up the side valley and Pocaterra and I climbed up the slide, taking our time. Above the trees we turned to the left, across the scree at the foot of the cliffs, round the point of the mountain and into the wind. Then, moving with infinite caution so as not to dislodge the loose rock, we worked up to a great square boulder the size of a small cabin. There we rested for a minute. Then I crawled up and stuck my head around the top end of the boulder—and there, level with us and not more than sixty yards away, stood the goat. He was looking down the mountainside into Adolf's valley. Cautiously I withdrew my head and nodded to Pocaterra who said in a low voice—and here you must remember that the wind was blowing quite strongly from the goat to us—"How far?"

I told him.

"Then shoot."

"I can't. This rock overhangs—and anyway I'm just balanced here. If I move I'll start half the mountain rolling."

"Then come down and shoot from below."

"For the same reason, I can't. It was all right coming up here but if I move down and around you I'll start half a ton of this loose stuff sliding and we'll lose him. You shoot."

"No—I want you to get him. You have never shot a goat."

"Don't worry about that—I've shot plenty of moose. Now, go ahead and shoot him."

"Very well, if you insist."

For Pocaterra it was not easy. It was a case of either shooting very awkwardly round the rock, or sliding down into the open and shooting quickly as the goat moved off. He chose the latter course: he slid in a clatter of falling rock with his rifle at the ready.

He checked himself skilfully and I watched him crouching there on the scree, tense and alert. But no shot came, and he turned to me: "I see no goat, Patterson."

Then it must have moved away while we talked. Perhaps it had seen Adolf. Throwing caution to the wind I gave a terrific heave and pulled myself up round the top side of the big rock. Down went a small rock avalanche which Pocaterra avoided with a leap, and we both moved forward. The scree was bare and open; there was no possible hiding place on that stony slope—and there was no goat. Puzzled, I looked upwards and there, moving along a ledge of the sunlit precipice that towered above us, was the goat. As I raised my rifle he disappeared.

Pocaterra came up to me. I pointed and we stood there in silence, watching. Suddenly the goat reappeared, to the left and higher up this time, heading in the opposite direction. As he came into view he stopped for a fraction of a second and looked down at us. Both rifles came up as if jerked by hidden springs, but before they touched our shoulders the goat had vanished again. He must have been climbing on a series of zigzag ledges or galleries that were mostly deep but occasionally narrow enough to throw him into view. As we saw it from below, the precipice ran sheer up into the blue of the sky without a visible foothold.

There we stood on that vast slope of broken stone, two tiny marionettes jerking rifles up and down but never shooting, while the goat climbed higher and higher. Occasionally he looked at us over some rocky ledge with a contempt that must have been as profound as it was irritating ...

Suddenly, from down below, there came the crack of a rifle shot. We had forgotten all about Adolf. What could he have run into? A grizzly? We looked, but there was nothing to be seen—only the deep, forested valley. I looked up again—and I grabbed Pocaterra by the arm and pointed.

High in the air, turning over and over as he fell, came the goat. For a fraction of time he seemed to hang there, creamy white and sunlit against the deep blue of the sky. Then he passed right over our heads, so close that we could hear the hiss of the air through his long wool; he struck the steep slope of the scree behind us and crashed and rolled down-hill, coming to rest hundreds of feet below in a straggling thicket of mountain ash ... Even as we looked a small figure appeared, climbing slowly upwards from the edge of the trees. That was Adolf. Seeing the way things were going he had placed himself below us and, being able to see the goat when we could not, he had made this magnificent shot directly over our heads.

This was the morning of the third day from the Elk Lakes where the mantle of the prophets had fallen upon Pocaterra. And yet he betrayed no elation. Indeed, rather the contrary, for, brandishing his rifle in the air, he bounded off down the dangerous slope with the agility of a chamois, crying out on a note of anguish: "Adolf has got our goat! Adolf has got our goat!"

I followed more cautiously. As I drew near to the kill and to the two men who were bending over it, the scarlet of the mountain ash berries

Adolf: active, capable and a good shot

caught the low October sun. The heavy clusters hung over the white goat, blending there with other scarlet. They flamed out against the blue-green forest of the valley, striking, in that quiet northern scene, a note of savagery that, even now, in retrospect, sounds as keen and clear as on that autumn day …

The seasons stood still for us in Nyahé-ya-'nibi. Once or twice the storm clouds piled up in the east over the main range of the Rockies—but the west wind drove them back and winter never came. Yet we were pressed for time, for with those storm clouds showing on the Divide we knew that our days in this old hunting ground of the Stoneys were numbered.

What we particularly wanted to do was to find a practicable horse trail out of the valley to the west, to the White River. The map showed an old Indian trail running through Nyahé-ya-'nibi—the one we had followed from Elk River. Beyond camp it went up the flats for a mile or two and then it swung aside up Abruzzi Creek. It followed that stream for about four miles and then it climbed in a series of zigzags to pass over a high col between Mounts Cadorna and Abruzzi at about 8,500 feet. From there it fell steeply to a small lakelet below the treeline, and from it to the White River.

Various known errors on this map, however, made us somewhat distrustful of it—especially when we came to study that wall of rock, which was snow-covered now and so often in the clouds. Just how any man could get horses up there we could not see, even when we scrambled up to a vantage point on the steep slopes above camp. And so we decided to try, first of all, the main valley.

Six or seven miles from camp, up the main fork of Nyahé-ya-'nibi Waptán was Cadorna Lake. We rode up there on a grey, sunless day, following the flats of the valley northwestwards. At the head of the flats and close to the trail we came on a trapper's cabin. It was very small—just a shelter, an outpost cabin. Roofed with sod and slabs of stone, it blended into its surroundings, lonely and forlorn and looking like some rock that had crashed down from the Aosta Range into these meadows by the stream. We went on, and within a mile we came to a small stream that came down from the north. If you follow that stream up it leads to a stretch of open moorland 2,000 feet above the valley—and from there upwards again, past springs of the sweetest water, to a stony col close under Mount Aosta. Six years later I came that way into Nyahé-ya-'nibi, alone and on foot, with the larches in their young green and the summer sun shining off the glaciers to the west.

It was at that stream that we swung to the southwest and first set eyes on the big mountains of the White River divide. High in the air there was a mist of fine snow through which the sun was now struggling. Seen through this drifting, glittering haze the peaks of Mount Cadorna looked twice their real height. Glaciers swept down from them, disappearing into the old forest at the head of Cadorna Lake. The three veiled peaks seemed to lean forward; it was as if they were reaching towards us through the dark green trees with chill fingers of ice.

We came to the silent lake in which the image of the giant mountains lay motionless as in a mirror. Even as we looked, the dark waters shivered a little in a sudden breeze and the image was broken. Then the breeze died down again and a profound silence fell once more on the lake basin.

Riding became dangerous. We slipped and struggled forward over slabs of rock that dipped steeply towards the lake, knee-deep in moss that was powdered with snow. Ptarmigan flew from the rocks below us; far away, on the cliffs towards the glaciers, a long file of mountain goats wound slowly along their thread of a trail like a string of small white beads.

We left the horses and pushed on on foot. We passed beyond the lake and up the creek flats into stunted, moss-bearded trees, and from them into a grey, stony wilderness of old moraines. And still the Three Giants of Nyahé-ya-'nibi barred the way (we found ourselves calling them that) and there was no vestige of a trail.

In the end, when the day was already fading, we fetched up against a high, snow-streaked precipice. Up it there was a way for a climber and above it there was, we had seen, an alpine plateau that seemed to lead to a high col between Mounts Cadorna and Abruzzi. But with that knowledge we had to be content, for this was the end of the day's trail. Far away, at the lower end of the lake, we could see the grassy hollow where we had tied our horses. If we could get back there before darkness overtook us we should be doing well. As for this wild basin in the heart of the mountains, the only horse that would ever pass out of it to the westward would be one possessed of wings.

☆ ☆ ☆ ☆

Meanwhile Adolf's goat was getting some of his own back. Our rule was that what we shot we ate—but that billy was the toughest thing I ever tried to sink my teeth into. Understandably so, of course, if you think of the years he had spent clambering around these mountains building up his climbing muscles. The soup was excellent, but what came out of stew pot or frying pan was nothing but a bunch of indurate rubber shock-absorbers. Adolf did what he could. He stretched the goat hide on a pole frame, and at odd times he would put in some work on it: he intended to make it into a rug as a present to his sister. Any time he got home ahead of us we would find, on our return, goat meat, cut fine with a hunting knife, together with dried vegetables and beans and anything else that was handy, simmering away in our biggest pot.

Adolf would be hard at work nearby on the hide, scraping—and the hide itself would be leaning against a dead tree, bang on the trail and just where it would be not only an offense to any visiting B.C. game warden but also a deliberate insult.

This simmering treatment Adolf called "giving old goat hell," and the expression was apt enough, for the product was truly infernal. In the end, I suppose, you got a certain amount of nourishment out of it—but it was tough work and you can understand why, on several afternoons, Pocaterra and I went prospecting down the creek after trout and fool hens, or hunting for blue grouse on the ridges.

Not only that, but it was also a chance to discuss, while we were alone, the possibility of my taking over the Buffalo Head. There was a little meadow of bunch-grass at the lower end of the flats, at the point where the quiet stream became the wild torrent of the spruce forest. It was a veritable sun-trap, and there we would boil our teapail and let our horses graze while we discussed the business that lay between us.

It was there, one sunlit noonday, that I saw Pocaterra twist round in a sudden convulsion and fling himself flat on the bunch-grass. He lay there for a second or two, breathing hard—it was most disquieting. A heart attack, I thought—and a nice mess we're all in now if that's what it is. He seemed to be in pain and I hurried over to help him … But he rose in triumph and tossed a fool hen down on to the grass. It fluttered once and then lay still. A few feathers drifted away on the warm breeze.

"How was that for quickness, Patterson? I was just taking the stuff off my saddle when I saw its head move behind that tussock. My God, they are stupid birds!"

They certainly are. Taverner's *Birds of Western Canada* says that this grouse has an "over-confiding nature." Even so, this sudden swoop of Pocaterra's was quick. What with one man snatching them out of trees at the lope and another pouncing on them in the bunch-grass like a hawk, the way of the fool hen was dangerous and hard and its days were short in the land with this outfit around.

When lunch was over we fished. We cut our willow rods and made our simple preparations, and when this was done Pocaterra went and got his horse, bridled him and mounted. He operated, as always, on the "where I go, I ride" principle, even in fishing: he rode off down the stream, dropping a line in each pool as he came to it. Sometimes he caught a trout and sometimes not but he never lingered. In this way he covered a lot of ground; and the amazing thing was that, even with his horse slipping and floundering over the rocks and stamping in the pools, he caught a lot of fish.

I came down on foot and I did very nicely, particularly with a certain spinner which seemed to be just the thing they were looking for that afternoon. Which made it all the more annoying when a big, fat trout broke the gut for me and then proceeded to tear up and down a long, rock-walled pool between two cascades with my spinner in his mouth, and I didn't have another one of that kind. Well, if he thought he was going to get away with that sort of thing he was mistaken. We carried our rifles on our wanderings in Nyahé-ya-'nibi; the reason for this being the mauling by a grizzly of some unarmed Indian in this country in the earlier days. Keeping an eye on the fish, I unslung the Mannlicher.

I slid a cartridge into the chamber, locked the bolt home and waited. All around me were the enormous trees. They leaned out from each side of the stream until, far overhead, they met, shutting out the sky. Here and there a golden spear of sunlight passed between the tree trunks, striking a patch of vivid green where it fell upon the moss and the bunch-berry leaves ... Suddenly the trout flashed downstream again and came into a small, round pool of sunlight. There he stayed for a moment of time—and in that moment I sighted and pressed the trigger.

There was an ear-splitting report, penned in and flung back at me by the giant trees. The heavy bullet made a hole in the water. Tiny drops sparkled on the huge tree trunks, and I leaned against one of them with my head singing. The roar of the waptán resumed its sway and the trout was nowhere to be seen.

From downstream I heard a faint shout. Soon Pocaterra appeared, with a sack of fish flapping from his saddle horn. He rode in and out amongst the trees or took to the water as it suited him, and he came to a splashy halt in the pool just below. He looked around, expecting to see some dead animal.

"You have wounded something, Patterson?" he shouted above the noise of the torrent.

"No," I said, perversely. "I was just scaring a fish."

"Scaring a fish? And with that cannon! I have heard you fire it before—but what a devil of a row it makes shut in under these trees! For heaven's sake, man, muzzle the thing—you are not in the Northwest Territories now!"

Fishing was at an end. We had caught enough, and we rode back to camp through the meadows and past the long, quiet pool that we called the Mirror of Nyahé-ya-'nibi. In its calm waters lay the cloudless blue of the sky, and in that lay the snowy summits of the mountains, serenely upside down … Smoke curled up from the campfire as we rounded the point of the last hill. Adolf had got home before us and already, apparently, "old goat" was in the pot and catching a bit of "hell."

"Shock-absorbers again for supper," I remarked, pointing.

"Not on your life," Pocaterra replied. "Trout and that careless fool hen. And, Patterson, you notice? There is that goat hide in the very same place as yesterday, leaning against the very same tree! I have said 'Keep it cached,' but I might just as well go and talk to Mount Abruzzi. It is indeed true that the Germans are a strong, persistent people!"

The Pass in the Clouds (1)

It was now obvious that to reach the White River we had to follow up Abruzzi Creek. However, the luck was not with us on our first attempt, for as we rode up the valley the high, snowy ridge for which we were heading became enveloped in cloud. This cloud ceiling did not cover the whole of Nyahé-ya-'nibi, for the mountains of the eastern wall were lit, all that afternoon, by the sun; and a weird, yellowish glow that threw no shadows was reflected from them back under the canopy of cloud … Seeing that the ridge had vanished we decided to leave the pass for a better day and, instead, to follow up a stream that seemed to come from a small tarn at the foot of the Abruzzi glaciers. So we forded Abruzzi Creek and started into the bush on foot.

After almost three miles of dense green timber the trees began to thin out and we saw, shining through them with a golden light, the waters of a lake. This was something entirely unexpected: in place of the insignificant tarn that the map showed, here was this lake comparable in size with Lake Cadorna. To it Pocaterra, in his *Italian*

Alpine Club Journal account of this journey, gives the descriptive term, "laghetto."

The lake was bordered by a forest of old and magnificent firs. We walked on through these splendid trees towards the mountain—and it was beyond the head of the lake, in an open glade, that we came on the ancient of days, the veteran of this old forest. He had fallen many years ago and he lay there, partly sunk into the moss, a monster almost of Pacific Coast proportions except for the quickly tapering trunk. How many years, we wondered, had it taken to produce this giant in this place of little summer, more than 6,000 feet above sea level and in the cold shadow of Mount Abruzzi? Hunting knives and an axe went to work: the growth, it seemed, had been incredibly slow: this had been a young tree when Columbus first sailed for the Americas—and in all the years since then no forest fire had come this way.

We went on through the last of the forest and over the alpine flats that lay between the trees and the steep terminal moraine of the Abruzzi glacier. Up this moraine we went, a breathless scuffle up several hundred feet of loose rock; and then the last man sent the last boulder bounding down on to the flats below as he heaved himself over the rim and on to the glacier. Then we turned and looked—and truly it was a sight worth seeing.

The stream emerged from an ice cave at the foot of the moraine and wound across the flats, disappearing into the dark wall of old firs that surrounded the lake. To the left, in the middle distance, the outlet stream tumbled away from the lake towards Abruzzi Creek; to the right and beyond the lake rose the peak of The Warship; and behind all this ran the sunlit eastern wall of Nyahé-ya-'nibi. But it was the lake that caught and held the eye. In its sombre setting of the fir trees it glowed like a sheet of burnished gold.

"Lago de Oro," I said—but Pocaterra said, "No. It is we who have found that lake. The surveyors can never have seen it: they must have put it on the map from some Indian report—and then wrongly, as we have seen. Let us call it Lake Marigold, after your wife. Her hair is that same colour of gold, and so it is fitting that we should name it for her ... "

On our way back to the horses that evening we saw a band of goats coming down the cliffs on the far side of Abruzzi Creek. There were

Lake Marigold, near the Pass in the Clouds

between twenty and thirty of them, including several pairs of nannies and kids. We watched them, passing the glass from hand to hand—and here, for the first time, I saw how the kids were taught to handle themselves on the face of a mountain … The mother would come down some steep and dangerous place to the ledge below. Then she would turn round and look up, obviously telling the kid that it was safe to follow. Nothing doing: the kid would stand there hesitating, looking down and not liking what he saw, timidly putting forward first one foot and then the other. Up would go the mother again to nuzzle the kid and tell him to have confidence—then down again to show him the way. Usually he followed then; but on one or two occasions a mother would have to demonstrate the climb as much as three times, and once a nanny gently bunted her unwilling offspring till he had to go. Once they moved, the kids were marvellously sure-footed. They had to be, for a slip in this place would have meant death.

The last day came. We had lingered almost too long and tomorrow was zero hour—time to get out of Nyahé-ya-'nibi while the going was good.

The day was cold and grey but the mountains were clear. Pocaterra and I rode away from camp with our horses' hoofs drumming on the frozen ground; the rim-ice shivered and tinkled as we forded Cadorna Creek. As we crossed the flats we looked back east towards the main range of the Rockies. Low streamers of cloud, leaden-hued and threatening, were creeping through between the summits from the Alberta side of the Divide. That was cold weather trying to get through from the prairies; it was not making much headway but the pressure was there; a switch in the wind and the snow would be driving down the valley of the Elk by nightfall. Time to hurry.

We rode fast up the Abruzzi Creek trail. It climbed steadily, and then, a couple of miles beyond the stream from Lake Marigold, it began to zigzag up the mountainside. It was faint and fallen-in, and it was a long time since it had been used ... As we climbed, the trees grew smaller. Then they vanished and we entered that wind-swept country of broken stone and patches of fine turf that lies between the timber and the barren rock. The trail was nothing but a goat track now and the rocks were snow-powdered. Still we rode upwards on a steepening slope—and then, as we topped a minor skyline and came on to a little grassy plateau, we found in front of us one lonely sentinel of the forest, a Lyall's larch.

The tree was old and battered by many storms. It had no business to be growing here, so far above all other trees. Yet it was strong and thriving and this year's needles lay around it, a powdering of fine gold upon the snow. To it we tied the horses and then we went on.

We climbed up to a spur of Mount Cadorna and there we hesitated, puzzled. To the right the ground sloped up more easily; it seemed to lead to a plateau. But in front of us, to the west, the faintest thread of a trail led upwards, across the face of a tremendous scree, to a high col. It was no more than a white line, picked out in snow across the broken rock of this dangerous slope. Yet it seemed that it had to be the trail to the White River, for if we took the easier slope to the north it would inevitably land us amongst the glaciers that lay above Cadorna Lake. We debated this for a minute or two and then we set out across the scree.

As we had expected to make merely a short reconnaissance on foot and then go back and bring up our horses, we had not bothered to take off our chaps. Pocaterra's were of sheep hide with the wool on, and mine were a very heavy leather pair that I used at that time. With these things on, and with riding boots on our feet, we were poorly equipped for that thread of a trail that was nowhere wider than six or seven inches, and often less.

Above us the scree stretched up to the rimrock. Below, the eye followed it in one unbroken sweep of 1,500 feet or more down into the head of Abruzzi Creek. A packhorse here would be in the same position as those mountain goats we had seen the day before: the first slip would mean death. A man, too, for there was nothing to hold on to, nothing to stop you until what remained of you fetched up in the stony bed of Abruzzi Creek, so far below.

Ahead of us there appeared a blackish thing protruding from the snow-covered scree. As we climbed up to it, we saw that it was a sheer limestone outcrop. The trail ran straight at it and vanished. There were signs that the goats came this way and got around by climbing steeply down to the foot of this little cliff and then up again; small twists of fine, white wool were caught on points of the solid rock where they had pressed against it as they passed. And then, beyond, we could see the thin white line climbing up to a snowy col, remote and desperately high.

Pocaterra stood there looking towards the skyline. "So it is a goat trail after all," he said. "No horse could get by here. We would have to put in a couple of hours' work around this rock alone, building a trail. Longer, perhaps, because a horse's pack would catch against the rock and throw him out dangerously far. Still, we can get around ourselves and go on up to the summit. We might as well make sure."

At this moment, by a lucky chance, I looked back. We had been intent on navigating this treacherous scree and our eyes had been all for the trail and the summit. Things, in the meantime, had been happening behind us ...

Nyahé-ya-'nibi had vanished. All that remained was a few summits of the eastern wall; the rest was hidden by a creeping mass of cold, grey cloud. We could still see the horses: they were standing motionless, facing each other from opposite sides of the old, solitary tree. The horses and the larch with its stout trunk and ragged crown stood on the edge of a drop. Below them there was nothing—only the grey boiling cloud that was climbing up towards them out of the depths. Silhouetted against it, they looked, from this height, like a child's toys.

There was no time to lose. Down we went, making haste slowly for a slip on these snowy rocks was even more likely now than in climbing up. And, as we descended, the cloud rose; it became a race to see which would reach the horses first. If we failed we might not be able to find them at all for there were other goat trails besides this main one, and in a fog or a snowstorm there would be little to guide us on this open mountainside. In the end it was a dead heat for we came to the horses just as the first streamers of frozen mist were swirling around them.

Somehow we got the horses and ourselves down into the timber and down through the cloud ceiling into the clear valley of Abruzzi Creek. The flats of the main valley, when we came to them, were chill and silent, as on our first evening, and heavy with the threat of storm. As we drew near to camp we could see the red flicker of a fire up on the knoll by the tepee: that meant Adolf was home. The firelit whiteness of his goat hide shone through the twilight and the grey mist of snow like a surveyor's beacon, provoking the usual comments on German pertinacity from Pocaterra. And already in the pot, which was suspended over the fire, a fresh ration of "old goat" was being toughened-up for supper—strong meat for mountaineers.

★ ★ ★ ★

When we came, on the following day, to the crossing of Elk River the frozen ground presented a curious record for our inspection. There were tracks of men and horses on top of ours and, whoever they were, they could not have failed to read the story of our crossing. We promptly took evasive action and made ourselves as nearly like shadows as it was possible for three men and six solid horses to become. Travelling by the old trail of the Stoney Indians we passed unseen over the Continental Divide into Alberta and, in four days' riding from the meadow of Nyahé-ya-'nibi, we reached the Buffalo Head.

The first part of this journey was made under light snow which helped to cover our tracks, but, when we reached the Highwood, we found there the blue and gold of Indian summer and we rode at our ease. One last weather change lay in wait for us, however, for when we emerged from the mountains by the Highwood Gap a blinding blizzard of wet snow drove down out of the north and blew straight in our faces.

For ten miserable miles we rode straight into the eye of the storm; the wet snow plastered our hats, chaps and Mackinaws; it whitened the horses and piled up in our saddles in front of us. We rode with our heads down and without speaking except to shout at some wandering packhorse. We suffered—and when the Buffalo Head corrals hove in sight we were all deeply grateful. Pocaterra said—prematurely, as it happened—"Thank God, that's over!" and at the same moment I, looking as usual for a shortcut, had an idea.

"Don't let's unpack in the usual place," I said. "Let's take the horses up into the garden. They can stand in the lee of the house by the kitchen door, out of this wind and snow, and we can take the packhorses one by one round to the east side, unpack them there and sling the stuff into the veranda. We can sort things out later … "

We did that, and it worked well—that is, for a time. It was the last horse that upset the applecart: just as we took the diamond off him a fierce gust of wind came along and flipped the canvas pack cover over his head—and there it stuck, securely held by the panniers under which it was tucked. The terrified horse rushed blindly round the corner of the house towards his friends, with the three of us in hot pursuit. Chaps flapped in the wind, somebody tripped on a big slab of river stone that was set in the grass, a hat blew off and the air was thick with comment …

This was altogether too much for Brainless who had been standing there quite quietly in a sort of a coma. Apparently under the impression that a pack of wolves was after him with murderous intent, he hit the trail at full speed, instantaneously from a standstill. He hit it in the wrong direction for he passed under a well-stocked washing line that the man in charge of the place had put out only that morning, before he rode away to get the week's mail. The horns of Brainless' pack-saddle took the washing line plumb in the centre and tore it loose at both ends. Away rushed the horse into the storm, tail erect and with anxious, prancing gait, hotly pursued on either side by a leaping, flapping string of shirts, towels, a tablecloth, silk scarves and assorted underwear. He galloped looking first over one shoulder and then over the other, trying to make out what it could be that was chasing him. Soon, however, he gave up looking as a bad job and concentrated on just galloping ...

We led the remaining horses down to the barn. I was in the lead with two horses, closely followed by Adolf with another two. Pocaterra brought up the rear; he was leading only one horse but he was swearing with fluency and skill in five languages. The wind was directly behind us so that nobody could possibly have heard a sound from the man in front of him, and yet I could hear every word of Pocaterra's performance and, at the same time, Adolf's roars of laughter. For my part, I was speechless and the tears were running down my face. I had got a sight of Adolf's crimson, compressed face in the garden and it had finished me.

A dark shape loomed up out of the storm. It rushed madly past, trailing behind it two bedraggled scarecrows, mud-coloured and horrible. The horses that I was leading swung round, backed against each other and stared anxiously ... This vision of Brainless seemed to inspire anew the two men behind me, for from Adolf there came an absolutely maniacal outburst of laughter, and from Pocaterra a coloratura solo the like of which mortal man will never hear again ...

And then silence. The curtain of memory drops and the scene vanishes as though it had never been. I have no recollection of catching Brainless—yet somebody must have done so because the little horse stayed sane and served us well for many years until some clumsy fool shut him in a log gate and knocked his hip down for him. Nor do I remember anybody getting shot by Pocaterra for all these wild doings. In fact I have set down here all that I can recollect of our homecoming.

Tale of a Game Warden

Brainless's frolic in the blizzard does not completely close the story of Nyahé-ya-'nibi: there still remain one or two loose ends to be tidied away.

We took the matter of Lake Marigold up with Ottawa. We were thanked for pointing out the error in the map and permission was granted for the naming of the lake. But first of all the Surveyor General required a fuller description, various data and a set of photographs.

We planned to return to the lake—but the years went by. A great forest fire swept Elk River, and a war came … Three times since that first trip have I been near to Lake Marigold, and in the end I managed to get a sight of it from the goat mountain to the northward. But on the map the lake is still, today, the nameless tarn in the shadow of Mount Abruzzi.

★ ★ ★ ★

Then there was that business of the trail to the White River that we had failed to find. This solved itself by the purest chance, before many months had gone by. Browsing through a very old number of the *National Geographic* I was surprised to find a full-page photograph of the Three Giants of Nyahé-ya-'nibi staring me in the face—and then a picture of enormous spruce by a mountain stream. Forgetting completely whatever it was that I was looking for, I read …

It proved to be the account of a long-forgotten expedition, the W. D. Wilcox exploration in the Canadian Rockies. The time was 1901; that area was then a blank on the map and the Wilcox party had lost its way. Missing an important pass, they had been driven south by the lay of the mountains until, eventually, they crossed a pass to the head of what was later called the White River, but which, to them, was just one more river running the wrong way.

Three Isle Lake in the Kananaskis Valley

They followed this new river—but again it led them south, and the way they wanted to go was east. So when they came, on the second day of their journey down the unknown river, to a much used Indian camp ground and a forking of the trail, they seized their opportunity and turned east towards a sort of gateway in the barrier of mountains that formed the curtain wall of their valley on that side. Fifteen hundred feet above the main valley they made camp by a little alpine lake, and from there, in the afternoon, Wilcox examined the Pass in the Clouds.

He went on alone, on foot, following a trail that "seemed from below a difficult scramble for a mountaineer," and eventually he reached the summit—not without excitement, for he had not the faintest idea what he was going to see on the other side.

The trail dipped over into "a valley of great depth ... a green valley." Wilcox found himself looking down into Nyahé-ya-'nibi, and beyond to the main range of the Rockies. "On either side of the pass," he says, "were imposing precipices three or four thousand feet above the valley. How the Indians first got their horses over this place surpasses comprehension. Part of the trail was covered by snow even at this late date, and the slope was so steep that the stones were ready to slide. If a horse ever lost his balance here, it would be all over with him ... "

In climbing Wilcox had observed that "the Indians in choosing a trail had most skilfully availed themselves of every little patch of soil and vegetation in a bare slope of limestone. On the upper parts, however, even these disappeared, and the trail was lined with sharp stones. A great deal of work had been done by throwing down the larger stones and paving a way with smaller ones."

The next day, August 12, the Wilcox party tackled the pass. Their horses, Wilcox writes, "hardly knew what to make of the tremendous climb, and the sharp rocks cut their feet badly. We rolled down tons of stones and repaired the trail as well as possible ahead of them ... A short rest and a precautionary tightening of cinches took place on the summit. Then ensued a still more difficult descent of 2,000 feet into the new valley. When we looked at the precipitous and snowbound pass from below, it seemed impossible that four-footed animals could traverse such a place ... "

Such was the crossing, by the Wilcox party, of the Pass in the Clouds in the days when the trail was used and maintained by the Stoneys. Thirty years later, when Pocaterra and I climbed up from the east, the trail had fallen into disuse and in places had fallen away. Only the feet of the mountain goat had kept some vestige of it trodden out and visible amongst the stones.

Later on in that August of 1901 the Wilcox outfit ran into the Stoneys at the Kananaskis Lakes. The Indians were on their way to British Columbia to hunt, and they questioned the white men, who were fishing in the lower lake, much as property owners might question poachers caught fishing in some private preserve. The Stoneys were still, in those days, free men and hunters, ranging freely through their mountain wilderness.

"They knew of the high pass which we had crossed on August 12," Wilcox writes, "and expressed the greatest surprise that we had gotten our horses over it."

Pocaterra told Paul Amos (whose Stoney name means "Spotted Wolf") where we had been. Paul knew of that pass, too. "O—Yetzkábi ta changó." "Yes—a Stoney trail," he said in a quiet voice that was full of memories. "That's ba-ad place. Stoney mens call um 'Umpabin-wah-giniangin.'"

And that means: "I-am-afraid-of-the-stones."

★ ★ ★ ★

There remains our departure from Nyahé-ya-'nibi and Pocaterra's avoidance of the main Elk Pass in our return to Alberta. Had this extra precaution been worthwhile?

Ten years went by before that question was answered—and then, one October morning, I drove with a friend to a little town of the East Kootenay to get our permits to shoot duck on the Columbia River. With some difficulty we found the game warden's office, and there we proceeded to fill out the usual forms for non-residents of British Columbia—names, addresses and so forth.

"Buffalo Head Ranch—where's that?" said the game warden.

"On the Highwood River, close to the mountains," I told him. "One day's ride and we can camp in B.C. on the head of Fording River."

"Fording River and Elk River used to be my district before I was transferred here. And I seem to have heard of this Buffalo Head Ranch. Have you been there long?"

"Eight or nine years. It used to be Pocaterra's, if that places it for you?"

"It does. And I knew Pocaterra, too. Where's he now? It must be ten years since I last heard of him, and that was when a message came to me that he'd taken a couple of dudes in, hunting, to the West Fork of the Elk. I went right after him and I thought I had him in the bag—but somehow he managed to give me the slip."

"He knows that country well."

"Too well for me—he and the Stoneys. Well, you're all fixed up now. Enjoy yourself and get lots of ducks."

"Thank you," I said and I went out to the car where my friend was waiting impatiently. A couple of dudes ... This was rich! If I ever set eyes on Adolf again, if the Gestapo hadn't done him in (for the war had caught him on a visit to East Prussia), how he was going to enjoy this! And Pocaterra, too ...

My friend's voice broke in on my dreams: "I've driven five whole miles now," it was saying, "and all you've done is sit there in dead silence and grin. What were you and that game warden getting so thick over? Have you met him before, somewhere?"

"Never," I said. "But I very nearly did meet him, once. A long time ago, now. On Elk River."

4

Bright Morning

Construction Period

That ride to Nyahé-ya-'nibi was the last of those eventful trips with Pocaterra. Other mountain trips were to come—but never again that perfect combination of two temperamental and volatile characters functioning with unpredictable eccentricity against the solid backdrop of Adolf's quiet persistence and absolute reliability. Never again did the lunatic incident loom so large in our camps in the mountains. For Pocaterra went away to his native Italy and did not return to Canada until the early war years; and Marigold and I took over the Buffalo Head, which, for some years to come, provided us with more than enough to do, leaving no time to spare for packhorse trips into wild country.

We took the place over on the proverbial shoestring because we loved it and loved the life that went with it. Quite what we proposed to use for money when we embarked on this venture I now forget; but in the end we somehow managed to climb out of the hole into which we had jumped so light-heartedly. That we did so was due not least to Adolf who stayed on the place as foreman for eight years until, in 1938, he made a visit home to East Prussia—and, in those dangerous years, lingered there a shade too long ... Through the war years he was put to work on the family farm; and when the end came he hit the trail westwards, one jump ahead of the Russians. Stowing away on a ship that was bound, as he supposed, for Sweden, he found himself, to his dismay, decanted at Kiel, right into the arms of the Gestapo who were curious to know what this man with Canadian papers was up to. At this juncture Montgomery's men arrived on the scene. ("Never has a uniform looked to me so beautiful!") The Gestapo went out of business and, after a period of energetic and successful poaching on an estate in Holstein, Adolf returned to Canada older by nine eventful years.

With the Buffalo Head we took over a large bunch of horses but few cattle. This was all to the good: there was plenty of beef on the place to eat, but apart from their food value cattle, in the years from 1932 to 1936, were worth next to nothing. It was a good time, therefore, to give the place the rest it needed and so to build up the grass—and it was a good time to buy calves. This we did, buying mixed bunches of steer and heifer calves at prices ranging from $8 to $12 a head. Any increase in the cow herd seemed, at first, to be far away in the future—but the years soon slipped by. In 1933, the first lots of calves became yearlings. In 1934 they were two-year-olds, and in that year the best of the heifers were bred, the steers and spayed heifers being sold for beef. And in 1935 the first calves were born from the cows that we had bought as heifer calves in 1932. Thus, without trouble or any great outlay, we built up a herd of young cows that had all been raised on the place—and built up the grass at the same time.

These young cattle gave very little trouble, and so we were free to tackle the rebuilding of the corrals, the making of new gates, repairing of fences and so forth—things that were all necessary to the ranch. There were also the various changes that had to be made in order to convert a bachelor establishment into a family home, and for several years a variegated gang of carpenters, painters, diggers and plain, brainless, strong-arm merchants seemed to be always with us. Adolf took to gate building. His skill was with an axe and in log work. He took a look around the country at the various types of ranch gate. He made notes of these and designed improvements. Spruce poles were cut and peeled, and Adolf, working with axe, drawknife and auger in a pile of sweet-smelling chips and bark, would put his gates together loosely on the ground. Then a wagon, loaded with trimmed poles and hewed and augered uprights, would be seen rolling out of the home meadow, and by nightfall another new and easily swinging gate, or perhaps two new gates, would have risen where, until then, the old ones had dragged and creaked through the evening of their days.

Back in the home meadow things were humming. New corrals were rising in place of the old, and the water line that was to bring gravity water into the house was creeping out of the woods and across the meadow. The water was to come from a well dug alongside the stream in the spruce coulee that was later known to us as Jimmy's Coulee. From there to the house was 1,300 feet and the pipe had to be buried seven feet to put it reasonably below frost level. This was by no means everybody's job, and I had got in touch with a character who did nothing but this sort of thing. He was known as Tony the Badger.

Tony turned up one busy day to look the proposition over and he made me a price on the digging. Thinking that his price was a low one, I pointed out to him, rather against my own interests but, at the

same time, wishing to make his contract a reasonable one, that he was running into something tough. He would be crossing the alluvial fan of Jimmy's Creek. It might be meadowland now, but beneath it lay, I was certain, every rock that Jimmy's Creek had rolled down from the Lone Pine pasture in thousands of years of cloud-bursts and melting snows. I said all that, but Tony didn't agree. Oh no, he said—it would be black soil, rich and deep; I would see. There was no saving the man so I let him make out his own contract, and then he moved in with two helpers and started operations. The Badger outfit, which camped alongside the stream in a tent that I provided, did its own cooking and bothered nobody but me.

Janet Patterson and the Buffalo Head Ranch main house

We maintained our own fences, and sometimes we built our new ones. But more often the new fences were built for us by the Stoneys, Paul Amos acting as head contractor. The routine never varied. After a large meal had been consumed by Paul, he and I would gradually get around, via hunting, mountain trails and the habits of the wild game, to the business in hand. With much gesturing the location would be clearly defined and understood, and then the price per mile. The next day, perhaps, the whole band would appear in the meadow—women, children and babies, old men, young men and maidens. Soon they would be riding away again with wagons, democrats and packhorses loaded down with grub, tools, wire and staples. And, if it happened to be in the fall of the year, He—by which pronoun Paul always designated his wife: "No *money*, Mr. Patterson," he would say. "He's spend um all. He smoke *too much!*"—He, I say, would be beaming all over her copper-coloured face at the gift of two enormous cabbages. The Buffalo Head garden grew monsters, up to 25 lbs., and He always went into fits of laughter at the sight of them.

The whole band would camp right on the job, and the fence would spring up at a tremendous rate—with time off for hunting and fishing as well. Adolf or I would ride up to see how things were going, and the scene that always comes first to mind with me is a camp of Paul's on the South Fork of Sullivan Creek, six miles west of the house. I was looking for the Indians, and I came on them suddenly as my horse topped a grassy rise. The tents and one tepee were set up in the shade of the cottonwoods down below, by the stream. Wood smoke from the cooking fires drifted slowly out across the flat, blue against the westering sun. Children were playing in and out amongst the trees and by the clear, brown water. From the camp, and from a belt of willows nearby, came shouts and laughter, the clatter of pots and the click of axes—supper was being prepared and willow posts were being cut and sharpened. The day had been a hot one but now, in the cool of the evening, everybody was at it: I could see the bigger children piling posts—and then suddenly, out of the trees with a rush came a girl on a pony skidding a bunch of posts caught in the loop of her lariat. She went at a run, through the loose horses that were grazing on the flat and up the hill to the fence. A man slipped the loop off the posts for her and she rode back to the stream again, coiling her rope as she went. Men were working along the fence, and there, away in the distance, came old Paul, riding slowly, supervising. Observing the way of the white man, he had learned that it is better to supervise then to toil ...

The impression was one of colour and life and light—shirts and scarves in the vivid greens, yellows and purples that the Indians love; the pinto horses set against the flowers and the bright green grass of early summer; the blue, drifting wood smoke; the laughter, and the evening sunlight that touched each shining tree with golden fingers ...

Days afterwards, when the Indians had departed and the grass was growing again, you would find, if you rode past one of Paul's old camps, a light pole stuck in the ground and, suspended from it by a bit of old moccasin string, a hawk's feather fluttering in the wind. It was a sign of some sort, like the gypsy patrin—a sprig of oak, as it might be, or a broken piece of fern.

Into the turmoil of the Buffalo Head kitchen in those early years burst Alberto. Pocaterra found him for us: "You will find he is a good man," he said. "He is from Friuli."

That settled that—and, as to cooking for us, Alberto was eminently qualified for the job by his previous occupation which had been the selling of magazines, postcards and souvenirs in the observation cars of the C.P.R. mainline trains.

Some of his first efforts in the cooking line were memorable. Some of his early loaves of bread would have made an efficient substitute for concrete. And the things that man did to beef! However, he learnt swiftly under Marigold's tuition, though he never lost his Italian frugality, and it was always a struggle to get him to set on the table the thick, rich cream which is part of ranch living. There was a frequent guest at the ranch who was a favourite of Alberto's. Observing her, one day, pouring some sky-blue, city-type milk into her coffee, I remonstrated with our cook.

"Will you bring some fresh coffee," I said, "and take that frightful stuff away and put some really thick cream on the table?"

Alberto bent over the lady to take her cup. "Madam," he said, gravely, "a word of warning: you don' h'eat too much cream, then you never 'ave the apoplexy!" He then disappeared in search of the real

stuff, having the solemn air of a man who has done his duty—and now
let the heavens fall!

Outside in the meadow the Badger was learning that things are not
always what they seem. A little knowledge of simple structural geology
would have saved his bacon at the outset—but he now found himself
stuck into a most terrible rockpile, and out of his trenches were coming,
not mounds of rich black soil, but rocks of all shapes and sizes from
gravel to small boulders. Progress was slow and the Badger's contract
was looking a bit sick.

All this time, behind the house, the plumbing party dug and delved
and built. It was a party of two—an Anglo-Irish concern—and it
moled away in secret with its own jargon and technicalities. Yet, in spite
of these strenuous efforts, the water got no further, in that Year of the
Badger, than the kitchen door. It finished up there in a standpipe from
which Alberto would fill, on warm days, by means of a hose, two large
drums in the kitchen. This system was by no means perfect, but it was
way ahead of carrying water up from the corral spring, and it can in no
way be blamed for the purely personal kink that Alberto threw into it
one sunny January afternoon. He had the golden touch if ever a man
did—by which I mean that, in his hands, the most ordinary situation
could be counted on to change headlong and without warning into
purest comedy.

This was the winter that Alberto, rummaging in a book shelf, had
picked up *The Three Musketeers.* He became absorbed. "By God," he
said, "they were surely men in those days!" and he followed d'Artagnan
right through the cycle of the three romances. On this particular
Chinook afternoon Alberto ran his hose through the open window
and into one of his empty water drums. He turned the standpipe valve
and he listened approvingly to the hiss of water that followed. Then he
sat down on a chair in a sunny corner of the kitchen, put his feet up on
a second chair and became lost to the world in *Twenty Years After.*

Perhaps twenty minutes later, "the Major," an engineer friend of
ours who made his home on the place, stamped the wet snow off his
boots and stuck his head in at the door. It was still the old kitchen
before we had rebuilt it: you stepped down into it as you entered, and
the Major just managed to save himself from splashing into a lake.

Paul Amos, the old Stoney hunter

Hastily he slammed the door shut, turned off the standpipe tap and went and bellowed through the window.

Startled but in no way put out, Alberto came back through the centuries, from Versailles and its sparkling fountains to the playful waters of the Buffalo Head. A man of action and resource, he had his plan immediately. With a shout of "I fix 'im, Major! I fix 'im," he splashed through the flood and opened the trap door of the cellar. For a second or two a green, curving cascade of water roared down the cellar stairs. Then a flick or two of a broom and the glistening floor was clear. And then the two of them knelt down and peered into the blackness of the cellar, dreading what they should see ... But there was nothing to worry about: only a few damp floor boards—that was all. The house was built on a natural terrace or bench of hard-packed river gravel, solid as concrete but porous as the desert sand.

Down there in the darkness lived a salamander. We saw him occasionally when hunting for beer or bottled fruit, but nobody ever bothered him. Down there, too, was Alberto's wine: a large crock containing an amber liquid that was based on dried figs, raisins, brown sugar, yeast—anything. It was the apple of his eye and we always knew when the brew was going well, for then he would be radiant and smiling from dawn to dewy eve. One morning, CMB came into the kitchen to find Alberto holding a glass of this golden nectar up to the light, examining it critically.

Flat Creek Valley and Mount Head

CMB had come to the ranch a year or two previously for a three-weeks' stay, to take care of our small daughter while Marigold and I were away. That, at least, was the original idea—but the place cast its spell over her and she ended by staying for twenty years. She was well-liked throughout the Highwood country; but on this morning Alberto seemed particularly glad to see her. "Mees Baldwin," he said, "I need your assistance. You drink this glass of wine for me and then you tell me just what you think of 'im." She took the glass and downed it. It wasn't too bad. It was faintly intoxicating, fruity, a little bit yeasty, perhaps ... She told Alberto all that.

"Ah!" he said. "You don't find anything wrong? That makes me 'appy. Last night I leave the cheese cloth off 'im by mistake—and what you think I find this morning? Two mice drowned in 'im! But I strain 'im carefully and now I think 'e must be all right ... "

Driving Cattle

Branding time at the Buffalo Head was early in June. A few days later, when the calves had recovered from their working-over, the she-stock, including the best of the two-year-old heifers, would be gathered down by the Fideli Ford and cut into their various bunches for the coming summer. The mountain bunch would then be driven a mile or so along the trail to a pasture at the mouth of Flat Greek. There they would be left to bed down while we rode back to the ranch—to bed also, most of us, for breakfast would be at the ungodly hour of 2:30 a.m.

A grumpy, silent crowd it was that gathered in the kitchen of the Buffalo Head on this June morning—which may be in any one of some ten or a dozen Junes. Outside in the starlit darkness the grass was crisp with frost and there were still no signs of dawn. Inside, in the light and the warmth, morose humans struggled with porridge and ham and eggs; the food somehow always tasted dry and unnatural at this hour. I, if there were guests in the house, or if there had been letters to write, had probably not bothered to go to bed; this gave me an unfair advantage over those who still fought with sleep and who, while they had obviously been to bed, had most certainly not been improved by it. Grumpiest of all was Old Henry, a cranky old Englishman. You could always count on getting a rise out of him, especially at this hour of the day.

"Not enough sleep, Henry? You should do as I do—don't go to bed at all, that's the way to handle the situation."

"Oh-h, hell! Sensible men sleep at nights, that's what I say—and I'll 'andle my own situation myself, thank you kindly!"

Boots were pulled on and lanterns lighted. They flickered about the home meadow like so many fireflies; then, gradually, they gathered at the corrals. Horses that one could barely see were saddled in silence. Dim, shadowy figures could be seen mounted, outlined faintly against a sky that was paling in the northeast. "Is everybody here? All right, then, let's go"—and the little party rode out by the Flat Creek gate.

The dark shapes of cattle rose to greet us, by the salting place, down at the mouth of Flat Creek, by the river. We sat around then for a while, motionless in our saddles, for it was still too dark to see in any detail. A match flared out some distance away from me and a humorous, weather-beaten face, crowned by an old-time Stetson, glowed red for a moment and then vanished again into a gloom that seemed deeper than before. That would be Sam Smith, the fishery warden of the Highwood district, a firm friend and ally, communing with his first pipe of the morning. The rest of us just sat and suffered in the darkness and the frost.

But soon it was just light enough to see and we counted the cattle out of the gate and headed them up the Flat Creek trail, a long line of heaving backs and gently floating dust with one rider in the lead. No protest came from the cows, for vague memories of last year and of other, earlier years were stirring within them—memories of sweet grass in alpine meadows, and of clear streams and cool nights at the foot of Mount Head and the Holy Cross Mountain, memories of a cow's heaven that was called, quite inadequately, the South Fork of Flat Creek.

At the head of the cattle marched (as she always marched in the latter years of the Buffalo Head) a big-boned, tawny-coloured, rough-coated Hereford cow with long, dangerous horns and an uncertain temper. Right at her tail trotted a stocky, well-disciplined calf, also of the same light colouring. Other calves of other cows might stray from their mothers—this one knew better than to wander, his mother saw to that and her calves were always models of obedience. Even if this martinet of a cow had not always produced a good calf we would still have kept her, for, on these June mornings, she knew exactly where she was going: the season of the year had come and she was headed for the valley of the South Fork. The sooner she got there the better, as far as she was concerned—and the herd followed her lead. In the same way, when the leaves had fallen and a white powdering of snow came creeping down the stony face of the Holy Cross Mountain—it might be in late October or in the early days of November—this same long-horned cow would call to mind the good grass of the Buffalo Head and would again be in the lead when the long strung-out procession of cows, with their big, seven-months' calves, grown strong and heavy in that happy valley, wound its homeward way down the Flat Creek trail at weaning time.

The shining whiteness of frost, with its winking pinpoints of light, still lay heavy in the low places. One could hear the slapping of chilled hands against the hard leather of chaps, and somewhere in the rear a rider was dismounted and leading his horse, stamping his feet as he walked. But the daylight was growing stronger. And then suddenly the cold, dead peaks ahead of us flared out against the western sky as the first rays of the sunrise touched the barren tips with liquid gold. Downwards this light spread, and the bare limestone glowed in its fiery radiance like a sunset cloud. The light lingered for a while on the rounded slopes of the Bull Creek Hills—then, with a rush, it flooded over the grasslands of the valley floor. Behind us the rim of the sun cleared the Knife Edge Ridge, flinging its first flaming shaft on cattle and riders; and Flat Creek valley leapt into sudden life in all the colours of the mountain spring—pale green of grass and poplar, darker green of spruce and pine, blue of forget-me-not, larkspur and pentstemon. This was the moment, above all others, that Marigold loved—when the hoarfrost stole away into the shadows and the soaring meadow lark poured forth a wild burst of song.

The cattle were travelling well. We passed the Chapman Coulee, named after an old wolf-hunter of the early nineteen hundreds whose cabin lies in ruins there, in a tangle of thick spruce by the bank of Flat Creek. Wolves had long been ancient history on the Highwood, but they appeared again in the late thirties and early forties and did much damage—monstrous brutes with great, long jaws like steel traps, and heads on them that were broad and black and heavy as those of bears.

At Bull Creek we stopped for a little while to give the calves a chance to "mother-up"; very soon every cow had her calf—and every calf knew what to do. They bunted, tugged and pulled; their noses ran white with milk and their skimpy tails twitched and wiggled with pleasure as breakfast went down. This halt lasted for about fifteen minutes; it also gave the riders a chance to tighten cinches and rid themselves of a few more blistering comments on early starts. But the thing that really mattered was the mothering-up; it meant that now, if we accidentally dropped some calf off in the bush, instead of going all the way home to the ranch it would come back here to the place where it had last sucked, and here it would lie down and wait, fully confident that its mother would soon return and find it.

The day grew quickly warmer; then it became hot. Tongues were hanging out now, and these April calves were tired and ready, with their mothers, to lie through the heat of the day by some shady spring of water until the evening shadow fell. The sun blazed down and tempers of man and beast grew short. The language flew: an angel hovering overhead, making entries in his notebook, would have gathered that all these matronly cows of the Buffalo Head were far from respectable in their ways while their offspring, besides being illegitimate, were possessed of every vice under the sun ...

We forded Flat Creek and turned up the valley of the South Fork. The drift fence ran down to and across the stream from outcrops of rock high up on either side, thus sealing off the valley at its lower end. The leader came to the gate, and she and each successive cow smelt it carefully and passed through. Riding and cursing, we pushed the bunch across the floor of the valley and got them as far as the beaver dams. That was always the cows' idea of a good place to camp for the day—trees, shade and water. In they wallowed, trampling over the lower dam for the most part, while the beavers, no doubt, sat in their houses trotting up the repair bill and cursing all cattle—a couple of hard nights' work, they knew, would be in store for them by the time this mob had passed by. Somehow, and almost with our last breath, we got the bunch out of the dams, up the hill and on to a knoll where a packhorse load of salt had been dumped for them.

The cattle surged forward, licking eagerly, shoving the salt around, slobbering with pleasure. More and more cattle kept coming from behind till the little stony hill was a mass of struggling cows and bewildered, bawling calves. For a little while they enjoyed the salt; then, in pairs and small groups, they moved on, scattering as they went, until the great slope of the mountain had taken them to itself and they were no longer to be seen. Only a few die-hards remained, licking steadily away at the salt blocks with a rasping sound coming from their rough tongues ...

The humans, too, were departing. A couple were hitting the trail for home. By the time they got there, around noon, they would have already put in more than nine hours in the saddle.

Marigold and Sam and I were riding on up the valley—we would go home by way of the Bull Creek Pass. But, first of all, tea—tea made from the stream that flowed down from the Mount Head Coulee, the sweetest water in the Highwood country. A mile went by, and then, very soon, the horses were grazing, Sam's pipe was going, and the teapail was singing over the fire. It was the same old place; we had made tea here last year and the years before that. We would make tea here always, I thought on that summer morning—and I lay there with my eyes almost closed, listening with half an ear to the movements of the horses, idly watching the pattern of sunshine and blue sky through the bare branches and the poplar buds above my head.

The Valley of the South Fork

It was a lonely place, this valley: the Bull Creek Hills guarded it on the east and Mount Head and the Holy Cross Mountain formed the western wall. Trails entered the valley only in three places, and these trails were only passable for cattle and for riders and packhorses—there was no way in for democrat or wagon.

You could come into the valley by following up the South Fork stream, the way we had brought the cattle. If you entered by this lower trail the mountains burst upon you suddenly as you rounded a gravelly spur of the hills. Blue-grey and hard-outlined in the brilliant light, they swept up a full four thousand feet above the valley floor which itself stood five thousand feet above the sea. Coulees ran back into the heart of the mountains, deep-shadowed even at noonday; one by one we explored them as the years went by, finding always something new in those green depths—old, bearded forest, mountain sheep, ice caves, the fairest of alpine rock-gardens, mountain goat in their incredible white breeches, bears; it was truly amazing how much of beauty this little mountain world could hold and hide.

Usually, in that happy climate, one came upon this sudden view in the full blaze of the sun, with the southwest wind swinging its white, spinning clouds over the skyline of Mount Head, and with the blue, rushing shadows chasing down the grassy slopes, sweeping across the flower-starred floor of the valley. But there were times when the black thunderclouds swirled about the mountains and the rain lashed down—and it was on one of these occasions, when I was riding alone up the valley leading a packhorse with a load of salt, that an appalling explosion split through the din of the rain. Simultaneously I saw the lightning strike full on the face of the Cross: fragments of rock rolled down the mountain and a puff of splintered limestone flew up as if a heavy shell had struck up there. Times too, in November, when a fine snow powder came drifting down; the sun would shine through it, copper-coloured, and the mountain outlines, those peaks and ridges where we had climbed on so many golden summer afternoons, would become blurred and indistinct in the glittering haze ... But never a time when one did not thank one's lucky stars for the gift of living and working with this lovely valley close by.

The valley ran south from the drift fence. It rose steadily for three miles of its length until, beyond the Holy Cross Coulee, it opened out into a wide grassy basin at about 6,000 feet. There was good soil here and the grass came early—but sometimes in May the young green would almost vanish beneath a purple carpet of shooting stars while, in June, great drifts of forget-me-nots and lace flowers would flood these high meadows. The blue and the white of these two small alpines were so dazzling and so perfect that it was as if one looked down from the saddle at a host of shining stars. Then, through July and August, grass took over the meadowland and the flowers were elsewhere—goldenrod, globe flowers and delphiniums by the stream; blue carpets of lupines over the high hills to the eastward, shining

Riders at Grass Pass, Mount Head in background

between the dark green of scattered clumps of fir. On the mountain slope to the west some stray spark from the fires of 1910 had caught and burnt a small wood of fir. Many of the gaunt, grey, lifeless trees still stood, a few more falling every year. Poplars and young firs were pushing upwards—and it was in this maze of grey and green that the fireweed grew, purple acres of it, softening the harsh devastation of the old burn, fighting with the raspberries and black currants that ripened there in their seasons.

Riding one day up the trail, which at this point was on the east side of the basin, Marigold and I saw a grizzly step quietly down out of the fireweed and the old, grey trees. The cows and calves were lying scattered about the meadows but the grizzly paid no attention to them; fresh from a feed of berries, he walked steadily towards us through the cattle who took scarcely any notice of him. A few calves ran to their mothers—that was all. We were riding two good horses. "Lets gallop straight at him," we said, "and see what happens." The horses leapt into sudden action; at the beat of their hoofs on the turf the grizzly stopped and raised his head and listened. But not for long: seeing two large things coming at him, he whipped round and fled for dear life back towards the down timber. The pleasant pastoral scene changed swiftly to tumult; cows bawled and ran; calves ran to them, bawling even harder. We might have gained a little on the grizzly in the open but it was when he hit the deadfall that we saw a real demonstration of speed and agility. He went through and over that stuff as easily as a moose would have done; we pulled up and watched him up the steep slope and out of sight, and his pace never slackened …

From this grassy basin the valley climbed, rather more steeply, for one more mile till it came to its head in the Grass Pass, a bunch-grass pass at 6,400 feet. From this pass two valleys, that of Fir Creek and that of the Pack Trail Coulee, led down to the Highwood River and to the wagon trail that ran up to the forest ranger station. Between these two valleys a grassy spur ran out, on a level with the pass; we called it Fir Creek Point, and from it the ground fell away very steeply on three sides—into Fir Creek, down to the Highwood 1,700 feet below, and to the Pack Trail. Away out on this point stood a very old limber pine. It grew, like all limber pines, almost completely in the rock, and beneath it, in July, the barren-looking gravel was alive with flowers. The old pine had been blasted by lightning; now, on its massive trunk, instead of a full crown it carried only a quarter of the greenery that once was there; and out of one side there reached two skinny, skimpy branches that somehow gave the impression of a witch's arms and claws. It was the Boundary Pine. We worked to prevent our cattle from drifting south of this old pine—from dropping down into Fir Creek valley or from wandering down the Pack Trail. Gradually we succeeded; strays were few, and that saved many a mile of riding and searching in October and November, around weaning time. And our bulls minded their own business and nobody else's and sired good X N calves.

There were good springs out on the Point and all that cattle could need in the way of grass. The little plateau sloped gently to the south in shallow steps, affording concealment. Once, on a still, warm day of mid-October, I came on three Buffalo Head bulls lying in the long grass just below the last step. The ground fell away precipitously for a thousand feet on three sides of them but they were in wonderful feed and there was water nearby; I never saw three more contented beasts. I had been hunting for them to take them home; it seemed a shame on a day like this, for Indian summer might linger on even into December. But one never knew: a switch of the wind, and in no time a fine, cold snow might be driving across the Point like blown sand.

It was at these same high springs on the Point that an old cowpuncher, Gordon Hall, and I stopped, one late October day, to make tea and eat our sandwiches. It was about ten above zero and a freezing mist was drifting slowly across the Point from the north, blotting out everything except the grey outlines of the horses, our two selves and the red, crackling fire. A puff of air revealed for a moment the rime-laden ghost of the Boundary Pine. Dimly seen, it put one in mind, more than ever, of one of Macbeth's witches with skinny arms outstretched, threatening ... Then the mist swirled in, thicker than before, and the grim old tree was gone and we were alone again by the fire.

We were gathering the cows and calves for weaning—or, rather, trying to gather them, for, though we could hear cattle moving around us in the mist, not a single head could we see. The scalding hot tea put new life into us and we sat there by the fire for a while, waiting for the mist to clear and thinking fondly, Gordon of the good Scotch whisky and I of the hot rum and lemon that we would drink when we got in to the ranch that evening—for it was Gordon's birthday, an annual fiesta which he always kept at the Buffalo Head. Around us in the swirling mist we could hear, now and then, the rattle of a falling stone or the soft note of some cow calling to her calf. But we could see nothing. Finally we gave it up and rode away, down out of the mists to pick up some cattle that we had seen around the beaver dams.

Whichever way you entered—or, for that matter, left—the valley of the South Fork, whether it was by way of the Grass Pass, or by the Bull Creek Pass, or by the gap through which the South Fork stream escaped, a lovely picture of valley and encircling mountains would suddenly unfold itself. Then—as always, when I crossed some high summit in this country of tremendous views—I would think of old Paul Amos, the Stoney Indian, Pocaterra's blood brother, and the words he spoke to me one day when he became eloquent on the subject of views. "Prairie *no good!*" he said, making a downward gesture of contempt with his hand. "See too much, see too far—teán-no! Always the same thing!

I'm *tired* looking too much one thing. Mountains—that's different. Mountains like picture book. Every time go round corner, turn new page—see new picture. *That* does my heart good!"

He was right. Riding south over the Grass Pass the jagged summits of the Lookout Range burst suddenly upon you, with the winding, shining, silver snake of Zephyr Creek wriggling down towards the Highwood River between off-shoots of those mountains, glittering against the sun. From the Boundary Pine the nearer summits of the Continental Divide came into view; they were only nine miles away in an air line. A V-shaped gap in the range showed where the trail ran through Fording River Pass to Fording River and Elk River in British Columbia, turning, if one followed it, many pages of old Paul's book of the mountains. The very sight of that pass made my feet itch; in a long day's ride from the ranch we could cross it and camp that night in the wilderness of the East Kootenay—a portion of British Columbia which, we firmly believed, had been created expressly for the benefit of the more active and enterprising spirits of the province of Alberta.

One way and the other, it was not an easy country for a born nomad to live in and keep his nose to the grindstone. Those distant mountains had a way of beckoning to you, and it was so easy just to saddle a couple of horses and hit the trail ...

Bull Creek

The most direct, though not the easiest, way home to the Buffalo Head from the grassy basin where we charged the grizzly was by way of Bull Creek. To reach Bull Creek one rode up the eastern slope of the South Fork valley and picked up a narrow hunting trail through a dense wood of old firs. Above that came alpine country, and above that again the stony, rounded summit of the Bull Creek Pass. That was above timberline. Rare alpine flowers grew there, and the mountain sheep grazed there in the wintertime.

The pass lay east and west. To the west the Holy Cross Mountain rose up across the gulf of the South Fork valley, carrying on its breast its white cross of snow. To the east Bull Creek, rising just below the pass in strong springs, ran down towards the Highwood, cutting through the walls of rock that had tried to bar its way. It was a lonely place; no one but myself ever went that way. It was on Bull Creek and in the deep coulees of Mount Head—but especially on Bull Creek—that I found, close to home, the true untouched wilderness of the wild hills. That, in times of stress, was what held me there on the Buffalo Head. That was what made a settled life possible for one whose conception of the perfect home was a camp.

On the east side of the pass, at the head of Bull Creek, there was a big stretch of excellent grazing. I wanted that grazing area for the Buffalo Head for use in October, and I wanted it now while the going was good and nobody cared; the time might be coming when there would be no more pockets of virgin bunch grass country like this that a rancher could have for the asking.

So I spoke to the forest ranger about it, pointing out that there was an ideal place on upper Bull Creek at which to stop the cattle—a place where the creek cut through between vertical walls of rock and where a short fence could be built, blocking this gap and so corralling the whole of the upper valley and the pass.

The ranger took a very reasonable view of things: "If I were you," he said, "I wouldn't put in a formal application to the office. Much better go right ahead and put the fence in and say nothing about it. I won't know anything and nobody'll be any the wiser ... "

So I cut out the old hunting trail up Bull Creek that Pocaterra had shown me years before, discovering in the process a waterfall that was the head of navigation for a teeming multitude of small troutlets. Not wishing to make a public highway of Bull Creek I cut out that trail in such a way that it would take a mind-reader to follow it: there were breaks in it and never anywhere did the trail do the obvious thing. Then, having other things to worry about, I let the Bull Creek fence business slide for a season or two.

And now it was spring and Paul and his band of Stoneys were camped somewhere up around Mount Head, ready to move in and build the Bull Creek drift fence. The arrangement was that I would pack in the necessary barbed wire, spikes and staples and drop them on the trail at the place where I wanted the fence built. Then, a week or so later, I could ride up, check the job, which would be done by then, and pay Paul in cash or in kind—usually in both, for the Buffalo Head storehouse was well filled and Paul had not failed to observe that the prices I charged him were lower than he would have to pay elsewhere.

We had some friends staying at the ranch from Toronto and I asked them if they would care to come with me. Of them only Nancy said she would; the rest had other plans—so the two of us went down to the corrals and saddled up. I rode Rex, and I packed Mollie with two spools of barbed wire weighing eighty-odd pounds apiece as side packs, and with the spikes, tools and odds and ends that Paul would want as a centre pack. Nancy rode some good, strong mountain horse, well able to plug through the snowdrifts that we expected to find towards the head of Bull Creek—and off we went.

About seven miles from home the trail came out of a belt of pines on to a very steep, open, bunch-grass hillside. We were entering the upper part of Bull Creek valley; and this bit of country was, and still is, a living memorial of what the foothills must have been before the white man came, measuring and parcelling, ploughing up, overgrazing with his cattle and horses. The bunch-grass grew there as it had always grown, with its roots protected from sun and frost by thick cushions of its own old growth. In summertime it bent before the onrush of the wind like a field of waving grain; its swaying seed heads made a rippling sea of silver light, splashed with the flaring colours of the summer flowers. In the fall the bunch-grass cured and ripened. Deer and elk passed by, and perhaps some wandering, pioneering cow and calf. But no herd came this way to break the quiet of this lonely valley. Then, through the lazy, slumbrous days of Indian summer, the grass hillsides would lie pale gold under the low autumn sun, shining with a light of their own against the dark rocks and the black woods of alpine firs, waiting ...

But this was May, and last year's grass lay dun-coloured and flattened by the winter snows. In this carpet of old grass the crocuses were flowering and the young green blades were poking through. The blue, snow-streaked summit of the Holy Cross showed to the westward through the pass, and down the valley sang the everlasting westwind. In the sun-warmed watercourses that wrinkled this hillside an early growth always started up, and the tender, juicy shoots of certain plants were already showing. One of these favoured spots lay about three hundred yards ahead of us and there was something very odd protruding from it—a pale-coloured, roundish shape through the edges of which the afternoon sun made a halo of light. I watched it for a minute or so. It was very busy, whatever it was, and it was scarcely moving. Then I saw—and I turned in my saddle and pointed: "Look, Nancy—a grizzly!"

"No!" she said, leaning forward. "Oh, where? Show me at once! Can we get closer?" Her eyes were shining with excitement.

"I think we can," I said, and we moved forward. The wind blew in our faces, straight from the grizzly to us, and, what with the rush and the roaring of it and the tumult of Bull Creek away down below, one could speak in an ordinary quiet voice without disturbing the bear. And the grizzly was feeding away from us into the wind; the round thing, which was all that I had so far seen of him, was a bit of his rump sticking up over the lip of the little coulee that he was grubbing in.

The trail was nothing but an old game trail, about a foot or eighteen inches wide. High above us on our right there was a belt of pines. Deep down on our left Bull Creek fought its noisy way through old snowdrifts and a tangle of twisted poplar and willow. It was a case of either up the trail or down the trail—there was no other place to run to if anything went wrong. And the outfit consisted of one optimistic rancher, one overloaded packhorse running loose, and one girl from Toronto, brimful of confidence (in what? I have often wondered) and breathless with excitement.

I had been reading Bryan Williams' book *Game Trails in British Columbia*. Bryan Williams had been a guide in the Kootenays and in the Cassiar, then, for thirteen years, head of the B.C. Provincial Game Department. If he didn't know what he was talking about, then who did? In his book Williams gives it as his opinion that a grizzly, when startled, will run in whatever direction he happens to be facing at that moment. Most of the "charges" attributed to these bears, Williams says, are due to the fact that, when the shot is fired or the grizzly is otherwise alarmed, he takes immediate steps to get away from trouble—and very often the quickest way to do that is to follow his nose and not waste time looking around.[11] And sometimes his nose happens to be pointing towards the hunter ...

This grizzly had his back to us and was fully occupied with his spring salad. I had full confidence in Bryan Williams' well-argued theory: never would there be a better chance of putting it to the test. And so we rode quietly up the trail.

There must be some minor deity whose special duty it is to protect the foolhardy, for, without any exaggeration, we rode to within twenty-five yards of that grizzly. I have often passed that spot since then and never without marvelling at the few short paces we left between ourselves and that bunch of living dynamite. It was not my old friend, the red-legged grizzly whom I often saw here. This bear was of one uniform colour, almost sandy with a touch of grey. He was very big and the wind was rippling his pale fur and sending small shadows chasing through it. He was grubbing away with claws and teeth in the soft earth, pursuing his tender mushy plants, and he was completely absorbed in his quest.

I turned round to look at Nancy. She was leaning forward in her saddle fascinated, absolutely entranced. The curious thing is that the sense of fear seemed to be absent that afternoon. The horses, too, were not alarmed; they were watching the bear quite quietly.

"What do we do now?" Nancy said, raising her voice just enough to cope with the wind.

The thing had gone far enough. "We speak to him," I said; and I turned and shouted, putting my trust in Bryan Williams: "Hullo, Bear!" It wasn't a particularly bright remark, but it worked like a charm. Without pausing to look behind, the grizzly lit out of there as if the devil was after him—straight the way he was heading, which was up and across the hill. The speed at which he moved was something of an eye-opener when seen from so close. He never stopped or looked behind him till he reached the edge of the pines above us; then he turned round, raised up on his hind legs to his full height, lifted his paws and let a roar out of him that could be heard by us down on the trail, even with that wind blowing.

"What do we do now?" Nancy asked.

"We get out of here quick," I told her, "and let's hope he isn't a she with some cubs somewhere up the trail." And we rode on up the valley, not slowly but not without dignity.

Nancy on the ridge between Mount Head and Holy Cross

The rest of that trip passed off without incident. We dumped Paul's stuff at the rock outcrops and went on to the pass. High up and to the south we saw a band of Bighorn sheep; they frequented the Bull Creek Hills at this season of the year. Facing us across the deep valley of the South Fork was the usual magnificent view of the mountains. Low down in the rocks where we sat and watched the sheep a small yellow saxifrage was making the first timid splashes of colour amid the melting drifts of snow … Home by way of the South Fork and Flat Creek. The others were very polite when we came in that evening and told our story—by which I mean that nobody actually accused us point blank of lying. But they seemed to think we might have underestimated the distance between us and the bear.

They were wrong; and I am convinced, after venturing that close, that Bryan Williams is right. The bear, I think, must act quite automatically on a blind impulse of panic. That bit of natural history is worth knowing and might well come in handy some day. At the same time I still think that I ventured a bit too far on that afternoon in order to prove the truth of it. It was indeed lucky for Nancy and me that Bryan Williams was a practical man and no armchair theorist!

Bull Creek runs from west to east, cutting across the strike of the rocks; the ridges and the rock outcrops, therefore, run transversely to the general direction of the valley. The western slopes of the ridges are open, and so there is nothing to stop the prevailing west wind from sweeping the snow off these grassy hillsides in the winter months and piling it into vast drifts on the eastern slopes, causing to grow there, owing to this extra moisture, groves and belts of trees.

Under these conditions, and given a heavy early snowfall, it is quite easy for cattle to get themselves walled-in by drifts on upper Bull Creek, and that is what a bunch of Buffalo Head cattle succeeded in doing one stormy fall. It was my fault. I had found them there in mid-November, up to their bellies in bunch-grass and watered by springs that never froze. It was a cow's paradise, and they were so content that I left them there, thinking they would wander on home in their own sweet time.

They didn't—and when I next rode up to see what was going on I found them drifted-in. There were ways of escape for them over the stony, open tops above timberline—but they had no intention of taking them; they were quite happy where they were.

I tried to get at them with a horse, but I couldn't: the snow was too deep. So I rode up again a couple of days later—this time with a pair of sixty-inch snowshoes slung across my back. I rode old Red as far up Bull Creek as I could, and then I tied him in a clump of firs well away from the trail. Then I put the snowshoes on and broke a trail through the drifts to the open slopes where the cattle were grazing—with old memories running through my head of winter trails on Battle River and in Deadmen's Valley. And then I approached the cattle from the west, brandishing a couple of fir branches and with the big raquettes making a horrible clatter on the bare ground.

Everything went according to plan. The sight of this strange-looking creature coming at them was too much for the cattle. They bunched and ran, and then wheeled and stared. Then a snort of fear—and they ran and wheeled again, coming to a standstill and staring anxiously. And then the whole outfit stampeded.

Down Bull Creek they went, hightailing it through the drifts, crashing through the bush; smashing off the frozen branches and fetching down dead trees, snorting, bawling ... it was as if a herd of elephants was tearing down the valley. I followed them for a time; I could keep pretty well up with them on snowshoes. There were cow trails in the snow all over the place at first; gradually they converged into one well-beaten path, and then they hit the trail that I had broken, and the uproar died away in the distance. I turned aside to pick up Red. The winter dusk was falling as I took my snowshoes off, and the hills looked desolate and forbidding through a fine, cold snow that was drifting down. Thankfully I swung myself into the saddle and rode away down Bull Creek in the gathering darkness and the oncoming storm.

5

High Noon

Dude Wrangling

Of the dry years of the Dry Thirties, 1936 was the last and the worst. This, of course, also had to be the year in which we chose to start our experiment in dude-wrangling. Pocaterra had made the name of the place known—a letter addressed simply to "Buffalo Head Ranch, Canada" would reach us safely. There, in the home meadow, stood the old cabins, scattered amongst clumps of trees, put to various uses. People kept on writing and asking if it was still possible to come and stay at the ranch—and finally, when, at the end of a very hard winter, Marigold and I had slipped away from the snowdrifts and gone down to Vancouver Island for a couple of weeks of spring flowers, a minor flood of letters came. With cattle worth next to nothing it seemed a shame to let these chances go by, and we considered the inquiries thoughtfully and to some purpose.

"I'll tell you what we'll do," I said. "We'll write to the pick of these telling them we have some very attractive cabins, unlimited water supply piped to them, showers, wonderful riding country, mountain scenery and first-class cooking. We'll give them a guide and saddle-horses at any hour of the day or night. They'll meet people who are strange to them, queer characters in ten-gallon hats—all this will spell romance. They'll love it, and when anything goes wrong we'll just give them a good Alberta-size drink and all pain will speedily vanish. We can get something printed quickly down here on the Island … "

"But we haven't got any beautiful cabins with water piped to them," Marigold broke in. "Or showers, or a first class cook. Just a bunch of wild-west characters, and that's not enough. And there's beds and blankets and furniture and saddles—I suppose it hasn't occurred to you that we might even need some money, too?"

"No, we won't," I assured her. "Calgary's bust flat, all the world's bust flat—and so are we, but no one knows it and our credit's good, which is more than many can say. We can have anything we want for the asking. Let's answer these letters now and tell them about all the lovely things we've got on the ranch, and then we'll hit for home and the snowdrifts again and put them there … "

So we did that, and on our return the Buffalo Head hummed with sudden activity. We had just over two months in which to make good all the lies we had told and there was no time to lose.

The old cabins which we planned to use were unroofed and stripped completely, down to log walls and floor. It was while they were in that unprotected state, about the middle of May, that a thunderstorm hit us and a deluge of rain came down. The old cabins got a thorough wash and started their new incarnation clean—and that was the last rain the foothills were to see for ten blazing weeks.

Construction then started. The cabins were re-roofed. The roofs were set at an attractive pitch and painted a dark green. New floors were laid on top of the old ones; the walls were re-chinked and made dark and shiny with linseed oil, inside and out; heavy slabs of stone were hauled up from the river and set into the grass outside the doors. New and bigger windows, and more of them, let more light into the dark, cool interiors where Frank Horrell was hard at work, with English thoroughness, building-in bedside tables, shelves and cupboards. He was doing a beautiful job of work—and it was when I commented on this that he told me what his real line of carpentry was: "Church work," he said. "Pews, lecterns, pulpits and the like … " Everything was grist to Horrell's mill, and a few days later I found the heavy plate glass of an old-fashioned Dodge windscreen fitted perfectly into place and doing duty as a dressing-table top. Horrell had noticed it shoved away in a corner of the old log-built garage.

Carried away by our enthusiasm we built one completely new cabin, over and above the renovations. This was a palatial affair, as cabins went, and as a result we found ourselves without time to build the promised shower house. So a large wall-tent was set up in a secluded corner of the meadow. A floor was laid in it and a bath, stove, table and chair were set thereon in barrack-room fashion. Outside the tent a large drum of water was set high up on a trestle where it would catch the sun and flow tepidly, when required, into the bath. The stove provided hot water and the outlet was via a hose pipe which wriggled away into the bush. This worked, on the whole, well. To be exact, better than well—for it produced, amongst a gay and light-hearted bunch of dudes, more excitement than any ordinary bathroom could have provided.

A colony of wasps took a fancy to the place. They were persistent and it was difficult to get rid of them permanently without either rendering the tent uninhabitable or destroying it completely by fire. Rumour has it that truly Arcadian scenes were enacted there among the tall white poplars, the purple fireweed and the blue delphiniums— nymphs running distractedly through the woods, casting away in their haste towels, modesty and anything else they happened to have with them. Running as if the devil were at their heels. Probably even harder, for the devil is supposed to be a gentleman while the wasps were quite obviously nothing of the kind.

The timing of the cabin job was perfect. Frantic work by all hands raked the last chip out of the grass, got the carpenters out of the way and the last bed made up precisely on zero hour. The dudes came up the valley and, not without apprehension, we watched them move into their new homes almost before the sawdust had had time to settle.

We needn't have worried. They loved their cabins and took the bath tent in their stride. Their outfits of bridle, saddle and blanket were dealt out to them: very soon it was "my saddle," and "my horse," and they ranged over the Highwood country from Mount Head to the Prince's Ranch, carefree and happy; the West had absorbed them with its easy tolerance and its open hospitality.

One blazing day followed another. The construction gang had now transferred its activities to the hillside west of the buildings and across the meadow. There, with a fall of about a hundred feet down to the house, a thousand-gallon concrete tank was built, sunk in the ground and well insulated from heat and cold. To this tank a high spring was piped, and from it a two-inch pipe ran down almost vertically and connected with the main water line from the spruce coulee. When all was ready a valve was turned—and the upper tank slowly filled with water that was ice cold and so crystal clear that, under the shadow of the tank roof, one could look down through it, six feet to the very bottom and never see that it was there at all. A valve on the two-inch line held this water in check until it should be needed, while the overflow ran out into a trough for the milk cows, in whose summer pasture the tank had been built.

This new water outfit was my brain-child—the making good of the "unlimited water supply" fairy tale we had broadcast from Vancouver Island. I had been convinced that, with this drought and with more people using the water, the old tank would prove inadequate and go dry. Which was precisely what it did, two days after the new system was ready—in the evening just after the men had finished their supper.

A wrathful calling upon strange gods came from the Chinaman cook; Adolf sent word to me and, feeling that once more we had dodged disaster by a hair's breadth, I walked off across the meadow towards the hill.

The heavy valve gleamed dully in its wooden box in the green shadow of the spruce. I turned it slowly and a hiss came from the pipes—then a vibrant, shuddering hum. A few seconds later a faint shout reached me from the ranch house which was about four hundred yards away. Something was happening down there ...

A little group of men was gathered on the stone pathway by the kitchen door; they called to me as I drew near. "Holy Moses!" somebody shouted, "just come and see her spin!" And from another: "Adolf's pretty near drowned—he's just gone off to wring himself out!" He had turned on a lawn sprinkler, it appeared, and, with the pressure at least quadrupled, the thing had almost exploded in his face. It was whirling there on the grass, just a blur of metal with no part visible, and with the water driven upwards and outwards in a mist that floated gently on the evening air. The shadow of the hill had already fallen, on the house; but far above the shadow—even above the tops of the big poplars—wreaths and streamers of moisture sparkled and flashed in the sunlight as they drifted over the shining leaves. A miracle, and I had wrought it.

A heathen scream from the kitchen proclaimed that the Chinaman had found there was water in his taps again. But he was not happy about it and he was shouting rapidly in his own tongue: he had tried to fill a saucepan, I gathered later, and a hydraulic jet, solid as a sword blade, had issued from the tap and dashed the utensil from his hand. Then the water had rebounded violently from the sink, overflowing in a cascade of noble proportions, while the frantic celestial, instead of doing something about it, danced raving round the kitchen.

Dude-wrangling, we found, was hard work but we got a lot of fun out of it and it was a success: financially it carried the place through several very difficult years. What pleased the dudes best was to be given something definite to do: "help" with cattle (sometimes they got terribly in the way); ride for the ranch mail, a twenty-mile trip that came round with every Friday—or whatever else we managed to think up. The annual stocking of the Highwood's tributaries was always good for a lively day. The dudes would go off with Sam, our district fishery warden, on the morning of the day the Fishery Department tank-truck came up the valley loaded with thousands—or it may have been millions—of trout fry for the stocking of Flat Creek and Sullivan Creek. The truck would go as far as it could; then the Buffalo Head packhorses would take over. The fry would be transferred into cans with ice containers and with wire-gauze, sacking-covered lids to allow the passage of air, and the horses would stand quietly while these were loaded on to them and secured. Things, however, always livened up a bit the moment the party moved off: the unaccustomed glugging of the water in the fish cans never failed to alarm and excite the horses who would tear around in circles on the end of their lead ropes with a horseman hanging on to each one, pivoting on his horse and trying to quieten him. Sometimes a frantic packhorse would wrap his lead rope and himself round a tree; or else two lead ropes would tangle and two horses jam together with the full equivalent of a typhoon on the Pacific taking place inside the fish cans. This annual circus of Sam's was always a popular event in the calendar—and, strange to say, the mortality amongst the fry was never very great. After two or three miles of some foothill pack trail the fish cans would be decanted into a likely looking pool. A few tiny bodies would float to the surface—but a brown cloud of swarming, active life would show for a moment in the clear water and then vanish, seemingly none the worse for their wild ride.

Back at the ranch our dudes found various employment, apart from the usual activities of riding, swimming in the home pool, fishing and climbing mountains. The blacksmith shop had a fascination for the gentler sex, and more than one girl spent a large part of her time there, turning the handle of the blower, keeping the fire at exactly the right heat and trying to do exactly what she was told. A curl of smoke would go up and the clang of hammer on anvil would ring out. Then, if one passed by, a fair head might be seen in the little log-built forge through an inferno of smoke and flame … Its owner would be at the handle, turning anxiously to the tune of an agitated "No, dammit, no! What did I tell you? If you get it too hot you'll burn the metal. Slowly, now—slowly … " from the wielder of the hammer.

A miscellaneous collection of old branding irons hung on the walls of the blacksmith shop. One by one they would be taken down and fingered curiously while somebody explained this queer alphabetical heraldry of the West. They were an odd lot: there was a heart and a diamond, an old buffalo head and an owl sitting on a branch; there were letters and figures and half-diamonds, and one large U that must have drifted up from the Bar U in Pocaterra's time … One well-beloved dude became so entranced with these outlandish devices that she insisted on having them branded all over her suitcases. I came in just as she was urging the Major on to do this fell deed: "Go on, Major Comey," she was saying, "slap them on. All of them—I want them all!"

"But good Lord, woman, don't you understand? It'll wreck this beautiful leather. And the porters'll think you're raving mad when you get back to London and decant yourself from the train at Waterloo—"

"Let them think it. Now then, for the last time—*put those brands on!*" And on they went!

Looking back on it all one comes to the conclusion that, by and large and on the hoof, it was a good time. Never, in all the rest of our years there, did we on the ranch get to see so much of the Highwood country. We got into strange and beautiful places that no man in his right mind would ever get into unless he thought strayed cattle might have gone that way, or unless he was trying to take a dude for a ride into entirely new country. Most of those places we never saw again.

It was an exacting life, because the regular ranch work had to go on alongside our capers with these summer migrants. But, quite apart from the friendships we made, it was well worth the effort: in those depression years running dudes was like having a small private gold mine on the place. Not only that, but we were lucky enough at that time to have steadily on the ranch the sort of help that a man might dream of now but never see, even in a lifetime of ranching—the perfect team. That made the whole thing possible.

The Elk Trail

Bit by bit things fell into place on the Buffalo Head and we were able to take once more to the mountains. It so happened that about this time I turned once more to an old project—the finding and re-opening of an old Indian trail across the main range of the Rockies to British Columbia. The thing became an obsession with me—but to understand it fully it is necessary to go back in time to the days when Pocaterra and I rode together in the mountains.

It was Pocaterra who pointed out to me the gap in the Continental Divide. That was the time he and I rode, with packhorses, from Mnogappa on the Kananaskis River to the Buffalo Head in two days; and it was towards evening on the second day, as we loped the horses over the High Meadows, that Pocaterra pointed suddenly towards the southwest and turned in his saddle towards me. "You see that gap over there, Patterson?" he said. "The one to the left of the Pyramid?"

I swung my horse towards him ... We were coming down the upper Highwood valley. We had the foothills of the Highwood Range on our left, and on our right, but hidden from us by grassy ridges with a scattering of pines, the Highwood River. Beyond the river and six miles away, the peaks of the Divide rose up against the low September sun. To the right of the gap at which Pocaterra was pointing the dividing range was pretty much of a wall; to the left and southeast-ward the range became more varied and broken by low saddles—more interesting. The British Columbia-Alberta Boundary surveyors noted this change in character when they passed that way in 1915: they called the unbroken wall in the northwest the Elk Mountains, and the peaks and saddles to the left of the gap the High Rock Range. The gap they christened Weary Creek Gap, for it led to Weary Creek which flowed down to Elk River. With that, and with the building of a few cairns and monuments, the surveyors departed and the silence fell once more upon those lonely places.

Above the thud of hoofs and the creaking of saddle leather Pocaterra's voice went on: "The Indians have a story about that pass," he was saying. "Long ago, they say, there were many elk on this side of the main range. Now, as you know, there are few.[12] They were very much hunted—too much hunted, they thought—and so they called a council. It was held somewhere way down the Highwood, outside the hills—and to it came the elk from all over; from the Bow and the Sheep Creek country in the north, and from the prairies; and from Willow Creek and the Old Man River in the south, they all came. At the council they decided that things were getting too tough and that they had better move away from their old range and find a new country. So they came up the Highwood, a great army of elk, and they turned up the creek that leads to the Pyramid. And they went, in single file, up and over to Elk River, through that gap that you can see. And they never came back. Just what lies at the bottom of that story, I don't know; but over there is Elk River and, my God, it's certainly rightly named! You can hear the elk calling all over the place there in the evenings. And here is the Highwood—a far better country and it has hardly a one. The old Stoneys tell me there's a game trail worn deep in the rock on the climb up to that pass below the Pyramid—so, they say, the legend must be true! There is Indian reasoning for you."

"If we could get horses over that trail it would be a wonderful shortcut to Elk River," I said. "And, if we didn't cut it out too much, nobody need ever know about it. How is it, do you know?"

"It would make a wonderful private hunting trail. Right close to home, too. But the Indians tell me there's some rock ledge or something that would need blasting out—some step that a horse can't make. I've never been there to see ... "

We rode down the winding trail that led from the High Meadows to the river flats. At the foot of the coulee Pocaterra pointed up to the right. "Not half a mile upstream," he said, "is the mouth of the creek that comes down from the Elk Trail. McPhail Creek it's called on the map but Bunk Creek is what the ranger calls it. There's an old lumber camp a little way up from the mouth; it was closed many years ago but the bunks of the old logging sleighs are still piled there."

The Elk Trail. That was it. The name alone was enough to draw one on ... We turned our horses' heads towards home. The sun had gone down now behind the mountains and the first touch of frost could be felt. We were still over twenty miles from the Buffalo Head—but the miles and the hours slipped easily away, and moonlight found us still playing with this new project of a hidden pass to Elk River and Nyahé-ya-'nibi.

☆ ☆ ☆ ☆

Other things got in the way and the Elk Trail had to wait four whole years. Then, one October morning, Marigold and I came riding at a good fast clip across the High Meadows, homeward bound for the Buffalo Head. The packhorses were in the lead, running loose. Behind them we rode at our ease with sleeves rolled up and shirts thrown open to the sun; it seemed a pity to hurry home on this perfect autumn day. I had just been telling Marigold the story of the Elk Trail and there, in the west, was the Gap, wide open from here and inviting.

"Let's camp when we get down to the river," I said. "As near as we can get to the mouth of this Bunk Creek or whatever its name is. We'll set up camp and we'll have lunch and then we'll take the saddle-horses and see what we can see."

So we did that—and early afternoon saw us following an old logging road that ran up the creek. Many years had gone by since the last sleighload of logs had come this way; the log bridges back and forth over the stream were rotten and fallen-in, and the road was blocked with fallen trees. We zigzagged around these obstacles, and splashed across the creek through deep pools and over gravelly shallows, with frightened trout darting away from the horses' feet.

Hook Ridge, overlooking the Elk Trail

The buildings of the old lumber camp were on a little flat on the right bank of the creek, tucked up against a low cliff. This silent place must have seen some lively times in its day, but now the bush was taking back its own again: the logs were rotting and the roofs were falling in; a young spruce was poking through one corner of the barn and the bunkhouse smelt to high heaven of packrat. The wide bunks of the logging sleighs from which the creek got its name were stacked outside the forge, and the forge itself was a museum—broken hames and tugs, fragments of logging chain, a bent kingpin, axe heads in various stages of decay, a prodigious quantity of horseshoes.

We forded the stream and climbed up onto the open bench that followed the valley towards the mountains. An Indian trail can be counted on to follow, wherever possible, the point of a bench, thereby avoiding the timber and gaining a good view of the valley. And there we found it—a well-used game trail that seemed also to have been used, long ago, by men. There seemed little doubt that it was an old Indian trail to Elk River that had been in use probably for centuries, ever since men first came into these hills, and then abandoned when the horse reached the Indians of the plains.

Late in November, I came again with Adolf. The excuse for the trip was the shooting of a deer, but what I personally wanted to do was to see the pass; Adolf was welcome to do the hunting for the two of us.

Morning came and with it the sun. Adolf took his rifle and a couple of horses and rode off northeastwards into the dry, grassy foothills of the Mount Head Range. My trail led southwest, into the snow and the green timber.

Nearly four miles up the main creek I came on a meadow. It was a lovely meadow: the stream flowed round it and it took in hillside and benchland as well. The bunch-grass grew tall there as it did on Bull Creek; it stood well above the snow. Down below on the flat, with the yellow grass all around him and looking just like a painting by Carl Rungius, a magnificent bull elk was feeding. The wind was in the west, from him to me, so I was able to come very close to him before he saw me; he had fourteen points and a fine spread of horn. I looked at him over the sights of the Mannlicher and he seemed better yet.

But this was the Elk Trail: that bull in his wintry setting of green and white and gold was a fortunate omen, a promise of good days to come. And then there was Adolf: knowing him, I felt certain that there would be meat in camp by nightfall. "Go with God," I said to the bull, and he went—northward, up the grassy slope and into the trees ...

Beyond the meadow the old forest began. The trail stayed, wherever it was possible, on the point of the bench. Where it rounded a grassy point or dipped into the coulee of a side stream it was beautifully graded and very plain to see—it was as if a shelf, sometimes almost three feet wide, had been cut back into the hillside. Here and there sizable trees had seeded and grown in the trail, and where this had happened a new trail had been trodden out to bypass them. How many thousands of hoofs treading through how many thousands of years, I wondered, had it taken to make this highway of the wild game? No wonder the Indians said that an army of elk had passed this way.

I passed between two enormous foothills into an inner basin at the foot of the Pyramid. There, in a little clearing which I thought might make a camping place for a two-horse outfit, the trail faded away. Ahead of me and only half a mile away was a 500-foot wall with a frozen waterfall coming down it close to the Pyramid. Somewhere the game trail went up that wall, but where?

On the right the wreckage of a recent avalanche that had fallen from the main ridge of the Pyramid barred the way—a wild tangle of uprooted and smashed trees. With more snow one could have snowshoed over that swath of ruin—with less it would have been feasible to climb through it. But perhaps the trail didn't go that way at all—and I headed over to the left where the slope was gentle and led to a series of rock ledges.

The sun came out from behind a cloud and lit the green forest of the basin and the stony ridges of the Pyramid. I climbed in the shadow, swinging myself upwards on the little firs. I hung my pack and rifle in one of them and crawled along a rock ledge, shoving the snow off it with my hands. Then up a kind of chimney affair with big blocks of stone jammed in it in the form of steps. I accidentally dislodged one of these and it went bounding away into the basin kicking up a tremendous clatter and smashing an old dead fir to fragments as it fell. I watched its antics, terrified.

The chimney led to a wide ledge, and that to a slope of rock that was solid but icy from the overflow of a small spring. Up that I went, scared stiff but hounded on by the desire to see. Then to the right again and up to the summit of a rocky ridge—and that was the end. I could go no further.

But that was enough. From the top of my ridge I could see over the wall that had barred the way. And what I saw was, first of all, a high basin thickly wooded with the dark green alpine fir. Then a second rocky rise—an easy one—and then a series of terraces, sparsely wooded with clumps of fir, leading to a summit. And beyond that summit, perhaps five or six miles further west, the peaks of the range that rose beyond Elk River.

So that was the Weary Creek Gap—the Elk Trail Pass of Indian legend. I swung the glass over it this way and that; every minute detail stood out clear and sharp in the golden light of that winter afternoon. There was a fascination to it, as there must be in any pass through a great range. Mountain peaks are all very well in their way and you can see the lay of the country from them very nicely; but a pass is different. It has seen so much. It has watched the migrations of the wild animals and the coming of the first lonely hunters. Men fleeing from their enemies have passed that way; tribes seeking new hunting grounds. The gap in the mountains says the same thing to them all: "Beyond," it says, "lies a new valley—a valley you have never seen. And beyond that again, somewhere, there will be another pass. Why just be content, like a cow in a patch of good feed? Why ever stop anywhere, however good it may be?"

The flicker of a movement showed in the glass. It was in the deep shadow of the Pyramid and the wall, and I looked again, carefully. Six mountain sheep, ewes and lambs, were making their way across the stony slopes above the wreckage of the avalanche. They were headed for the 500-foot wall and, now that I came to look closely, I could see the thin threads of game trails crossing the great, barren screes towards the precipice. I watched the sheep curiously. They might, if they felt so inclined, give a man a line on the trail.

Sure enough they dipped down towards the foot of the wall. Then they began to climb at an angle on a wide ledge; and then they disappeared from view behind small, dwarfed trees, vanishing into some gallery in the rock. They reappeared higher up, going in the opposite direction, and then they came to a very steep place up which they bounded one by one. And so they went, zigzagging up the face of the wall, now in view, now hidden, keeping always to the right of the waterfall, until one saw them for the last time as they walked sedately over the crest of that barren rampart and vanished into the darkness of the firs.

Now I knew all I wished to know—thanks to the sheep. High time too, for the shadow of the wall had already fallen across the basin. The nameless mountains beyond the Elk showed darkly against the green radiance of a cold sunset. Far above their snowy summits a few lingering clouds were turning slowly to amber in the turquoise lake of the evening sky. It was time to be getting out of here and pounding the trail back to camp and whatever Adolf had shot in those tawny open hills that still were catching the last rays of the sun, so far away to the eastward and yet so clear to see.

Elated, I put the glass in my pocket and made a move. I hurried— and in my haste I slipped and skidded down the whole of the icy slope, fetching up on the lower edge more by good luck than good management. After that I moved more carefully ...

There seemed to be no end to the dark forest, but at last the light of the tent appeared in the distance and the sound of the bells drifted up the valley on the frosty air. That was good; Adolf was home and all would be in order. I hailed him as I drew near: "Hullo, Adolf!"

"Hullo! It is late—you must have been far. But you have timed it just right; the hotel is putting on a special celebration dinner tonight: deer's liver with bacon, and potatoes mashed with butter. And that is only the main dish—by God, we will surely founder ourselves if we go on like this."

Oh no, we won't, I thought, as I undid the hooks of the mosquito-screen door. At least, one of us won't. I was hungry and Adolf's menu sounded just the thing. Time enough to worry about foundering after we had eaten. And I lifted the screen and stepped, with pleasurable anticipation, out of the moonlit snow and forty degrees of frost into the dancing light of the candles and the genial warmth of the stove.

The Hill of the Flowers

It was full-leafed summer before I came again to the Elk Trail. I came in the evening, by devious ways and with much log-hopping, to the meadow where I had found the bull elk feeding in the snow, and there I made camp.

From the meadow back towards the Highwood I cleared out the trail in such a way that no very obvious sign of my work remained for anyone to see. The lower end, towards the river, I left blind: that is to say that no cutting was done at all; I merely made a winding round through the jackpine by dragging out of the way the major obstacles. Nothing was left in plain view that one year's growth of grass and fireweed would not obliterate.

Above the elk meadow I left the trail blind for some distance into the old forest. After that I cut it out into a good pack trail as far as I could in the time that I had. This brought me to the gap between the big foothills that guarded the inner basin. There I stopped in an open glade, a good place for tying horses. From below came the noise of a waterfall—but I left that for another day and spent the evening climbing the 8,000-foot hill to the north of the trail. Though this was the end of June, the snowdrifts were still deep up there and the larches were still only in bud. But where the snow had gone there were signs of an amazing variety of alpine flowers, a few already in bloom. In ten days or so, if this hot weather held, the whole summit of this butte was going to be a solid carpet of flowers—a blaze of colour that would outshine anything I had ever seen, even in this Highwood country.

Marigold would enjoy seeing all this in bloom, I thought, as I sat and watched through the glass a couple of elk playing down below on the flats of a creek that spread out there into water meadows—the sort of place where one might well expect to see a moose feeding. Truly this small corner of the mountains had everything within a few short miles. All we needed now to make it perfect was a lake—and some mountain goat, if that was not asking too much. The circling of the elk became larger and wider. Then, suddenly, one took off into the bush with the other after him and I saw them no more.

The sheep trail up the cliff to the pass was plainly visible from this hill: but it was still blocked by a huge snowdrift at the foot of the waterfall, into which the water plunged and vanished from view.

Back at the ranch we busied ourselves with the preliminaries of haying. Then we took the bulls up to the valley of the South Fork, starting, with them, as usual, in the small hours of the morning. When that was done I could see four free days ahead before haying started, and I broached the subject of alpine flowers to Marigold ...

I sorted the outfit for our trip the evening of the day we took the bulls up to Mount Head. I had not gone to bed at all the night before and, when I strolled over to the storehouse with the list in my hand that evening, I had been without sleep for over thirty-six hours. This was to be the grand finale. Then an early bed.

Soon Marigold came over with a list of stuff that the cook wanted. "You're half asleep," she said, "better let me put up that outfit."

"No. I know where everything is and I can do it in half the time. But I'd be glad of a hand when you've got your stuff for Alberto."

So we went at it together and, one by one, the various items were placed in the panniers and struck off the list. After years of putting up outfits for the bush one becomes skilled in the art and quick. Not for us the pitfalls that ensnare the week-end picnicker—matches left behind, salt in the sugar, sugar in the salt and so forth. We worked together there in the twilight as one, quietly and efficiently. It was darkish, but with practice one can tell by the feel of things what they are. I picked up a cotton sack and pinched it: the granules gritted harshly against each other—it was sugar and I added some more to it and crossed it off the list. Marigold held up a small sack and asked what was in it.

"Has it got a blue string?" I asked her. "Then that's salt. But it's not quite enough; better shove some more in it."

She did.

☆ ☆ ☆ ☆

Late the following afternoon Marigold and I swung our horses off the main Highwood trail, forded the river and plunged into the trees that hid the lower stretches of the Elk Trail. It was hot and we had ridden fast from the Buffalo Head, and now the dry, gummy pollen was flying from the pines as we brushed against their branches on the blind part of the trail. Pollen and dust and sweat—how good it was going to be to off-saddle, stick one's head in the creek and then drink great mugs of steaming tea!

"How much further to this elk meadow of yours?"

"Oh, I don't know. A couple of miles, perhaps. Not very far. Soon be there."

And I pushed on through the trees with the packhorses close behind me, kept up by an occasional wrathful cry from the "arriero" who was riding in a cloud of pine dust and expressing her feelings with abandon. Soon the trees began to thin out and we were riding into the open against the full glory of the evening sun ...

The bunch-grass had grown since I had last seen it. It was four feet high now and the rays of the sun struck through it in a glittering maze of shifting light. Wild roses grew at the edge of the pines, and low down in the swaying bunch-grass the heads of flowers showed— larkspur, wild geranium, yarrow. Summer clouds drifted lazily out of the west across a summer sky. Mountains and forest, too, had known what was expected of them: never had they looked so fair and so beautiful.

I pulled up Black Jack and checked the packhorse that I was leading. "There!" I said, with a magnificent sweep of my free hand. "Look at that!" And though I had had nothing to do with the creation of this landscape, it was not without a certain pride that I drew attention to its beauties.

But the dust and the pollen of the pines and the heat of the day had got in their fell work and I might just as well have shown this glowing vista to the Sphinx. Moments of heavy silence went by on leaden wings and then a flat, expressionless voice came from behind: "Look at what?" it said.

Look at what? My God! There was Wessex for you, speaking—and my cherished view might just as well have been a burnt muskeg in Saskatchewan! A tough lot these Saxons, I thought—no wonder the Normans found them difficult; no wonder the armies of Europe broke against their solid squares! No wonder ... And I fetched Black Jack a crack with my quirt that made him leap forward from a standstill, almost dislocating the neck of Bozo who was hitched to Black Jack's saddle horn and dreaming sleepily of oats.

Up the slope we pranced, and then down to the camping place—the horses all up in the air, tails up, ears cocked. Off flew packs, panniers and saddles in record time, thudding down on to the grass. Bozo, the master mind, was hurriedly secured to a tree; the other horses moved off to graze. A minute later the smoke of a fire curled up and drifted away downstream. Soon the teapail was singing, then it boiled. I threw in a handful of tea and set the pot off the fire. We were both too furious to speak and I was vexed that I had laid into Black Jack with my quirt; tea was what we needed, and soon—tea the great healer ...

With chilly smiles of recognition we raised our mugs. I was about to drink when I saw a look of horror come into Marigold's face; she flung her mug from her as if it had been a scorpion and rolled over face downwards on a great cushion of bunch-grass. Then, without a word, she got up and fled for the creek. Now what? It seemed there was no pleasing anybody today, whatever you did—and, determined not to be stampeded by my partner's antics, I took a prodigious swig of tea. Then I understood—and I followed Marigold to the stream.

Brought together once more by common disaster, we analyzed the situation, on our hands and knees by the water's edge. The system had broken down, that was obvious—and soon we had the reason for it: Adolf and I had taken a sack of coarse salt out with us for the salting of trophies on a hunting trip; it had been left in its pannier and, when pinched through the sack, the stuff felt exactly like granulated sugar. That explained that—though not why the second sack, the blue-stringed one, was also found to contain the same disgusting mixture. And now we could spend four days without salt or sugar and, another time, be more careful.

"Do you remember how witty we were, yesterday evening in the storehouse, about comic week-end campers?"

"I do. I think perhaps we'd better forget about that, don't you? And look here—not a word about this when we get back to the ranch. For the honour of the firm ... "

I put in a day's work on the trail and then, the following morning, we set out for the pass taking our two saddle-horses to the end of the cutting. There we tied them and went ahead on foot. The day was sultry and silent—not a break of air was moving in the bush and thunder clouds were gathering round the Pyramid. The clouds thickened over the Divide and came lower; the rocks above us and the cliffs by the waterfall turned a sickly yellow in a feeble light that came from the eastward—from the Mount Head range on which the sun was still shining. The storm caught us as we were struggling across the tangle of the avalanche slide—a few heavy drops of rain fell, and then came a dazzling flash and a tremendous bang: lightning had struck the Pyramid. Down clattered some fragments of rock which came to rest in the upper end of the slide—and it was about then that we saw a little band of Bighorn sheep crossing the face of the scree above us, headed for the Horned Mountain and moving with less than their usual dignity; they were getting out of range of the falling stones. We, too, felt that this was no place to be—we clambered frantically forward at the rate of about one mile an hour over the smashed and fallen trees. Lightning split the gloom, thunder crashed and echoed in the pass, rain came down in torrents. We heaved ourselves over the trunks of ancient firs; dead, broken branches that were like steel springs tore at our shirts or stuck themselves through the straps of our packsacks. Somehow we got through the slide and on to the game trail that ran up the cliff (the big snowdrift had almost gone), and there we found a refuge beneath an overhang of rock a few feet from the waterfall—a green place of glistening moss and small, curling ferns. The spray sometimes came drifting into this shelter on an eddy of the wind, but that was nothing to what was coming down outside. We just sat there in the moss and watched the grey, streaming curtain of rain.

The storm lasted for about an hour. Then it rumbled away down the Highwood valley leaving behind it rags and tatters of cloud and a cold wind rising. We could hear the rush of the wind above us in the pass; masses of grey cloud came driving through; they tumbled over the edge of the precipice like water, only to be swept upwards again by some warmer air from below. Down beneath us grey, ghostly wisps and streamers of vapour trailed over the sodden forest of the basin; plainly this was no day to drag a wife, however willing, over the cold, wet backbone of North America. Sadly we hit the trail for camp, crawling through the avalanche debris like a pair of bedraggled beavers, hoping to God the horses were still where we had left them ... And in the night it stormed again.

That left us one whole day—one lovely, rain-washed, shining day. Bright and early in the morning basket ropes were taken from the packsaddles and strung from tree to tree. Soon they were decorated with all the odds and ends that had got soaked in the storm, and then, when that was done and camp chores were seen to, we went and saddled the horses ...

Sometime early in the afternoon we came to the first larch on the big 8,000-foot hill that guarded the inner basin. It was a Lyall's larch, and Lyall's larch rarely grows below 7,000 feet in the Highwood country. That meant we were getting close to timberline: the trees were thinning out; meadows were appearing; and this larch and the alpine fir were taking over from the other trees. We pushed on, upwards. Rock outcrops appeared; they ran northwest and southeast in parallel ridges a hundred yards and more apart. The character of the hill changed; it became wholly alpine; on the northeast side of the rock outcrops, snow was still lying and out of the snow grew black, wind-twisted hedges of alpine fir. The rush of the southwest wind sounded through the broken rocks and through the barrier of these old, dark trees like the steady roaring of the sea; but down in the shelter of the snowdrifts and the outcrops there was only an eddying breeze.

Close to the melting snow the anemones grew, their blue and white flowers in striking contrast to the brown, bare ground beneath them from which the snow had only just departed. Further away from the snow the tall seed heads of anemones that had already bloomed and faded caught the sunlight in their silver threads. Right out in the open the tall, old larches stood. Their reddish trunks were two feet and more in diameter and from their widespread branches and their twisted crowns there sprang a mist of tender green, for, though it was July, it was springtime for these ancient trees, set there so beautifully in this open alpland as though some forester had planted them with loving care.

But everywhere, in the open and beneath the thin, green canopies of the larches, there grew, massed as a flower should be for effect, the golden snow lily. Except for the anemones by the snowdrifts there seemed to be no other flower; this most beautiful of all alpines had this slope of the larches to itself and it covered the ground with its golden acres of nodding bloom. It was impossible to walk without treading on these perfect lilies; we had caught their short season at its peak—and caught the larches, too, at the high moment of their spring. In three months time these young, green needles would be golden and falling

Overlooking the Elk Trail to Mount Muir

on the early snows. Then nine months winter—and then once more this gorgeous pageant of colour ...

We looked down this vista of the larches and the lilies to other hills and other snow-streaked ridges—to mountains beyond that faded into the blue, sunlit distance. To have all this within a day's ride of home—was there such a thing, we wondered, as too great good fortune? But we would come here often, we said, always at this season of the lilies, and make our peace with the old gods of the hills. It would be a pilgrimage to the very altar of Pan ...

We went on and, as we climbed, the larches thinned out and became smaller until at last there were no more of them and the firs crouched lower and closer to the ground or huddled together in clumps for shelter from the wind. Then they, too, vanished—but we still plodded on, over ground that was becoming gravelly and over scattered patches of fine turf. We swung to the left and up the last rise; mountains, jagged and snow-streaked, rose suddenly into view to the westward. There, too, lay the Elk Trail Pass. But it was only later that we had eyes for these things for, as the summit of the hill opened up, we saw that it was one living, shimmering carpet of many colours: here, by God's truth, were flowers beyond all imagining—flowers such as we had never seen. It was the kingdom of the flowers, the garden of the gods.

There was no shelter on this windswept hill. A mile and a half away across the intervening gulf was the wall of the Divide, broken to the left of the Pyramid by the pass. Snow lay in the hollows and cirques; shining streams of water cascaded down the grey, forbidding slopes, sparkling in the sunshine. Over the ramparts of the Divide the southwest wind whirled great masses of spinning summer cloud. They swept over the range, sunlit, soft-outlined and glorious—and then they hit the drier air of Alberta, shredded into torn fragments and vanished against the royal blue of the summer sky. Not one faintest wisp of cloud reached the hill on which we were standing—only the wind came on. It leapt the gulf at our feet and boarded the hill with a rush and a roar, a keen, sharp wind straight from the snows, tempering the blazing sun.

Down in the gravel and behind small stones the flowers shook and quivered in the gale. All the dry-country alpines were here; this was no place for globe flowers or the small, white rhododendrons of the Rockies, or for anything that needed shelter. The things that grew here had to hug the gravel and take cover from the wind—but how they liked it and how they grew! Small, golden potentillas, forget-me-nots with their intense blue that always seemed to have in it something of the stars; dwarf asters with great purple flowers an inch and a half across, set on stems that were only half an inch high; purple cushions of pentstemon, carpets of rose-purple moss campion, cream coloured androsace, saxifrages, bright blue campanulas—they grew, not one or two, nor here and there, but in drifts and acres of flashing colour. Amazed and delighted we wandered on, shouting to each other above the bellowing of the wind ... We halted at last by a drift of erigerons while Marigold pulled her raincoat out of my packsack to use as a windbreaker. The small golden erigeron sat snugly down on the gravel, but its braver cousin, a white daisy, yellow-centred, raised its head a few inches and caught the wind. Together they made a field of gold powdered with small, white, trembling stars.

The big hill had no name. That was, perhaps, all to the good, for the Rockies must surely be the worst named range in the world. If you look carefully at the map you can find there, enthroned in stone, a collaborator, a traitor to his country, sundry generals of dubious merit, and a demagogue who, for his own ends, wrecked a way of life which had taken centuries to perfect—to cite only a few of these ill-named mountains.

They managed these things better a hundred and fifty years ago. Those old voyageurs of the North West Company—if those men had chanced to pass this way, they would have been in no two minds about the naming of this hill: they would have called it, quite plainly and simply, La Butte des Fleurs—the Hill of the Flowers.

From that day we knew it by that name.

The Roof of America

Haying, that year, went without incident and with good weather. Congratulating ourselves on that, Adolf and I sat down and planned a hunting trip up Bunk Creek. The arrangement was that Adolf would take charge at the ranch while I rode up to the elk meadow with two horses. From there I would cut trail onwards as far as I could and then, in some suitable spot, build a cache. When that was finished I was to leave the outfit in the cache (which would be useful to us as the years went by and we opened up this bit of country) and return to the ranch. Together Adolf and I would see to the salting of the cattle and various odd jobs, and then, in the calm that comes before weaning, we would take ten days or so and ride up to the cache. There we would off-saddle and turn four out of our five horses loose. The saddles and horse outfits would be put in the cache while we and one horse—probably Bozo—would freight our camp on into the basin in two trips, horse and men carrying, each time, all they could stagger with. The clearing in the basin would provide grass for one horse for a week which it certainly would not do for the whole bunch, and we should not have to disturb everything with wandering horses and the din of bells. Having one horse on picket we could always somehow round up the other four when we needed them.

So off I went in late August, and for two days I cut trail on into the old forest till I came to an ideal site for a cache. I felled various trees that were in the way, leaving three standing that I planned to use

Bozo, a good packhorse and a "comical old devil"

to support the triangular platform. Then I made a ladder and cut my three trees off about fourteen feet above ground level. I peeled these three uprights so that no small animal could find a hold for his claws on them, and then I spent the rest of the day cutting crosspieces and slats for the platform. Everything had to be exactly so with this cache because I could see it playing a considerable part in the dude business as time went on, and I wanted to make it a good one.

I then succeeded in cracking a rib for myself—cinching a horse up too tight and too quickly first thing in the morning, and then having him rear up, cinch-bound, and come back over with me— and very nearly on to me. That put me in rather a fix. I couldn't put a big pack on to Bozo because I couldn't reach high enough; and I couldn't leave the camp where it was for every bear and wolverine in the country to romp with. I just *had* to build that cache and get the stuff into it.

It kept me busy for the next two days—painfully hewing and fitting, and then hoisting the materials fourteen feet into the air and setting them into place. But it was a beautiful cache when all was finished—all white and shining, with the green shadows of the living trees moving over it. I admired it from every angle; and then I went down the valley and broke camp and brought the stuff I was leaving up to the cache and somehow slung it in. And then I made ready to go.

I put Bozo's little pack on him and turned him loose. Then I got Black Jack up against a sidehill from which I could practically step on to his back: one brave swing and a desperate curse and I was there. And I was there to stay: it was twenty-five miles to the Buffalo Head and I had in Black Jack the fastest walking horse on the ranch; I would travel the whole distance at a walk, open and shut the few gates from the saddle and not get off till I got to the corrals.

It was late evening when I started. It was dark when I passed the ranger station and there was no light showing. Two miles further on I passed a man sitting by his campfire having a late supper; he was down by the river and his tent was set up beside the fire. I saluted him and passed on without a word, never stopping. The moon rose as I came out of the mountains and I rode down the silent valley in the silvery light, past groups of sleeping cattle, over shaven hay meadows and through black pools of shadow from the arching trees. And about two in the morning I rode into the corrals, unsaddled my horses and turned them loose in the meadow.

By this time I was hungry and I tiptoed hopefully into the kitchen, occasionally grunting with pain but doing my best not to rouse Alberto who slept nearby through a single door. What I wanted was coffee and cake, fruit and cream—and I was doing very nicely when the combination, in the larder, of moonlight and a booby trap of Alberto's betrayed me. A shallow pan of thick cream was balanced on top of a jug of milk, and the jug was standing on a small tray that covered a deep bowl of freshly made butter. I fetched the whole lot down with an appalling crash and, in an effort to save something from the ruin, sent a large roast of beef to join the mess that was already on the floor.

Alberto was used to people coming in late and helping themselves, but this was stretching hospitality a bit far. From somewhere nearby I could hear an outraged Italian voice asking 'ow the 'ell a man was going to do a day's work if every drunken son of a bachelor in the country was going to dance a fandango in the larder in the middle of the night and juggle with the grub. "And the next time you come, 'ooever you are," Alberto shouted, "be sure and bring your 'orse into the 'ouse with you! 'E will be just as quiet and we will be very 'appy to receive 'im! And now—eat till you burst and no one will be sorry!"

I ate. And in the morning I made my peace with Alberto.

As for the man who was sitting and eating by his campfire—he went up to the ranger station in the morning to get a permit to camp and fish. He asked who it was who had passed his camp at midnight, riding a black saddle horse and with a bay packhorse running loose.

"What was he like?" the ranger asked him.

Sitting there and listening intently was the assistant ranger. He was a firm believer in the Lemon Mine—a lost goldmine that was supposed by many to exist somewhere in these southern Rockies and for which a man called Lemon had murdered his partner, Black Jack, turning up alone with their joint clean-up of gold somewhere in Montana. As the fisherman described me and my horses, comprehension was dawning on the face of the assistant ranger. Suddenly he leapt to his feet and smote the table with his fist. "That's Patterson!" he shouted. "So *that's* what he's been going into that country for! He's found the Lemon Mine, and now he's snuck out at night so that he can collect all his friends and get in to Calgary and record his claims. Oh God, why didn't I get a sight of him?"

He went on and on about it, the ranger told me, and it was only with great difficulty that they prevented him from taking the forestry truck and tearing in to Calgary, to the Mining Recorder's Office, in order to ascertain the exact location of this new bonanza ...

There are some spells of weather so beautiful that you remember them forever afterwards, sunlit islands in the everyday pattern of rain and wind and shine. They remain apart, cut out of time like walled gardens, secret and hidden—gardens to which there can be no returning. Of these were the first ten days of that October. Never a breath of wind came to break the autumn stillness, and not even the faintest wisp of cloud came drifting across the limitless blue of the sky. Every night, reaching down from the glittering stars, the frost laid its iron hand on the basin, and the rustle of the stream would take on a harsher note as ice formed in the eddies and on the stones. Every dawn was pink and grey and silver—but soon the blazing light of the sunrise would flood the Pyramid and pour into the meadow. Each tree, each shining blade of grass, even elephantine Bozo, would be picked out in the cold, winking fire of diamonds. But not for long: soon the soft warmth of Indian summer would send the frost stealing away into the shadows. Scent and the warm glow of colour would come back again to the basin: scent of the firs and of wood smoke and dead willow leaves—brown and green and gold colouring of the forest, grey and mauve and blue of the mountains. The priest can talk of his paradise. What has he to offer compared with this?

Adolf and I climbed up by the waterfall, the way the sheep had gone that winter afternoon, almost a year ago. We passed over the rim into the upper basin, and there, feeding the waterfall, was a little lake—a tarn. The black firs were mirrored in it and across the bottom of it, plain and sharp through the clear water, were the tracks of a cow moose and calf. We went on up the gentle slope of the pass. The country became more open, with small meadows and outcrops of grey limestone; the firs began to huddle together for shelter from the storms. Suddenly Adolf stopped and pointed high up and to the left: "I see one goat," he said. "Mrs. Patterson wants a white rug for her blue room. You should shoot it."

"It's your goat, Adolf."

"No. I got your goat in Nyahé-ya-'nibi. You should take this one; it is your turn."

This was like old times—arguing as to who should shoot the goat. However, history failed to repeat itself. Adolf sat down on a rock in plain view of the goat who was lying up there on a grassy ledge and feeling very secure. I disappeared behind a screen of firs and then, crouching and crawling behind rock outcrops and using small, grassy hollows, I climbed up the southern wall of the pass until I was well above the level of the goat. Then I traversed to the west along a ledge until I thought I was directly above him—and then I began to descend, very quietly and carefully and all eyes. That was the difficult part; each limestone step or terrace looked the same from above, and I was beginning to wonder if I had made a mistake when I saw a creamy object on a ledge of rock some hundreds of feet below. It was the back end of the goat who was still lying down and still watching Adolf. Now, if I went on down, there were some loose rocks that I would start rolling. The head of the goat was hidden from me by a huge rock and I couldn't move to the left to get a sight of all of him because my ledge broke off sheer. It was now or never. I raised the old Mannlicher—and then I found that, for some reason, the stalk had excited me and I couldn't aim. I rested the carbine again and waited. Then I raised it once more and fired, aiming behind the shoulder. The goat rose to his full height, rising in the same way as a cow rises. For a second he stood. Then he collapsed forward again into exactly the same position as before—stone dead. Not one kick; his feet never moved and he never knew what had hit him.

We converged on the goat, photographed him and admired the head which was an unusually good one. Then we skinned him and carried the meat, hide and head down into the shade of the firs. Then we went on, and soon the summit hove in sight. In the centre of the pass a huge rocky knoll, almost a small mountain, was heaved up. There were low divides to right and left of this knoll but the lowest and the one that the game trail followed was to the left or south side. We went up on to the knoll, passing a strong spring of ice-cold water that welled up out of the rock into a little meadow. Suddenly the green valley of the Elk and the walled fastness of Nyahé-ya-'nibi lifted into view—and a sea of unknown mountains to the south. Out of them towered one very high mountain that carried a hanging glacier way aloft against its peak. There was no map of that country, and that mountain was an old puzzle: we had often seen it from Mount Head and we could never quite figure out where it was. Perhaps I could see from here—and I sat down on a square block of limestone that lay right on the water parting and pulled out the glass. Adolf had rambled away to the north somewhere, nosing into this and that.

This was the ridge-pole of the continent. A drop of rain might fall towards this limestone boulder and the smallest shift of the wind would decide its fate—whether it would come in the end to the cold shores of

Hudson Bay or whether it would follow the mighty Columbia River to the Pacific. I sat there utterly content, sorting out the far ranges as best I could: Forsyth Creek, the White River, Bull River, the Palliser—a lifetime would hardly be enough for all this...

Adolf's voice roused me: "There surely are grizzlies in these parts," he said as he walked towards me. "Over there, digging for marmots—the ground is all torn up just like a kitchen garden. An acre, perhaps even more. Never have I seen the like of it ... "

Evening found us sliding ourselves and the goat meat and the trophies down the sheep trail by the waterfall. Then came the avalanche slide. We each had a load of meat and we took head or hide by turns. I don't know which was the surest way to break a leg—teetering along a spiky log six feet above the ground with the green, sloppy goat hide doing its best to slip out of its leather thongs, or with the equally heavy goat head on your shoulders and a horn like a dagger stuck into the back of your neck or prodding you in the ear ... The grand finale as we came into camp was quite spectacular: the first thing that Bozo saw was a man's head parting the green branches of the firs on the edge of the meadow. That was perfectly normal except that, sitting on the man's shoulder, there was the ghastly white head of a mountain goat, horns and beard and all complete. A horrid-looking sight—and Bozo, whose nerves were all on edge anyway owing to the absence of his fellow horses, let a frightful snort out of him and leapt to the full extent of his picket rope. The pickets pulled out and the horse careered madly across the meadow on the homeward trail. A staggering run by the two exhausted sportsmen just managed to catch up with the tail end of the picket rope as it was snaking out of the meadow and into the trees.

Suppertime drew near. From the tent came the soft glow of candle-light and the pleasant aroma of coffee which was making on the stove. Outside, over the open fire, two large frying pans sizzled and spat—one full of potatoes and onions, and the other of goat's liver and bacon. There had been some debate about this—would we try it or wouldn't we? The meat, we knew, would have to hang for about a week at this season of frosty nights—but just how would a big old billy goat's liver taste? However, it cut so well and looked so good that it seemed a shame not to use it. And now all was ready and we carried our heaped-up plates through the open door of the tent and sat down by the stove.

"Good, Adolf," I mumbled with my mouth full. "Nothing wrong with this."

"Surely good," he replied, munching away.

Then we swallowed—and then we sat there looking at each other thoughtfully.

"I don't know that I altogether care for that," I said.

"There's a certain something that it leaves behind in the mouth. Notice anything?"

"I do. And I do not think I really like what I notice. I cannot go it. What a pity—it looks so good. I shall have to throw mine out; the trout can have it. Do you think we could cook up some eggs or some ham? And tomorrow I will take Bozo and go down to those grass mountains east of the Highwood and bring us back a moose or a sheep or something. We must have meat in camp. I will be back here by nightfall."

"You do that—it fits in well. I'm going to take my eiderdown and a lean-to and grub for three nights or so, and camp up by that spring we found today—the one near the grizzlies' kitchen garden. Then I can really get to see that country up on the Divide and perhaps get a sheep as well."

☆ ☆ ☆ ☆

For three perfect, cloudless days I probed around in the heads of Weary Creek, following the old trail down towards the Elk, clambering over the stony screes of the Pyramid and Mount Muir. I saw sheep on the Pyramid but nothing worth shooting—small heads only and I was not shooting for meat. I knew Adolf, and if he had said there must be meat in camp, then by now meat there would be. But the more I saw of this alpine country, the more I liked it. It was just what we were looking for. Two shots of dynamite properly placed in that sheep trail by the waterfall and we could get horses up here. Then I could throw a drift fence across the head of the sheep trail where the waterfall flowed out of the little tarn, and the whole of the Weary Creek Gap would be our private horse pasture. A paradise both for the dude wrangler and the hunter, and only one day's ride from home. And the run of two provinces!

The nights were silent and starlit and with a moon nearing the full. After supper, when all was tidied up and stacked away under the lean-to, I would go, past the small gurgle of the spring and through the huddled, wind-twisted firs, to the limestone boulder on the Divide. It was only a few hundred yards from camp but the frost, which whitened the grass around the spring, flowed away from this high point. There for perhaps an hour I would sit in the quiet of the autumn night, watching the moonlight flooding over a sea of nameless mountains, looking down into the black depths of Weary Creek and Elk River. All the surge and uplift of the continent from two far-off seas had culminated in this block of stone on which I sat.

On the last day of that high camp I headed for Carnarvon Lake—a lake that lay right on the Divide in a low saddle about three miles southeast from camp. That sounds simple but the way was difficult and devious and there was a precipice to climb. At last I found a way up—and then I turned east into a long, steady climb, keeping the edge of the precipice on my left and a barren, boulder-strewn slope on my right that ran down into one of the heads of Aldridge Creek. All this had taken more time than I could well spare, so, to speed things up a bit, I laid down my rifle and packsack on a rock and went on with only a bar of chocolate and the field glass.

The drop on the left rapidly increased. I approached the edge gingerly and looked down 1,500 feet, almost sheer, into the head of Weary Creek. As I did so I heard, on my right, a sort of a snuffling snort, and I looked up to see, less than twenty yards away, an enormous billy goat standing on the brink of the drop, watching me. He had been asleep in a little hollow that was right on the edge and was dead ground from below; I must have disturbed him by kicking some loose stone.

We stared at each other without moving. The goat that I had shot in the pass was a big one—way above most of the recorded North American heads. But he was small compared with this monster which must have carried almost, if not quite, the record head.

I cast a glance back down the mountain, but rifle and camera were half a mile away on any one of a thousand rocks. That was a pity, for the goat had no intention of moving; he was standing facing me with his head slightly lowered and his feet bunched together, and he would have made a magnificent picture. Unless threatened, it would not be in his nature to open an attack; and, for my part, the last thing I wanted to do on the edge of this precipice was to tangle with those dagger-like horns and that tremendous mass of neck muscle. I moved down the rocky slope and circled around the goat at a respectful distance of about thirty yards. The billy pivoted slowly so as to face me all the time, keeping his feet close together as I have seen goat do on narrow ledges. And there I left him watching me as I moved away along the edge of the drop—motionless, a white statue of a goat, growing smaller and smaller until he was hidden from view by a fold of the mountain.

I got a sight of the blue waters of Carnarvon Lake from 2,000 feet above them, but the day was too far spent for me to go down there and return. Even without doing that, it was a tired and hungry traveller that plodded up Weary Creek in the twilight. Rarely had camp looked so good.

I breakfasted and broke camp in the darkness, intending to get back to the main camp and set Adolf's mind at rest before he got away on a day's hunt. Down the pass I went in the greyness of the frost, with the dawn unfolding over the Mount Head Range—down by the ice-rimmed waterfall, down over the avalanche slide. When I came out into the meadow in the basin I stood for a moment in the shadow of the trees. The early morning sun blazed down on camp and all was perfect peace. Bozo was standing sleepily in the centre of the clearing with the frost still steaming off his hide. At the far end of the meadow the fire smoke curled lazily upwards, blue against the black wall of the trees, while Adolf, seated on his bedroll in the sun at the tent door, was downing a late breakfast. He had been busy from an early hour, he told me later, clearing more ground for Bozo and doing all the evening chores so that he could make a long sashay north along the foot of the range and return as late as he pleased to camp.

A very pretty domestic scene, and I admired it for a minute or so. Then, suddenly inspired, I gave my celebrated imitation of the snort of an angry bull moose in the rutting season. I did better than that: aided by the frost and the silence and the encircling trees, I surpassed myself: for one moment of time I *was* an angry bull moose. Only in that way could I have produced that perfect sound.

The picture changed. Still-life became action. Bozo's snort of terror rivalled that of the angry moose. The big horse leapt a full ten feet and fetched up at the end of his tether, shaking like an aspen leaf. Adolf's plate of bacon and eggs flew into the air from off his knees and went I know not whither. In one swift movement the man executed a roll and whipped something out of the tent—and I found myself looking down a rifle barrel from a paltry hundred yards' distance. Had Adolf been a townee sportsman he would probably have fired at the sound or at some faint movement, and my saga might well have ended there and then. Being a countryman he waited, peering with screwed-up eyes into the shadows and against the sun.

"Don't shoot, Adolf! Don't shoot! It's only the old bull moose come back to join the herd again."

"By God, I am glad to see you back even if my breakfast has gone all to hell! I surely thought it was a four-legged bull that time—and fighting mad from the sound of him!"

✫ ✫ ✫ ✫

All we needed now was a lake.[12] So my thoughts had run, back in the summer, as I sat on the Hill of the Flowers and watched the elk playing on the flats of Bishop Creek. The day after the return of the "old bull moose," Adolf and I stood on that same Hill watching a bull elk and some cows in the same meadows down below. Gone was the summer wind and gone the gay carpet of flowers. A warm breeze blew gently from the Divide, rustling the dead seed heads and the dry herbage— and it was to this fortunate breeze and the low October sun that I owe the granting of my wish.

We had come up the Hill of the Flowers looking for sheep, but Adolf was now staring intently towards the southwest into a cirque between the Pyramid and the Horned Mountain. Without taking his eyes off the cirque he reached out his hand: "May I have the glass?" he said. "Surely there is a lake in that coulee to the right of the Pyramid. I can see the sun sparkling on the water … "

We looked carefully through the glass and, sure enough, there *was* a lake—well over 7,000 feet up and almost level with us. But all one could really see was the flash and glitter of water. We looked on the map that night after supper but there was no indication of any lake—only a coulee with a large scree and some very prettily executed contour lines.

The following morning I came to the foot of the slope leading to the cirque and the lake. It was a nasty-looking proposition: it was high, smooth and very steep, and there was nothing to hang on to—a couple of small trees widely separated, a patch of grass, a bit of wild rose and a bit of buck-brush, that was all. If ever one started sliding or rolling, disaster waited at the foot in the shape of a grove of small larches interspersed with huge blocks of limestone that had crashed down from somewhere up above.

Up then, gingerly, on fingers and toes; a rest behind one tree and a rest behind the other—and then a delicately balanced scuffle up to the summit of the dam. For a natural dam was what this slope proved to be—a limestone dam connecting the two arms of the cirque, steeply sloped on the outer side and absolutely vertical on the side that held the lake. One could take a white stone and set it in the water close to the edge of the dam; then release it and watch it settling into the green depths until it was out of sight. I tried several stones and not one ever touched the dam in its descent, nor was there any sign of the bottom.

I walked along the dam and then along the northwest shore of the lake into the heart of the mountain. The shore was littered with one kind of fossil—some sort of a sea beast, it seemed, and the shape was that of a horn. The Lake of the Horns, perhaps? The name was an apt one, for above this northern shore towered the Horned Mountain. The lake was about 600 yards long by 400 yards broad—bigger than Carnarvon Lake. Deep into the cirque and beneath the cliffs of the Horned Mountain were a few stunted firs. There I found a few dry sticks and with them I made my noonday fire by the water's edge—the first fire, probably, for there was no sign, and indeed no likelihood, that this lake had ever been visited by men.

There was a feeling of utter remoteness about the place. It was complete and it was perfect, and yet there was not one single thing in sight except the ordered chaos of the mountains. The blue water stretched away to meet the low black line of the dam, and beyond the dam all that could be seen was the serrated crest of the Highwood Range ten miles away to the eastward. Of all that lay between there was nothing visible; my whole world was this hermitage of the cirque with its giant screes and towering cliffs, its soft alpine turf and tiny stunted firs. I lingered in this place till the shadow of the mountain, falling on the lake, told me it was time to go.

As though on a giant sundial, the creeping shadow of the Pyramid marked also the passing of the seasons: summer had come to an end and the warning was already in the eastern sky. When I came back to the dam I could see, through the Highwood Gap, a cold grey wall of cloud hanging over the foothills, motionless and threatening. That was winter pressing in from the north and east against the west wind. Plainly it was time we were hitting the trail for the Buffalo Head and the workaday world again.

The clouds came into the mountains in the night and the dawn was grey and sunless. We spent the day relaying the outfit and the meat of three wild animals down to the elk meadow; and there, in the evening, the wind from the northern plains caught us, bringing with it a blinding whirl of snow. We woke next morning to a silent world; a smack on the tent wall produced a minor avalanche; there was no enthusiasm for early rising and we lay warmly in our eiderdowns for a little while longer, half dreaming of the ten golden days that were just ended, planning new ventures to the mountains of the Elk Trail.

How were we to know, on that snowy morning, that the door of the garden was already locked against us, and that, inside a year, the key would be thrown away and lost forever?

6

The Fiery Cloud

Fire over the Foothills

There comes, sooner or later, a peak in the life of all things. Somewhere, as in the trajectory of a shell, there is a culminating point and, beyond that, decline. It was that way with my years on the Buffalo Head: the summer of 1936 saw that high point reached and passed, never to return.

Things were bone dry in June of that year and a week's solid rain wouldn't have been a bit too much. But apart from that we had the world by the tail on a downhill pull. Things were pretty well fixed up on the ranch, there was a nice bunch of cattle building up and there was nothing wrong with the horse bunch. There was a good cover of grass on the place, the help was fine, and we had enough dudes lined up to take care of the low cattle prices and still leave a good profit. It was amazing how much you could do with a dollar in those days, and we seemed to have enough of them. Some day, too, the Depression would end and beef would be worth money again—there was always that to look forward to. In the meantime, with dudes, we were sitting pretty.

And who else had a private hunting park in the mountains and the trail to it well concealed? No—I wouldn't have changed places with any man just then. It was a good life in a good country and in my carefree way I thought it was going on forever, world without end ... But that was not to be, and already, far away in the mountains, disaster was preparing.

The thing showed its ugly head for the first time in the early days of July. We had climbed up, four of us, to a little plateau on the southern spurs of the Holy Cross Mountain. The place was a look-out of the mountain sheep, a grassy ledge where the Bighorn like to lie, secure from their enemies and with the world at their feet.

The afternoon was blistering hot. The everlasting sun blazed down, the grass was burnt and crisp, the flowers were shrivelled and the small pellets of the sheep droppings were dry and crumbly. From below there drifted up to us the warm scent of the firs. The faint up-draught that carried it was scarcely to be felt; no breeze was stirring. The rocks quivered in the heat and all life seemed to be standing still; only from nearby, from somewhere amongst the stones, came the harsh, hot snapping of a grasshopper's wings. Away in the southwest, beyond the nearer ridges, beyond the heads of Cataract Creek, the jagged peaks of the Divide thrust into the inane blue of the rainless sky. And from beyond them, from somewhere in British Columbia, rose the cloud.

It was far away. It might have been on Fording River but it looked even further than that—Elk River, I thought, probably, and I reached for the glass.

"There, you see," somebody said. "It can rain, after all, somewhere. Look at that thunderhead … "

But that was no thundercloud. It billowed up, cumulus-fashion, only to flatten out on top, and a thin, nasty streak that could only be smoke stretched away from it into the northwest. It was a forest fire that had taken a good hold—in thick, green spruce most likely—and it was burning hard.

That was the first sight we had of what is now known to the British Columbia Forest Service as "the Phillips fire." We watched it for a while and then, with the afternoon shadows lengthening, we dropped down again into the valley of the South Fork where we had left the horses.

The hot, dry days went by with never a sign of rain and the cloud hung in the southwest like a portent of doom. Sometimes the burning east wind would blow in from the prairies and the air would clear and the cloud would be gone. But it always came back again when the wind switched and blew, however gently, from the mountains. Then, early in the mornings when all was still and cool, the bitter scent of burning spruce would lie heavy on the air. And as the sun topped the Knife Edge River you would see that it touched the poplar trees on that steep hillside with a strange, new beauty: a blue haze of wood smoke filled the valley, lying motionless in gently undulating waves and streamers, giving depth and a rich colouring to the folded hills and to the long dawn-shadows of the woods and trees. That smoke, you knew, was the green forest of Elk River, burning—the forest you had last seen from the little spring on the Elk Trail Pass, covering the great trough of the Elk valley like a velvet cloak. And you hoped against hope that the fire might not reach Nyahé-ya-'nibi and the Kananaskis country; that there might be something left ...

And then the Chinook wind began to blow. It blew day and night out of the southwest, and it blew strongly as in the fall or wintertime. The Chinook Arch, even, formed in the western sky—that curious standing arch of heavy, streamlined cloud that, in any normal year, is never seen in summertime. The Arch stayed still over the mountains and through it screamed the Chinook; it was as if the gates of hell had been flung open. The blistering wind sucked dry what little moisture was left in the country; only in the deep woods and on the northeast slopes did any green grass remain. Even the poplar leaves began to wither.

The Highwood went dry for a short distance above the ranger station, and the North Fork of Sheep Creek was dry where the Calgary trail crossed it. Further on, Fish Creek and Pine Creek were dry and dusty as any roadbed. Sam and I sat gloomily in the living room one evening after supper and he told me then of former dry years, and how old-timers had told him of summers when there was no water for man or beast on the Macleod Trail between the Old Man River and the Highwood, and again between the Highwood and the Bow. This summer was supposed to be the driest since that of 1886, fifty variegated years ago—years of drought like this one and years so wet that you could bog a wagon in the middle of a rocky flat.

It was under these conditions that CMB and I took a climbing party of dudes up to the crest of the ridge that joins Mount Head to the Holy Cross Mountain. We left our horses down in the timber and pushed ahead on foot to the junction of the two streams that drain the Mount Head Coulee. Then upwards—through old, bearded forest, past moist alpine gardens, alive with sparkling water and the vivid

The remains of a fire-killed forest

green of moss; sheltered there, in the heart of the mountains, from wind and burning sun ... Upwards again to the green plateau where the marmots and the rock-rabbits live and conduct their methodical and orderly haying operations—and from there up a spur of the main ridge, with the valley of the South Fork 3,000 feet below and the Bull Creek Pass sinking lower and lower till it became nothing but a hollow in the rounded, stony Bull Creek Hills. Climbing in the deep shadow of the ridge where the Chinook thrummed through the crannies and the crevices, until the last set of legs had safely kicked and struggled itself over the crest and into the sun and the bellowing wind ...

The party spoke as one. "My God!" it said in tones of awe—and then was silent for a time.

Four thousand feet below lay the valley of the upper Highwood inside the first range. The valley was without habitation; there were no ranches here—nothing but two or three deserted and ruinous lumber camps of long ago. An abandoned wagon trail, fast degenerating into a packtrail, wound its way up the grassy flats. From here and there came the flash and sparkle of water; the poplar bluffs showed green against the tawny yellow of the grass, and beyond the river the unbroken green of the conifers swept up to the dividing range—dark green of old spruce and fir; paler green of jackpine.

Facing us, nine miles southwest across the valley from where we sat, was a U-shaped gap in the Divide. The gap had no official name but Pocaterra and I had once spent two cold February days trying to reach it on snowshoes from the east; we failed in the end for lack of an ice-axe but, as a parting shot, we christened it: we called it the Gunsight Pass. Right in the pass and right on the Divide there was the little lake which I had tried to reach the day I met the goat on the precipice, Carnarvon Lake; and from right behind the U of the Gunsight there boiled up the mountainous smoke cloud of a raging forest fire. It was far worse—and much nearer—than I had expected. Imagine about four of the worst thunderstorms you have ever seen; pile those thunderheads together with a wild and jagged range of mountains just in front of them, light the whole dreadful scene with the lurid glow of smoke-blurred sunlight—and you will have some idea of what we saw.

The smoke cloud was climbing thousands of feet into the blue. The Chinook was getting stronger. It was sawing off the top of the cloud and flinging the smoke in a yellow arch across the Highwood valley and far over our heads. Fine ashes and burnt spruce needles were falling beside us on the rocks of the ridge. That fire was evidently roaring up the Elk valley at a most ungodly speed. How long, I wondered, before the up-draught flings a glowing coal over the Divide into the green forest of the Highwood? And I looked over to the crescent-shaped sweep of ancient trees that led to the Elk Trail Pass: their feathery tops would be bending before this roaring wind as they had bent before so many winds in the last few centuries—but now so tinder dry that they were almost ready to explode.

And then, suddenly, I thought: what if this Chinook drives the fire through the pass and down by the waterfall into the green basin of the Elk Trail? In my imagination I saw it happen—and I felt afraid.

The same thought had just occurred to the worried forest ranger. He was new to the Highwood and new to mountains. All he had seen, till last fall, was the little hills of his native England and the tamarack swamps of Lesser Slave Lake. But he had brains and energy, that man, and right at this moment he was somewhere down below us in that green and tawny valley, riding like mad for the ranger station. From there he phoned a message to be relayed over the forestry line to Calgary. Then—since there was no direct communication by telephone between the ranger station and the Buffalo Head and since he could do nothing till a fire crew arrived—he saddled a fresh horse and proceeded to warm up the fifteen miles of trail that separated him from the ranch. He rode in, they told me, just when supper was over—in a muck sweat, man and horse—and straight away he asked for me.

He had an idea. Between great swigs of tea and mouthfuls of cold beef he told Marigold and Sam what was happening behind the mountains. His quick, eager voice rose slightly as he pointed out the danger to the forests of the Highwood that lay in that lonely, unwatched gap by the Pyramid. And I had some hidden trail that went in there—a sort of private hunting trail. He knew that because the outgoing ranger, his predecessor, had told him. And now that trail to the gap by the Pyramid Mountain was far too well hidden—where was I? When would I be home? Because the ranger's idea was this: I would take one or two men, however many I thought sufficient, and ride up to the pass and stay there. He would come himself if he could but he didn't think he would be allowed to leave the ranger station area. It wouldn't matter so long as I had a couple of good men. Once up on the summit my party would be in position to deal with any spot fires caused by burning brands carried by the wind from the main fire, or with any ground fires that might come creeping through the heather—we could get after them and probably put them out with shovels, axes and wet saddle-blankets.

Fishery warden Sam Smith was a "firm friend and ally."

It was a good idea—to go to meet the fire before it came to you. But it was already too late ... The summer dusk was falling now and, as the ranger talked, Marigold and Sam could just see, from the house, the movements of my climbing party down in the corrals where they were turning their horses out. One by one the sunburnt and thirsty mountaineers drifted up to the house and sat down to supper. Between bites they described what they had seen from Mount Head—and that, coupled with what the ranger had seen from the valley, filled out the picture. Things didn't look so good, and the country was bone dry—ripe and ready to burn.

About the same time, but ten miles away, I was fastening on the bells and picketing for the night two saddle horses and one cranky old packhorse—Bozo—on a little flat at the foot of Mount Head. To the music of the bells and the noise of the stream I walked back to camp where, over a tiny fire which was all we had dared to light, a girl was busily frying eggs and bacon. And, if my memory serves me, burning the bacon. Camp was already made and the tea water was boiling; very soon supper was ready and we doused the fire and sat down on the kini-kinik in the last of the twilight, hungry and ready to show the grub—burnt bacon and all—the trail home.

To the north and to the south the stars were coming out, but overhead they were hidden by the monstrous arch of drifting smoke that now reached far out over the foothills, eastwards. The underside of the arch was lit with a wavering glow from the flames of the fire that was still ten miles away and still behind two ranges of Rockies. Three thousand feet and more above camp the heavy outline of the mountain loomed darkly against the firelit canopy of smoke. A truly Wagnerian setting, fit background for tragedy and doom.

The jangling of the horse bells was ceasing now, sure sign that the day was over. Soon, in the queer half-light of the fiery cloud, the camp was sleeping. Only the west wind remained awake, fanning the fire for the terrible day that was to follow, roaring down the mountainside in savage gusts and whirlwinds, sweeping on eastwards over the valley of the South Fork.

The Rock Paintings

The reason for this camp in the mountains was, literally, far to seek. It was to be found in Ottawa and its name was Marius Barbeau. Dr. Barbeau was, at that time, Dominion Ethnologist and a moving force in the National Museum. He had written to me, quite recently, regarding some Indian rock paintings that I had heard of from Pocaterra but which I had never seen. Would I visit them, Dr. Barbeau had asked, and let him know what I found? And he added some detail of these paintings as given to him by the Stoney Indians in 1923—and much embroidered, it seemed, with legend.

The pictures, the Indians said, varied with the seasons: you might find anything there, from mounted men in war bonnets hunting buffalo on the prairie, to a lone hunter after bear or sheep in the mountains. The pictures were not the work of human beings at all, and as the years went by they kept moving higher and higher up the cliff face. One thing you could count on meeting there was a high wind, and if you were fortunate enough to see a representation of the moon with seven horizontal lines under it, that would give you a vision of things to come and would bring you good luck.

That letter of Dr. Barbeau's, I had read it out loud to a little party of our guests who, I thought, would be interested. And afterwards, this girl, who was sleeping now in the little tent that strained and flapped so wildly in this crazy, unnatural wind, had said: "Will you go soon to look for those paintings? And may I come?"

And here we were … The walls of the tent sucked in and then blew out, in a frantic gust, with a report like a pistol shot. Not wishing to see the girl go sailing off, tent and all, into the dark valley down below, I got up and got a lariat from my saddle. Quietly I flipped the loop over the centre-pole of the tent; the other end I tied securely to the base of a little fir. That looked as if it would hold—and I rolled in again and went back to sleep under my tree.

The ranger slept that night of July 22–23 at the Buffalo Head. He hit the trail at sunrise and breakfasted ten miles away, at the last ranch up the Highwood valley. Three miles further on he passed the foot of the Pack Trail Coulee—just about the time the girl and I must have been coming over the Grass Pass, 1,700 feet above him. But the ranger didn't stop. He pounded his horse on towards the ranger station, for the Forest Service was sending out a fire-fighting crew from Calgary and he had to be on the spot and ready for them. That settled for good and all our chance of defending the Elk Trail Pass against the fire, assuming that any chance had still remained to us. It seems more probable that it had already vanished and that, even if I had been at the Buffalo Head when the ranger arrived there the evening before, it would still have been too late. By using the greatest speed and energy, but allowing time for the gathering of fresh horses and some sort of a primitive fire-fighting outfit, we *might* have arrived in the forested basin at the foot of the waterfall just in time to perish with it in a tearing blast of flame: for there was no refuge there and no living thing escaped, as will be seen.

The girl and I dropped down to the Highwood trail and forded the river. We rode up the little flats of Zephyr Creek. The wind had dropped a bit since breakfast, and now the day was getting steadily hotter. By riding south we had come out of the shadow of the smoke-cloud and into the sun; the bare ground threw the heat back at us, for the valley had been grazed-off clean as a whistle and what little grass there might have been was gone. So, too, were the cattle and there was no life—only the hot, overgrazed grassland, the dry stream-bed and the parched trees.

A gap appeared in the eastern wall of the valley and we turned our horses into it. Its stream, too, was dry and we rode slowly along beside the stony watercourse with our eyes wide open and focussed for rock paintings large, high and magnificent. They should be here, on this rock wall on the left—but they were nowhere to be seen. A roaring gust of hot wind swept into the gap behind us, sending the horses' tails streaming forward; that part, at least, of the Indians' tale had come true.

The gap opened into a kind of rocky, waterless cirque. We rode around this basin rather hopelessly, wondering if it was the right place and getting rapidly hungrier and thirstier. Finally we gave it up and turned back towards the gap. As we passed through, bending our heads against the wind, I heard the girl call out to me: "That couldn't be what we're looking for, could it?" she said, and she pointed to the rock wall.

There *was* something there, it was hard to see exactly what—certainly nothing very big. We dismounted and dropped the lines. Then, leaving the horses in the dry creek bed, we scrambled up a short slope of broken stone to the foot of the cliff.

There, done in some red pigment (it was probably the usual iron oxide clay) low down on the cliff face, was a small representation of a house with gables and a pointed roof. Smoke rose from the chimney, and in the left foreground stood a cow—an obviously white-man cow and no buffalo. The whole thing looked like the work of some Indian child and we stared at it disgustedly.

"This can't be what Marius Barbeau is talking about," I said. "Is there nothing else?" And we backed down the slope a few paces to get a better sight of the cliff above us.

And there, about twenty feet up, were the paintings of the nomad hunters of olden time. They were old and much faded now; it must have been the full glare of the sun on the cliff face that had rendered them invisible when we first rode by. One could quite well see how legends might grow around them. There were figures of Indians scattered about, some of them hunting buffalo—and above them shone the sun, or possibly the moon. But nowhere could we see any trace of the seven lines. To reach that high point on the rock face the old-time artists must have built themselves a scaffold of poles lashed together with thongs.

I made a few notes of these paintings for Marius Barbeau. Then we slid down to the horses again and rode away.

To get grass and water for the horses we had to go right up to the springs at the head of Zephyr Creek. There, high up, there was grazing and some greenery by the stream. To the north, facing us as we drank our tea and ate, was the Grass Pass and, behind it, Mount Head. The pass and the mountain lay in the shadow of the smoke cloud, which was thicker now than ever and starting to fan out and veil the sun. The Chinook was back, blowing with redoubled fury. A long spur of the Lookout Range cut off our view to the westward, but from the smoke that was going up it was obvious that all hell had broken loose on the Continental Divide. And with this wind—what next?

"I wish we could see what's happening," I said. "All we've seen so far of that fire was yesterday from the ridge. It might be that we should hit for the ranch—there are things that will have to be done if the fire comes to the Highwood."

"Could we get the horses up this coulee?" the girl said. "Could we see then, if we got on top of the range?" And she pointed to a frightful-looking shale and sandstone couloir behind us that led up the mountain ridge …

We packed up and went at it. We hung our chaps on our saddles so that we could climb quickly and lead our horses—and keep ahead of them, for a horse comes up a steep slope with a rush. Since he would never have stayed alone all day at camp our packhorse, Bozo, was with us, running loose; he was the chief danger. He always liked to be in the lead, and he somehow got ahead of us in the couloir which narrowed and steepened as it went up. I came next, leading my horse, and all I could do was to watch that monstrous rump up above me, clawing and scuffling away at the mountain and hurling down rocks which we below had to dodge. I urged Bozo on with horrid threats and with my quirt whenever I could reach him, because, if he hesitated and fell, he would sweep the whole lot of us with him to perdition. And there was no question of turning back; I don't think a horse could have turned round on so steep a slope and with so poor a footing, let alone go back down it. Up we went, hoping. It was all we could do—and fortune provided a way out at the top on to a gravelly, rocky slope where no horse had ever been.

From the rocks of the Lookout Range the upper Highwood valley was a terrible sight to see. There could be no doubt about it now— the fire had crossed the Divide into Alberta. The big foothills became fainter and fainter till they vanished into the smoke; the Divide and the Misty Range were completely hidden. From the upper valley and from the forests of the Elk Trail a stupendous column of smoke was rising. It boiled up in successive waves as fresh groves of timber went up in flames. Its billowing summit was still climbing, sharp-rimmed against the blue. It was snow-white where the sun's rays caught it, dark in the shadows. This smoke cloud must have been piled up to at least 9,000 feet above the valley floor, for it reached far above the peaks of the mountains. Towards us the smoke was fanning out at a lower level, drifting across the sun. Except for the summit of the great cloud the whole dreadful scene was lit with a yellowish light from the smoke-veiled sun, and we sat there watching it with awe, appalled.

On that day this one fork of the fire travelled fifteen miles, from Weary Creek in British Columbia to Sheep Creek in Alberta. On the other side of the Elk Mountains the flames were racing on up the Elk valley, towards Nyahé-ya-'nibi and towards the Elk Lakes. The whole country seemed to be on fire. Wood ashes and burnt spruce needles were falling in Calgary, fifty-five miles as the crow flies from the Elk Trail pass ...

Two thousand feet and more below, a truck lumbered up the valley towards the ranger station, trailing behind it a yellowish cloud of dust—and then a second truck. The glass showed men in them, fire-fighters—at least in name. Poor material, some of this was, for the ranger to work with, for few of these men had the slightest interest in seeing the fire brought under control. Rather the contrary: times were hard and this job meant fire-pay. There were devastating fires in the Hungry Thirties that were purposely set in order to create fire-fighting jobs, and we shall never know how much of beauty and of value went up in smoke in this way.

"What would you do with a man who deliberately set out a fire?" I asked the ranger, one snowy afternoon the following winter.

"By God, if I caught him alone I'd throw him back into his own fire, that I would. And I mean it. But all I could do last summer was weed the bad ones out and fire them, and replace them, and go on doing that till I got a crew of good men."

The trucks vanished round a spur of the hills and the dust cloud settled. We got up, the girl and I, and walked down to where we had left the horses. We had seen enough—and what we had seen we would never be able to forget.

"Well, that's that," I said, wiping out with those simple words a host of cherished plans. "Now we'd better get down out of this if we can find a way—because we surely can't go down with the horses the way we came up, that's a cinch! And then we'll hit for camp and sleep there tonight and be at the Buffalo Head for breakfast in the morning. The fire might get into the head of Flat Creek, and we'll have to move those cattle down from the South Fork before that valley goes up in smoke with them trapped in it."

We swung over on to the eastside of the mountain and there we found a way down—an affair of rock ledges, moss-covered and insecure, a zigzag trail which led us, at one point, to the sheer head of some remote glen that I had never seen and never saw again, some feeder of the Middle Fork. During this performance we were again in constant danger of being wiped out by Bozo, the individualist, who, this time, followed us but on a line of his own. He always fancied himself as a short-cut artist but lacked the brains to back this up: the things he did up above us on that almost vertical mountainside went beyond the bounds of reason—some angel must have had us in his care.

We came down off the face of the mountain into a little wooded basin between two bare limestone ridges. There was no underbrush there and the firs were of an even size and beautifully spaced; we led our horses through these trees, thinking to find a way down into the head of Zephyr Creek. And then, in the middle of the wood, we came on an open glade. The glade formed a gentle hollow in the centre of the basin, and to it the rains of centuries had brought a depth of rich soil. It was completely covered with asters, tall and pale and scarcely moving in this sheltered spot—no other flower grew there. Walled around by the dark green firs the asters shone, in the unearthly yellow light of this smoke-clouded evening, like their namesakes, the stars.

The girl was strangely moved. She bent down over the flowers for a moment and when she raised her head her eyes were shining. "I don't think I've ever ... seen *anything* ... more beautiful!" she said. She spoke always with a slight hesitation in her voice but, even without that emphasis, you knew at once that this came straight from the heart.

"The fire can't come here, can it?" she went on. "It can't burn this? Oh, say that it *can't* come here!" And she bent once more over the asters which shivered a little as a hot, roaring gust passed high overhead, and then were still again.

Chaos

They put a hundred men on the Highwood fire but there was not much they could do with it in that 1936 drought except herd it a bit on the flanks. And, even at that, they had some lively times. One bunch of men got cut off on the trail to Fording River Pass by a switch of the wind that sent the fire racing through young jackpine in a sudden burst of flame; the bunch scrambled and hacked their way through old forest down Lost Creek, crossing dry-shod over what had been, five weeks previously, the Highwood River, to reach the safety of the valley trail. Another shift in the wind sent men riding and racing for dear life up Storm and Misty Creeks, leaving their camp behind them to be devoured by the flames. That was the limit of the fire on the upstream side; downstream it came almost to the ranger station—and the shape of it was that of a giant fan spreading out from the Elk Trail Pass through which it had come.

On Sheep Creek, helped by the lay of the mountains, they held the fire. But the smoke cloud spread till it covered the sky; by day it hid the sun, and by night the underpart of the cloud glowed with the flickering light of the distant flames. No place was safe. If the fire ever got out of the mountains it would come raging through the foothills with the speed of the wind, destroying ranch buildings, roasting cattle on the hoof, stampeding horses and hunting men. Bar U, Seven U, E P, Stampede and Buffalo Head—big and little, we would all be in its path and only the lucky would escape.

And the drought continued, and no coolness or dew could come to the earth with that canopy of smoke overhead; and the west wind, the Chinook, the friend in wintertime but now the destroyer, screamed over the foothills day and night like some mad, tormented thing. I see, from a letter written that August, that it was "so dry that even the weeds shrivelled, the grass dried and broke off under foot and the leaves were falling."

Ashes went on falling, too, on Calgary and High River, and they were swept up daily in the Buffalo Head veranda. They fell in the Highwood and they marked out clearly, in neat parallel lines on the rocks at the bathing pool, the gradual shrinking of the river ... At the Flat Creek gate Adolf, riding home, found a piece of glowing charcoal lying in the powdery mixture of dust and horse droppings; a little smoke was rising from it. The nearest fire was ten miles away, and so ten miles or more was the distance that brand had come, carried aloft on some red-hot whirlwind, and then swept through the upper air by the Chinook to fall in the home meadow of the Buffalo Head. Spot fires—small, isolated fires—were caused by things like that; God only knows why we didn't have more of them. And what use as fire guards were rivers and mountain ranges and the puny hackings and slashings of a fire crew when that sort of thing could happen?

There was a further hopelessness about that blazing summer of '36 in that this kind of thing—drought, fire and high winds—was not confined to the Highwood and Elk Rivers; it was happening all up and down the mountain West. Fires were chasing the cattle down out of their forest and mountain range and on to the dry, overgrazed ranchlands which should have been saved for winter. And, anyway, if the coming winter should prove to be a tough one, there was no feed. The hay never grew and the crops just came out of the parched ground, took one look at the flaming sun and shrivelled. And in many places there was no water. Soon ranchers in dried-out areas began to throw their cattle on to the market—most of them in terrible shape. That put the lid on it and bang went the price to rock bottom—and even before this happened it hadn't been anything to shout about. Now you couldn't even see it, it wasn't even tobacco money.

So, faced with the alternatives of being burnt out and bust or just bust, we waited to see what would happen next. We didn't have to wait very long …

I saw it happen. It was well on in the afternoon, and for once the wind was quiet and the smoke had drifted away towards the north—we could see the Mount Head Range. I had crossed the river with two of our dudes and we were riding towards the Miller Gap in the Knife Edge Ridge. We had our supper with us, on our saddles, and we were headed south for Pekisko Creek.

On the crest of the Gap we checked our horses and looked back west towards the mountains. All afternoon the clouds had been gathering around the head of Flat Creek and north along the range. It looked as if a good sousing downpour was about to descend on Upper Flat Creek and make that bit of country safe for some time to come.

Hopefully we watched the storm gathering. The thunder clouds were settling down on the peaks—when suddenly it came: one blazing flash of forked lightning against the blueness of the storm and the shadowy Dog Tooth Mountains. That was all. And then the mountains vanished with a rumbling growl of thunder into the greyness of the rain and we, not recognizing this new danger, were pleased with what we had seen.

Lois, a dude from England with a light heart and a startling mop of unruly hair, was the first to speak. "You've not got your slicker with you," she said. "You'll get soaked if the storm comes this way."

"It'll be a pleasure," I said. "I'll never get soaked in a better cause." And we rode on towards Pekisko Creek.

Late that night I heard the wind rising. It rose and it blew like fury for two days, varying between west and southwest; it drifted the smoke from the mountain fires all over the country and once more the Mount

Bert's cabin near the headwaters of Flat Creek

Head Range was blotted from view. And then, on the second evening,
I saw Sam tying his horse at the hitching rail.

He stamped in, obviously upset and covering his feelings with an
abruptness of speech. "Flat Creek's afire," he almost shouted. "Afire and
burning beautifully. Got a nice hold. Up around Bert's cabin the fire is.
Must have been that thunderstorm a couple of days ago. Let me get at
the phone." And he stamped out into the veranda.

This new fire was on our doorstep, and the only barrier left now was
the 6,700-foot High Rock Ridge, six miles west of the house. Hell broke
loose promptly and the Buffalo Head was right plumb in the centre of
it. We were the nearest ranch and the nearest telephone and so we
became the base of operations against the new fire. A second fire crew,
this time of fifty men, came in and disappeared up Flat Creek; trucks
growled up the lane into the meadow and our garage became a dump
for fire-fighting equipment—shovels, grub-hoes, axes, saws, gasoline
in four-gallon cans, a pump, packsaddles ... The hitching rail never
seemed to be without horses as men came and went with messages; the
kitchen table was rarely without some hungry and thirsty horseman,
dusty and streaked with the black of charred trees. You never knew

how many there would be to breakfast. I counted twenty-three one morning and that was a fairish average.

There is not much "even tenor" about ranch life at any time but, during this period of danger, the Buffalo Head lost what little it had ever had. It was haying time and something had to be done about that because, fire or no fire, we could bank with certainty on one sure thing—and that was winter. So we sent two men with seven packhorses up to the fire, and then, back at home, we somehow hayed and somehow got the cattle down from the South Fork.

The dudes revelled in all this excitement. They rode like mad hither and yon, they carried messages, they hounded cattle and they even got their faces well smeared with charcoal, as certain unprintable photographs go to show.

Meanwhile, in the mountains towards the head of Flat Creek, a lively time was being had. It was the wind that kept things on the move. The valleys of the upper Flat Creek country run in all directions, biting deeply into the Highwood Range and Mount Head, with the result that the west wind, leaping over the mountains, comes eddying down in savage whirlwinds, blowing this way and that as the spirit moves it. We of the Buffalo Head knew that Flat Creek wind of old. Now the fire fighters had to contend with it and it kept them on the hop. One bunch had to move camp no less than three times in one night, hunted out each time by a change in the direction of the fire. They were hungry and tired and just about all in, and they would have given much for a bite of supper but they couldn't even get that. They nearly got it at the second camp—and they would have got it if it hadn't been for the bull-cook, the cook's enthusiastic helper, Ole. There was a vast mulligan slung over the campfire in a thing like a witches' cauldron. All it needed now was another bucket of water and then boiling up again; very soon the welcome cry of the cook would be heard: "Come and get her, boys! Stick in till you stick out!"

Ole climbed down into the darkness of the little canyon below camp and dipped out a bucketful of Flat Creek, complete with ashes and burnt spruce needles. With this he staggered back to the campfire and raised his bucket, ready to pour. Alas! Blinded by the firelight after the darkness by the stream, he had failed to observe that the lid had not been removed from the cauldron. Warning shouts came too late; Ole let fly and a frightful sizzling explosion of steam and ashes erupted from the cauldron lid and the hot rocks by the fire. In one brief second the campfire was practically extinguished, Ole was fleeing down the trail just one jump ahead of a furious cook, and supper was further off than ever.

But, before the cook could catch Ole and kill him, a switch of the wind drove the forest fire straight at camp. All feuds were temporarily suspended and the outfit had to up stakes and go, supperless, to some safer site, taking their cauldron with them.

Headquarters had to be evacuated, on another occasion, for an even more pressing reason. They were working with the gasoline-driven pump along the fork of Flat Creek that runs under the Dog Tooth Mountains. With the jet from the pump they were soaking everything they could reach from the little stream, thereby creating a fire guard that, with any luck and barring the outbreak of spot fires, nothing could cross.

Away up the mountainside, across the stream from camp, the fire was creeping upwards. It was coming to a very old burn, the result of some lightning fire of long ago. Wood stays sound for many years in that dry climate and many of the old, fire-killed trees were still standing— gaunt and grey, tinder-dry and sound as a bell. Lodged behind them— and behind many of the green forest trees also—were boulders and great fragments of broken rock that had been split off by the frost and the sun or dislodged by heavy rains. Now these trees were burning and so was the humus around their roots. Soon the trees began to fall or were burnt through, releasing the heated rocks that they held. These came bounding and leaping down the mountainside, gaining speed at every jump, smashing their way through the burning forest, dislodging other boulders that were even bigger than themselves. Very soon red-hot chunks of rock, in assorted sizes, came leaping across the stream; they hummed through the air and buried themselves in great drifts of fireweed and delphinium; they shivered to fragments any wretched tree that barred their way, and then fell in the ruins of it. Old-fashioned warfare this may have been but, none the less, it was effective. Tanks would not have been improved by this bombardment, let alone human

beings and the simple packhorses of the Buffalo Head—Bozo, Brainless
& Co. As luck would have it no man or horse was hurt. Nevertheless,
the fellows didn't feel much like staying there. They packed up and got
out of that camp. In a hurry.

Bozo had some narrow shaves. His job was to pack the pumps and,
when they were in use, the gasoline for them. Bozo was big; he could
pack a lot of weight and, provided he was led, could easily handle it.
Adolf was up there one day, riding across the face of a steep hillside
and leading Bozo and two or three other packhorses, all tied head to
tail. Suddenly an eddy in the wind brought to Adolf's keen nose the
unmistakable smell of gas. He dismounted quietly and went back to
investigate; and, sure enough, it was Bozo—Bozo absolutely stinking
of gas. Something was leaking.

This was a bit of a nuisance. Adolf didn't want to go on with the
stuff slopping out all over the pack pads and blankets—and he certainly
wasn't going to go right up to the fire with Bozo all ready to explode
at the first spark. He didn't know quite what to do: there were no trees
just there to tie the other horses to, and he didn't want to unpack Bozo
with the whole bunch tailed because, if anything happened, if a pack
cover flapped in the wind and scared them, they might go bucking off
the trail and crash down the hillside all tangled up together, and so kill
or lame each other.

So he mounted again and rode on, down on to the creek flats over
which the fire had already passed, heading for a little "island" of grass
and trees that had somehow escaped and which stood out bright and
clean against the sombre desolation of the burn. Arrived there, he
untailed his horses and tied them to the poplar trees. Then he took
Bozo's top pack off and poked around to see if he could find the leak.
One side of Bozo's pack pad, he soon found, was saturated with gas and
giving off a highly volatile essence.

At this point in his investigations Adolf heard a crackling sound
and there came to his nostrils the smell of grass smoke. He whipped
round to find that his island of dry grass and poplars was on fire, and
that the fire was heading straight for his horses. The main blaze was
not far distant and some hot whirlwind had carried a brand from it to
start this spot fire.

Adolf got himself and his horses out of there in record time—just before the new outbreak gathered speed on a rising wind and swept down and consumed his island. Having learnt that lesson, and not intending to be caught the same way twice running, he rode to the next clump of poplars—which was black, charred and completely immune to flying brands and red-hot charcoal. He tied his horses to the burnt trees; and as he did so he noticed a rider coming down the valley towards him.

The man was weary and blackened. It was days since he had last shaved and his buckskin coat was full of spark holes. He dismounted and threw his lines down. "Mornin', Adolf," he said. "Having a bit of trouble with that pack?" Then he turned his back to the wind and busied himself with cigarette papers and a sack of Bull Durham … When he had things fixed to his liking he went over to help Adolf. "I guess if a man can't smoke safely in this black desert," he said, "then he can't smoke safely no place," and, before Adolf could stop him, he struck a match on the crotch of Bozo's packsaddle, within three inches of the open gas can nozzle—for Adolf had located the trouble and was just about to jam home the cross-threaded plug. Adolf's peace of mind was shattered completely; and he told me that the whole morning went on like that: just one damn thing after another— every possible hazard of a mountain fire. Why Bozo failed to go up in flames and burst with a tremendous bang no man knoweth to this day and Adolf, when speaking of this afterwards, gave it as his opinion that "a fire is no place for a man to be. A man is undoubtedly safer mowing hay." An understatement which nobody ventured to contradict.

Down at the Buffalo Head certain routine precautions were taken. The meadows had already been cut close and now, around the buildings, sprinklers were kept running night and day in an effort to keep the grass green. Hoses were laid out in readiness and drums of water were placed at certain strategic points with sacks dipping into them for the putting out of grass fires. Our forty-odd remaining horses were gathered and kept handy so that, if the need came, we could chase them across the river—for what that was worth. What cattle we could get our hands on were kept close.

Mount Assiniboine, British Columbia

In the middle of all the confusion I took six of our dudes and went off into the mountains, to Mount Assiniboine. I had been going to take them to Elk River but that was now impossible, so I took them up to Banff and we went with a Banff guide's horses and part of his outfit and part of mine.

Before I left I had a conference with Sam and Adolf—to go or not to go being the subject of discussion.

Finally Sam said: "You might just as well go. Six head of dudes out of the way'll be something gained, and all that can be done here has been done. If the fire comes we'll save the buildings and we'll save the cattle and horses. That's all a man can say, the way things are."

So I went. We had perfect weather on that Assiniboine trip, and we were out of touch with all news for about a couple of weeks. Sometimes I thought of the ranch and wondered if it was still there—or if the fire had got into the valley of the South Fork or Bull Creek. If that's gone, I thought, I'm going, too! There's still room in the West and I'll not live my life out in the ashes of the things I've loved. And I would look up at the sky and ask what curse it was that lay on the country that it couldn't rain.

But more often I never thought of the ranch at all, having the faculty of concentrating on what lies nearest to hand and being able to put out of my mind distant things over which I can have no control. Capable men were in charge down there and nothing was ever gained by worrying. And so we moved from camp to camp through the mountains, ten people and twenty-three horses. And the skies were clear and blue, and the sun shone down on us from dawn to dusk, and never a drop of rain.

Which made it all the more odd, when I came back to the Buffalo Head, to find it also under the same bright blue sky and the smoke cloud gone. I got out of the car and stared at the little flat in front of the garden gate. All the broken grass and the dead wreckage of the wild flowers had been washed and swept by water into long, curving rows such as one sees on a beach at high watermark. And the hills had a faint touch of green on them, and the house, where the sprinklers had been running, stood in a neat pocket-handkerchief of bright green grass, vivid against the tawny yellow of the meadow. What could have happened here? A deluge?

That was exactly it, they said—a deluge. Just when it was most needed, too. And they told me the tale ...

The fire had chased the fire crew down Flat Creek to the mouth of Head Creek. There the wind had switched and driven the blaze back west again—this time up Head Creek, a deep, V-shaped valley that cut in behind Mount Head, densely forested with thick, green spruce. Thank God no man was caught in there for the valley exploded in a roar of flame and a gigantic upheaval of smoke. The whole sky was hidden, and on that last night and day of the fire there was no sun nor moon, nor were there any stars. A beastly, unnatural darkness settled on the Highwood country and the lamps were lit and placed on the table at midday at the Buffalo Head. This was it, they thought—and they braced themselves, much as a man does who expects to receive a blow.

It was on that day, too, that there came to the ranch a refugee. Across the river, almost a mile distant from the ranch house and well up on the slopes of the Knife Edge, there was a cabin. It stood on land that had once belonged to the Buffalo Head, land that had been sold by Pocaterra, years ago, to some people who built this cabin there for the sake of its magnificent view of the mountains.

Alone in the cabin in the semi-darkness of this hellish noonday was the cook; her employers were away. Stuck there for days on this lonely hillside with the bunch-grass all around, knee-deep and tinder-dry, this woman had watched the Flat Creek fire. So appalling had been the hideous spectacle by day and the glowing clouds by night that her nerve had been slowly giving way. And now this.

No more of it for her, she decided—she was through. Hastily, in the gloom, she collected one or two things—her rifle, a few personal belongings. Then she took the steep trail down to the bathing pool, waded what was left of the Highwood River and proceeded at speed across the flat and up the lane to the Buffalo Head. The sound of other women talking was what she wanted to hear—and quickly. And, after that, the first car down the trail to High River, or anywhere out of this cursed valley, would be just the thing.

And that was not a woman who panicked easily. Some years later she was out hunting for deer on a hillside not far above the ranger station. The rifle she had with her was a high-powered .22. Suddenly, from behind a big log, a grizzly rose and confronted her. Most unpleasantly close he was—a matter of a few yards, that was all. But it was the grizzly who had come to the end of the trail, for the lady shot him through the eye, in a very businesslike way, with the .22 and he fell dead at her feet—an object lesson in game-getting to the expensive sportsmen of the Cassiar and elsewhere, with their hard-hitting magnum rifles, their telescope sights and their happy prattle of ballistics.

The darkness thickened as that last day wore on, and who could tell that, above the smoke, the rain clouds were gathering? Then the first great big drops came down through the smoke, and tired men, men who had been without hope, looked up and wondered if this was real or if it was only a part of some weary dream. But the skies opened and very soon the rain was drumming down in blinding torrents. The gangs ran for shelter amongst the rocks or hit the trail for camp—and gradually the smoke was washed down out of the air and the mountains appeared once more with their heads in the storm clouds and their flanks streaming with the blessed rain. And the fires choked and steamed and spluttered—and slowly died. And that was the end of it.

Grass

The original estimate by the British Columbia Forest Service of the loss caused by the Phillips fire was 1,700,000,000 board feet—a board foot meaning a piece of lumber twelve inches square by one inch thick. Further inspection and trips into the burnt areas, however, revealed that the destruction was not so complete as had at first been thought: valleys and pockets of green timber remained—bright oases in the blackened ruins of the forests. The final estimate of loss, therefore, was cut down to 900,000,000 board feet, a figure which amounted to 30 per cent of the entire cut for 1936 in the forest province of British Columbia. And since a figure of that magnitude has but little meaning for most of us, I have reduced it to a measurement that even I can understand: it represents, in lumber, a solid floor one inch thick laid down over an area of 32 square miles!

Those giant spruce that grew by Nyahé-ya-'nibi Waptán—a hundred years will not replace them. Indeed, a thousand years will not suffice to make good some of the damage that was done. There was one beautiful flat on the upper Highwood from which the river washed away three and four feet of the finest black loam. Nothing remained but a waste of shingle—and that was all due to the river overflowing its banks in high floods which were the result of fires, and then flowing down a deeply cut cattle trail. The old mat of grass that might have partly saved the meadow had already been destroyed by overgrazing.

The evil that men do lives after them: it is a sobering thought that the lonely half-wit who sets fire to a forest in order to make fire-pay in hard times, or to work off a grudge against some railroad or logging company, leaves behind him a memorial as enduring as any of those achieved by a prime minister of Canada backed by the resources of the whole country.

☆ ☆ ☆ ☆

Over the Highwood country crept the colours of autumn. The first light frosts came and the first splashes of red and gold flared out in the green woodlands. The days wheeled past under sunny skies—and then, at the proper intervals, as if to make up for the terrible summer, fell the autumn rains. Bare, gravelly knolls turned green again; here and there crocuses, thinking it was April, pushed up and flowered a second time, and in the woods the partridges began to drum their messages of spring ... Fire crews, dudes, summer help, guests—even our small family—departed from the valley, and a tremendous peace fell upon the Buffalo Head. It was as if a bombardment had ceased and it brought with it the same feeling of relief.

As we sorted out the cattle and the horses and returned them to their normal grazing grounds we soon got a rough idea of what had happened, and it was curious to see how, in the two places where the flames had threatened us, we had been saved in the nick of time—once by a shift of the wind and once by the final rain. The downpour had come just as the fire was climbing over the shoulder of Mount Head into the valley of the South Fork. High up at timberline a few scattered firs were burnt. But that was all. An hour or two later and the east slopes of Mount Head would have been swept by the flames.

It was not until the following summer, that I had time to go up to the lake in the wooded basin at the head of Flat Creek. I left the ranch at sunrise. It was still cool when I passed the desolation of the Dog Tooth Mountains and entered the narrow upper valley of Flat Creek, crossing and recrossing the stream. The little grove where we always left out horses had not been burnt; I tied my horse in the shade there, greased him against the flies and went on. I climbed over the barren shoulder of a mountain, browsing on wild strawberries; there was a fresh goat track, I remember, in a patch of clay and just beyond that there was an outcrop, a high wall of rock. I climbed over it—and that was the end of the burn: at this point the rain had fallen, and beyond it, the dark green mantle of the firs covered this cirque of the mountains as it had done for ages past, through generations of old, slow-growing trees. I went on to the lake, up sloping avenues between the firs, wading through great drifts of tall asters, blue delphiniums, crimson Indian paint brush ... The lake was, as ever, a garden of small alpines, alive with shifting colour under the sun and the wind. It was here, the very first time we saw the place, that Alberto had his vision, as it were, of the perfect life: "God, but it is beautiful!" he called out to Adolf and myself who were ahead of him. "Why do we waste time with a garden down at the Buffalo 'Ead? 'Ere is our garden for the asking. We move up 'ere and we are 'appy all summer long among these flowers!"

It was on the way up to the lake, on this summer morning, that I first noticed what was to me a new thing. Crossing a burnt hillside on a game trail some six inches wide, I found the track hidden by a tremendous growth of wild rye-grass. It was anywhere knee-high and in places it came up to my hip. This was very odd, for there had been practically nothing there before in the way of grass. What was going to be the end of it? I wondered. A frightful fire hazard, as the years went by and the grass piled up? Or what?

That same summer, the year after the fire, Marigold and I, with one man and eight horses, crossed Picklejar Flat on the upper Highwood on our way to the Palliser River and Joffre Creek. That was on June 26, and the rocky, barren-looking flat—which never had anything much in the way of grass on it—was coming green very nicely. Beyond noticing that, we paid no attention to it; but when we came back that way, homeward bound, on July 24, the scene had changed with a vengeance. The rocks were all hidden and a magnificent growth of rye-grass was swaying in the wind with dark, rippling shadows passing over it such as one sees in a field of grain. It was a lovely sight and we all three exclaimed at it. Could it be that the fire, which had destroyed so much, had in some obscure way improved the grasslands?

The thing puzzled me and I pursued it through books on grass and trees until I found the answer, which is this: a fire, given certain conditions, can make available to a barren soil a sudden supply of nitrogen and potash. In a grass country, and where the grass roots have not been killed, a flush of grass is the result—but this flush represents the stored-up fertilizers of years, and after this sudden effort the soil is left bankrupt. It must speedily revert to its original barren condition.

It did. The year 1938 saw the end of that sudden growth of grass: Picklejar Flat went back to its normal barren condition—only slightly worse than before—and when I last saw it a gopher would have starved to death on it. And that hillside on upper Flat Creek produces a blade of grass here and another blade there, just as it always did; and the game trail across its barren face is once more plain to see. But that is not the end of the story: others had seen that flush of grass on the upper Highwood and had jumped to the conclusion that it was there to stay. Very few cattle, anyway, had ever pastured in the upper valley and the grazing, therefore, had always been in very good shape—much as the Lord made it. Now it was even better. Soon the word got around that there was a whole world of grass on the upper Highwood to be had for the asking. One way and another, the time seemed ripe for that ceremony which, above all others, is most dear to the Anglo-Saxon mind: a public meeting.

Those of the assembled ranchers who fancied themselves at handling their tongues, promptly let fly with speeches. After all, this was an occasion: it was not every day in this cramped century that unspoilt grazing came, as it were, on to the market. Optimism was the keynote of those speeches—optimism and a total disregard of the fact that mountain grazing can be quickly ruined by overpasturing. Grass for a thousand head, some timid soul opined. They jumped down his throat. A thousand head! Why, that was nothing—make it fifteen hundred, no, two thousand, anyway ... And the figure went on climbing as if the meeting were an auction sale.

Three of us sat together and held aloof from the general uproar. We were very nicely fixed the way we were. With our cattle packed away in separate valleys at the heads of Flat Creek and Sullivan Creek we just minded our own business and mingled with nobody, not even with each other. An ideal state of affairs, and we had no desire for this Highwood grazing; we were only at this meeting to make sure that nobody tried to interfere with us.

As for me, I was seeing the thing from an angle of my own. The forest fire had cut a big hole in my dude-wrangling country and I had been toying, for some time, with the idea of a hunting ranch far in the wilds. Now, if it panned out so that I had to share the South Fork of Flat Creek with anybody, I would up stakes and go. To be a dyed-in-the-wool cattle rancher you had to have a single-track mind; your one idea of a fine view had to be the back end of a cow lined up between your horse's ears—and nothing but. It might be my good luck or it might be my bad luck, but I had seen other things in earlier years—things that kept getting in between me and that cow. They lingered in the mind's eye, just out of reach and just over the horizon's rim, but always there: a green upland with the blue cloud-shadows sweeping over it and the white sheep of the north grazing into the sun; an unmapped river driving down from God knows where between scarlet-topped, snow-powdered mountains that had no name; the dawn flooding over an unbroken, unfenced prairie that was furrowed with the buffalo trails of

Holy Cross from Mount Head

yesterday ... There were parts of the Northwest where already I, even in my short years, was known as an old-timer—and there were parts of the Northwest where there was still room to turn around without bumping into somebody. And I knew the way to them and it wasn't too late to hit the trail.

I just sat there, listening with one ear but thinking hard.

The "grass without end" section of the meeting got its way and crowded all the cattle it could muster on to the upper Highwood with the full approval of the authorities, who at that time, it would seem, saw grass not as a part of the natural balance but purely and simply as a fire hazard. Their worries were soon ended. The grass cover was eaten off until, on the bare ground that remained, a fire would have had about as much chance as the proverbial snowflake in hell. Two years later it was hard to find a good camping place for an eight-horse outfit. Ten years later Marigold and I, riding away from the Buffalo Head for the last time, packed with us oats for our horses.

Counting the Losses

I climbed the ridge between Mount Head and the Holy Cross one September afternoon, a bare two months from the July day on which, from this same spot, we had first seen the fire raging up Elk River. A vast expanse of blackened forest met my eyes: the Elk Trail was burnt and, with it, much country on the far side of the upper Highwood. There seemed to be dark masses of green near the top of the Hill of the Flowers: that would be the old firs up at timberline—and perhaps some of the big larches and the meadows of the snow lilies had survived as well. But it was hard to see; against the sun dark green and black look very much alike; one would have to make a trip into that country to be certain.

Smoke from a couple of spot fires drifted up out of green forest. Even yet these fires were burning, in muskeg, in rotten logs—a constant source of anxiety to the ranger. Men were watching them, digging round them, isolating them—for it was possible for a fire to smoulder away in the peat of a muskeg all winter, under the snow, and then break out with the first high wind of spring and set the whole country ablaze again.

I swung round to the south to see what had happened to a goat which had climbed up on my left, a little below me and up an impossible-looking precipice. With his feet bunched close together he was pivoting carefully around on a tiny and quite invisible ledge. Slowly he walked along it, and then, at the far end, he raised himself up with a smooth, careful and seemingly effortless pull from those marvellous shoulder muscles. From there it was easy: a few rocky steps, a slope of broken sandstone—and then he walked over the crest of the ridge and into the sunlight with the westwind ruffling his long, creamy fur. He never looked back. He walked slowly down the easy slope towards the ranger station and vanished from view. The precipice he had climbed, deep in the shadow and apparently sheer, one would have thought to be impossible even for skilled mountaineers with the benefit of hands and ropes and pitons.

☆ ☆ ☆ ☆

That October I went over the Elk Trail for the last time. My plan was to climb the Pyramid and then, if there seemed to be any point in doing so, to go on down to Elk River, cross it on a raft if I couldn't wade it, and go up into Nyahé-ya-'nibi. The trip had to be made on foot because the burn had probably been complete and, even if it had been possible to get horses over that pass, there would be no feed anywhere along the trail. It would be a hard trip, and so I made careful preparations: I took a light cord for raft building, a 1 1/2 lb. axe, a light tarpaulin and a single blanket. A pistol and ten cartridges, a caribou knife, field glass and camera completed the outfit. The rest was all grub, with teapail, mug and frying pan, fish hooks and a toothbrush. I packed the stuff into my lightest packsack, got somebody to drive me as far as possible up the Highwood and then hit the trail. After a couple of hours walking I waded the river and climbed up on to what was left of the Elk Trail.

Never have I seen such a complete burn. The old cushions of bunch-grass were gone from the elk meadow; here and there young green blades were poking through, but I wondered if most of the roots had not been destroyed as well. Even the kini-kinik, the little crawling plant of the

stony benches, had been burnt and the fire had followed the roots of the
ground cedar deep into the gravel. There was *nothing* left alive—not
even a green willow by the stream. Bunk Creek clattered down through
the burnt and blackened forest, sparkling in the sunlight with the hard,
soulless glitter of a diamond. It made more noise than formerly, for
there was no greenery left to muffle the uproar of the water. From the
dead trees there came no longer the continuous, friendly sounds of the
bush, no gentle rustling of the branches—only a lifeless silence, broken
now and then by the dismal moaning of the wind as it found some
split trunk or loose piece of bark and sounded through it. Sometimes,
too, one heard the dreary creaking of two dry, fire-killed trees rubbing
against one another. But there was no living thing: no bird, no animal,
no green tree. And very likely, no fish.

Nothing remained of the cache except the three trees that had
supported the platform. There they stood—three gaunt, upstanding
rampikes of charcoal with the humus burnt away from their roots. Of the
ladder there was not a trace, and even the rocks were burnt and blackened.
It was there, by the cache, disgusted with all I saw, that I made up my
mind not to rest or sit down until I came to some patch of green.

I plugged on—past the ruin of the meadow where Adolf and I had
camped, over the ashes and the fire-scorched rocks that now showed
where the avalanche debris had been, right to the foot of the waterfall.
I followed the old game trail up the cliff. Already, even it was not so
good as it used to be, for the rain had been getting to work, washing
away the unprotected soil. My pack, too, seemed to be getting rapidly
heavier and, in one or two steep places, I went up without it, hauling
it up after me by the line. Then, beyond the little lake at the top of the
waterfall, I found my green spot and rested there ...

Here and there in the pass there were clumps of green firs and
patches of unburnt meadow; and on the way up to the summit it was
easy to see how the fire had travelled. The westwind must have been
blowing at gale force on that day, for one could see where whole groups
of firs had burst into flame—and then, as the flames raced up the trees,
burning the stems, the recent growth at the very top had snapped off,
still blazing, and had rolled as a fireball down the pass, scattering and
spreading the fire. There were signs that this had happened often; and

there were one or two places where the burn narrowed down to such an extent that a couple of men, stationed up there in good time, might have stopped the fire from spreading into Alberta. In those places the flames had crept through light alpine growth on a front of only a few yards between bare rock and water; the most primitive equipment would have been quite effective and the victory might have been gained—always provided that there had not been too dense a volume of smoke driving through the pass. However, that was all water over the dam now. I went on to the summit and found my old camp ground by the spring an oasis of green in a desert of charred trees.

In the morning light the valley of the Elk presented a picture of utter desolation. Dusk had softened it somewhat, but now, with the hard, clear light streaming out of the east, the ruin of the once-beautiful valley could no longer be hidden. Here and there a patch of green timber could be seen—but it only served to accentuate the blackness. I looked at it with a bleak, frozen memory of all that it had been, and all the vivid similes that I had ever heard came back to me: "black as the ace of spades," an old trapper friend used to say; and a fellow homesteader of the Peace River: "blacker than the Earl of Hell's waistcoat." That hit it off to perfection, that last one. I spat out some charcoal dust and turned away from it all towards the blue sky and the clean stone of the mountain.

Almost 2,000 feet higher I was still climbing up a steady slope consisting of big blocks of broken sandstone. I had not stopped to rest. The widening view showed only more desolation and there was no inducement to sit down and admire it. Moreover, my thoughts were far away and I clambered over the tumbled rocks in a kind of dream: I was considering the sale of the Buffalo Head (if that were possible in these hard times) and a trek into the wilderness in search of a good hunting country. Northern British Columbia, perhaps—and, at that point, a great shadow flitted over the rocks just to my left and the quiet air was split by an appalling sound: it was as if an 18-pounder shell had swished past, right over my head. I flattened and clutched the face of the mountain in sudden terror. Then I turned my head just in time to see a second enormous bird flash past about ten feet away, making the same tearing sound as it banked and turned.

So that was it—eagles. I watched them anxiously, knowing nothing of their habits. They were obviously annoyed and they swooped down on me again and yet again, turning away at the last moment. The peak of the mountain was narrowing and I was on the crest of the last ridge with a deep gulf of nothingness to right and left of me. It might have been fun for a trained ornithologist to watch that much bird coming straight down at him like a dive bomber, all beak and talons—it was no fun at all for a poor, ignorant rancher. I jammed myself in between the rocks, pulled out my hunting knife and vigorously flapped the linen-mounted sheet of the Boundary Atlas at the eagles; these things were the only weapons that I had. Soon, however, the eagles tired of the sport. It might have been that their curiosity was satisfied; in any event, they circled away northwest along the range, becoming smaller and fainter until at last they vanished into the blue.

I crawled on upwards over the big rocks. I had almost come to the end of them now, for the ridge was becoming too narrow to give them a resting place. Only one large one remained, cocked up amongst the smaller stones. I could go to one side or the other of it—or over the top or underneath the cocked up end. The sides gave me the jim-jams merely to look at them: on the south, sliding rock and then a drop of 2,000 feet down to my lean-to shelter which I could see shining in the sunlight in its little oasis of green trees; on the north, a steeper and longer drop into a barren, stony coulee. Over the top looked a bit airy and exposed for me, and I decided to play it safe: I crawled rapidly and successfully underneath and out the other side. As I drew my feet out from under I thrust hard against some smaller rock. It moved a little with my weight—and it must have disturbed some delicate balance, for I heard behind me a slow grinding noise and then a heavy "Chug," and I felt a small vibration in the mountain. The big stone had fallen. It had dropped into place as a deadfall drops that is set for a bear. Had it moved a second earlier, or had I moved the smaller rock on my way through, I should have been trapped there with my legs crushed beneath all that weight of stone.

The idea was not a pleasing one—lying there helplessly, fainting and coming to, waiting ... And the eagles—what were their habits? I knew that the bald-headed eagle ate dead salmon. These were golden eagles. Were they more particular? Or less? And another thing—did they wait patiently for their meals? Or were they, like some people, always in a tearing hurry? The way of an eagle would be a fine and a wonderful road to take—but, for choice, not inside the bird. Better by far the humbler way of the horseman on the winding mountain trails.

Thinking of the eagles, I had been climbing steadily upwards, away from the deadfall that I had escaped. And now I had come to the end of the solid rocks; only 200 feet remained of the mountain, but here the ridge was like an ill-made road. It was composed of friable and sliding sandstone; one could only adhere to it by friction—and not much even by that. With the moral support of a companion and a well-belayed rope I might have got to the top; but alone, and after the eagles and the moving stone—no. I sat down and made myself comfortable. The day was perfect and life was sweet.

From this altitude of about 9,500 feet, green patches of forest could be seen that had been invisible from below. One could see from here right into Nyahé-ya-'nibi: the old and magnificent spruce by the Waptán where I had fired at the trout was gone, but there was green forest ten miles beyond, towards Cadorna Lake. Up Elk River itself the fire had died at the mouth of Tobermory Creek where a crew of men from Alberta had met and fought it. That meant that the Elk Lakes were safe, and the head of Nyahé-ya-'nibi; the White River and the Kananaskis countries were green, and all the country that lay beyond. There were still the green fastnesses, even if one had to ride further and traverse a burn to find them.

I swung the glass on to the Pass in the Clouds. A sea of mountains lay around and beyond it—mountains without end, it seemed. And then I looked more carefully. There *was* an end. At least, there was a gap and then a new beginning. You could see that there had to be a gap there, for the last mountains visible in the glass were not the Rockies at all; they were a wild-looking, sharp-peaked range; they were of a deeper blue and incredibly far away. They were the Purcells, the mountains west of the Columbia River.

Marvelling at this, I turned and looked eastward over the shoulder of the Pyramid. There, through the Highwood Gap, beyond the foothills, lay the prairie. It was dim and remote, for the smoke of burning stubble lay over the flatlands and the horizon was not to be seen: the plains

Patterson on the trail up Cataract Creek

faded imperceptibly into the sky. This, too, was a marvel—that, from the Pyramid, the gaps in the mountains were so arranged that a man could swing his glass, in a second, from the prairie in the east, all the way westwards to the jagged peaks of the Purcells, a distance of a hundred and forty miles.

All the Rockies lay in between. But there was an older name for these ranges than that: Duncan's Mountains the Northwesters had called them—the name is written clearly on the great map that once hung in the mess hall of the North West Company at Fort William. It can be seen on that map today.

The name had something of youth in it. Something of the youth of the west when the Purcells were known as Nelson's Mountains, and when the Kootenay was called McGillivray's River after this same Duncan. And these mountains were still young. A thousand valleys, a thousand meadows gay with flowers—they were waiting there beyond this blackened valley of the Elk, and few had travelled them. They beckoned, and, as I looked, I knew that there would be no sale, then, of the Buffalo Head: it was home, and it was a good place for a man to be—with Duncan's Mountains at its door.

There remained the Cataract Creek country: had it been burnt? Or had it escaped? I had to know—but other things got in the way, and it was not until the shortest day of that year of the fire that I rode off up the Highwood.

I left my horse at the mouth of Fir Creek, crossed the river on the ice, and began to climb. I followed a spur of the Lookout Range, plugging through drifted snow, over ice-glazed rocks and round projecting pinnacles. Three hours of this sort of thing brought me to a viewpoint from which I could see that no fire had touched upper Cataract Creek. That was something to the good: there was still an outlet there for hunting trips and dude activities.

I wasted no time in admiring the view, for it was already time to be getting down again to the river. I kept to the ridge for part of the way back; then I swung over on to the east slope, getting into a lot of deep snow for my trouble but losing height quickly and easily. One snow-covered slope seemed familiar—and soon I saw that it was the way the girl and I had come down with the horses the day the fire jumped the Continental Divide. I plunged and slid down the steep slope, carrying with me a miniature avalanche of snow. Then I went down through the trees to the glade in the centre of the grove through which we had passed on that smoke-clouded evening of the hot wind. It was cold in that hollow now, and utterly still. The dark wall of the evergreens seemed to intensify the sunset light that was reflected from the snow of the little clearing. Here and there, brown against the carpet of white, a seed head of the tall asters still poked through. They had survived; and so the girl's wish had been granted—though narrowly and precisely and with nothing to spare, for the fire had been extinguished by the rain just as it crept over the rim and burnt the first outlying tree of this little grove of firs.

7

Gone West

Wartime

The years slipped easily by in the ordered routine of stock raising. Calving, branding, haying, weaning, wintering—and, by God's truth, it seemed you'd hardly had time to turn round before April was on you again with its green grass and purple crocuses and the cows once more calving! Sometimes you managed to fit in a mountain trip. That would be either just before haying or just before weaning—unless, of course, one went off somewhere in the way of business with the dudes. It was a good life—one of the best—and the months and the years were not marked as on any ordinary calendar: there was "the November of the big wind" and "the winter of the big snow." Or it might be "the fall we ran into that big bunch of elk on Fording River" or "the summer we took the outfit away down the Palliser." Any life that has only natural things like these for its landmarks has nothing wrong with it; a man should realize that and be content with it.

But the nomad is never content. Always, in the mind's eye, there is that one more pass to the westward. If you could just see what lies on the other side of it! Who knows? it might be something even better …

Then Hitler's war started. I had been reading for some years past all I could lay hands on that had to do with the steppe and desert countries of Asia—Mongolia, Turkestan, the Gobi. How I wished that I might get a sight of those far places while the going was good! And now, here was a reason ready-made. This war would spread far away from the narrow roads and the little fields of Europe. Before it ended the armies of England were going to need men who knew what it was to travel in rough country—men who could handle a truck in snow, mud or sand, and then, if need be, switch to wagons, packhorses or riverboats. I could do all that and I didn't care where I went: I only hoped that it would be wild, wide open and far away from made roads and cities. And, if fortune smiled, in the empty spaces of Asia. And so, with Marigold's permission, I started the ball rolling on the opening day.

I pulled what strings I could and awaited results. One rode for the mail in those days not without excitement. Every Friday, over the grass hills of the Bar U, past the Chinook Ranch to the little ridge by the mail boxes at English Corner. There you sat while your horse grazed around you and the westwind rustled the dry grass of autumn—straining your eyes into the blue distance for the moving speck that would be the mailman's car. But all that fall and winter, and all the following summer, there was no word: you flipped through the ranch mail, just on the off chance, and then you slung it into the mail bag, hitched the bag to the saddle horn and rode back west towards the mountains, eleven solitary, deflated miles.

Almost a year went by. And then, one afternoon of late summer as I strewed the mail out on the grass at English Corner, I saw, lying uppermost, a letter from the War Office. The mailman had gone and I was alone. I tore the letter open in a state of wild excitement, expecting my marching orders. I found, instead, that I had been placed on the "special reserve of officers." Now what did that mean?

It meant, I realized as the years went by, that I had been swept into the centre of the official Sargasso Sea, that I had reached the fabled Isle of Dead Ships along with all the other wrecks. It meant that I was so old and decrepit that my proper vehicle was not a horse but a wheelchair. It meant the end of all my dreams of Turkestan.

Having been put in my place by the War Office, I settled down to it and hayed. Through the wartime summers I stacked hay on the Buffalo Head—and, as time went by, with increasing difficulty. For one thing, starting with 1937, the summers got wetter and wetter till I actually saw (as Sam had described it to me years before) a wagon bogged down on a rocky flat. In that year, if a cloud the size of a man's hand appeared over the Rockies, two hours later it would be covering the whole sky. Soon men and teams would be running for shelter from a torrential downpour, blazing lightning and thunder like the crash of guns. I got enormous tarpaulins made so that we could cover an open butt of hay, but even with that the work was doubled and so, too, was the time taken. Then, as if that wasn't enough to drive you raving, the better men gradually drifted away into the armed forces or into wartime construction work, and you got by with what help you could get—old men, young boys, girls. Even R.C.A.F. officers, week-ending with us, gallantly forked and tramped hay into the stacks. Sometimes these mixed crews worked well together. Sometimes not so well, and there was one summer when I had to listen to two ancient men quarrelling foolishly and incessantly with each other, and all the time complaining bitterly to me sweating on the stack.

"How the devil can I sweep it clean when that old fool's raking it like that?"

And from the other, bawled out as he drove by: "Look at 'im, will you? What the 'ell does 'e think 'e's playin' at? Scattering my rakin's from 'ere to breakfast time! I've a good mind to quit!"

We carried on always until the dew began to fall. Then the hay would become limp and soundless instead of crisp and rattley; teams would be unhitched and the procession would start for home—some riding in the democrat and leading an extra team over the end-gate; somebody riding a harnessed horse and leading his team-mate; others walking and driving their teams in front of them. It was a quiet picture that never failed to please me—with the purple outline of the mountains in the southwest, the sun sinking towards the shining rim of the Bella Vista hill, green pools of shadow flooding out over the meadows from the poplar clumps. The din of no engine broke the evening stillness—only the jingle of harness and the thud of horses' feet. Soon we would be swilling the dust out of our throats with tankards of cold beer. Then supper. Then showers and bed. A day's work had been done.

Those were good days: never in all my life have I worked up a finer thirst. But that summer of the two snarling ancients and the drenching thunderstorms—that was another thing entirely! Only the valley of the South Fork kept me sane: there were no frantic greybeards there, thank God, just a bunch of sensible cattle and some nice quiet bears.

Into that valley I rode one August Sunday with a light heart and a packhorse load of salt. It was towards noon and the country lay empty under the sunshine and the blessed silence of the mountains. Not even a cow was in sight ... I rode on up the valley, calling them. Soon they began to appear, high up on the slopes of Mount Head. Soon they were streaming down the mountain towards me. I waited until the leaders were close enough to get a smell of the salt in Mollie's pack; then I rode on towards the upper basin with the whole mob strung out behind me—bulls, cows, calves, they came silently and without fuss. After a mile or so and a stiffish climb I dumped the salt out for them on some rocky ground in a belt of dwarf pines. The cattle crowded up to it, pushing, shoving, licking hungrily. I moved off a little way, fixed up Mollie's pack and turned her loose. Then I swung on to Rex and looked the cattle over. All was well; and it was surely nice to see something on the place that was contented and not raising hell about its fellow creatures; it was too bad one couldn't have a haying crew composed entirely of cows.

And now the summer's day was all mine to use as I pleased. I whistled to Mollie and rode down on to the meadows, heading for the little flat at the entrance to the Mount Head Coulee where I had camped, seven years ago, with the girl on the night of the fiery cloud.

☆ ☆ ☆ ☆

The sun was in the southwest by the time I reached the peak of the mountain. The afternoon was hot and still, and I was hot and dry and hungry; I made myself comfortable in a hollow of the rocks and then I opened my packsack and arranged things neatly on a flat stone—map, field-glass and camera, sandwiches and a thermos of tea.

It was some years now since I had climbed Mount Head. Down below, in the upper valley, the Highwood flashed and sparkled, as of old, against the tawny grass of the meadows. But beyond the river the old forest had gone and in its place stood the gaunt grey rampikes of the 1936 fire, the skeletons of burnt trees. Here and there in the greyness was a mist of young green: that would be the trees returning to the attack—the pioneer growth of poplar, willow and jackpine that would pave the way for the forest that was to come. But not in my time: I would not see that forest tall and green. For that one would have to go westward now, into British Columbia—and I lifted the glass over the Divide to mountains that lay beyond the grey desert of 1936.

Gleaming in the far distance, I identified them one by one: peaks of snow and ice that rose from the very head of the North Kananaskis, from the Elk Lakes, from the heads of Nyahé-ya-'nibi. And there, a little west of south and far away, was the mysterious mountain with the hanging glacier nestling against its peak. It towered above its fellows and you could see the glint of the sunlight off the ice. There was still no map of that country but there would be the old trails of the Stoneys, they ran everywhere. If only I had the time to take the horses and go and keep on going till I came to the foot of that mountain!

I looked to the left, along the ridge to the Holy Cross Mountain and beyond, over the Highwood Gap and along the Lookout Range. A thunderstorm was gathering there, an island of billowing white cumulus in the summer sky, dark-shadowed and threatening. If it came this way I would have to get down quickly; I had seen the lightning strike these summits like 18-pounder shells. But, even as I watched,

The Eden Valley

there came a flash and a rumble of thunder and the storm started to move out over the foothills. To rain on my hay, I thought—but no, the storm went down Pekisko Creek. Lightning flashed again and a grey curtain of rain slowly descended, blotting out Snake Lake and its valley. That would be Thorpe and Cartwright's hay catching it this time; the Buffalo Head had had a soaking yesterday. It was nice to know that these favours were distributed impartially. I watched the storm for a while as it drifted down towards the E P; then I moved round to the east side of the peak.

Some hundreds of feet below me a goat walked across a spur of the mountain. His hide was red with the dust of the sandstone; he had been rolling in it as goats often do in the summertime, but whether that was to get rid of loose wool or whether it was an instinctive form of camouflage I was never quite certain. The goat walked on over the neck of the "head" from which the mountain got its name and then he disappeared from view—the individualist, the very emblem of freedom, the finest mountaineer of all time.

Nearly 4,000 feet below and a couple of miles away a small knot of cattle was milling, with the aimless persistence of insects, round the salt. Others were coming out from amongst the trees where they had passed the heat of the afternoon lying in the shade. They came out singly and in small groups; sometimes there would be a large red insect with a small one walking beside it—a cow with her calf. Then out on to the meadow would come a group of calves with their mothers moving behind them more slowly. And then the massive bulk of a Hereford bull; even at this distance you could spot the bulls with the glass. I watched the cattle for a while to see if they would drift back down the valley—but they were content, they would give no trouble. Then I scrambled back on to the sunny side of the peak to get the stuff I had left there. I came suddenly out of the shadow into the full blaze of the sun and the glory of the western mountains.

It may have been that sudden vision of the Shining Mountains or it may have been the sight of that goat, free as the wind to go and come as he pleased—whatever it was, the years of wartime restraint vanished into thin air. The thunderstorm was away east of the Bar U now, blotting out the prairie with its shadow and its skirt of rain; if no more storms came, if we could get our hay up and the stacks fenced without further hindrance, I would take a couple of horses and go, westwards beyond those furthest mountains to some valley where men never came—to the White River, it might be, for which Pocaterra and I had set off so gaily years ago and which I had never seen. And I would go alone.

With that settled in my mind I slung my stuff into the packsack and lowered myself over the rim into the shadow of the mountain.

Rex and Mollie

Summer mellowed gently into autumn and no more rain fell on the Buffalo Head. The end of September came. Things had gone, if not merry as a marriage bell, at least not so crossways as before: all the work was done well up to date. And so, with an easy mind and with no small pleasure, I kissed the ranch goodbye and rode off up the Highwood.

There was nobody at the ranger station, and that suited my mood exactly. I met not a soul on the trail, and that was better yet. The old landmarks slipped by: the Pyramid, Misty Mountain, the lick on Storm Creek. Bighorn sheep were there as usual; they scattered as I came in sight. There were more sheep above the Highwood Pass, and more again high above my camp of the second night on Pocaterra Creek. In all that distance there was not much grass for Rex and Mollie; the old days had gone and where once the bunch-grass had swayed in the wind there now was bare ground.

Riding on in the early morning towards the Kananaskis Lakes I got a fine view of the weird mountain that the Stoneys call Waka Nambé. Waka is the Great Spirit; Nambé means Thumb. Freely translated, you might call it The Hand of God for it reaches from behind up and over the glaciers of the Divide, above the Aster Lakes, like a mailed fist. The peak is wholly in British Columbia, yet it is higher than the Divide, from which only a low saddle separates it. No snow can rest on the overhanging precipices of Waka Nambé and the mountain hung there that morning, black against the blue of the sky, reaching out over the icefields at a fantastic angle. On the map it is Mount Warrior and the beautiful Indian name will soon be forgotten.

The Kananaskis ranger was at the Lakes cabin. We talked for a while and I left my rifle in his keeping. The Kananaskis country was a game reserve and I was headed for British Columbia: in neither place could I lawfully shoot anything. We both agreed that it was unwise to venture into the heart of the Rockies at this season without some weapon for camp protection: the rutting season of the moose was on, the elk were just coming to it and both were on the fight. And over all this high country roamed the unpredictable grizzly bear and his comic poor relation, the black bear, who thinks nothing of tearing a deserted camp to shreds once he has smelt the bacon. I had never met anybody on the Palliser River on previous trips, but it was five years now since I had been that way—things might have changed. If I ran into a B.C. game warden, would he be reasonable about a rifle? Or would he be official and want to confiscate the whole outfit? Better play it safe and take a chance on the wild animals—so we put the rifle in the cabin and the ranger showed me where he hid the key. And I went on, fording the Kananaskis River, past the upper lake into untravelled country. In a couple of weeks and well over two hundred miles of trail that ranger was the only man I saw.

I camped early that day in a tree-ringed meadow where the bunch-grass came up to the horses' bellies. Rex and Mollie had earned a rest and a real feed. I put them both on picket for the last time and they put in a glorious afternoon, ranging up and down, cropping at the seed heads, growing visibly fatter, their bells jangling against the roar of a distant waterfall. By suppertime they were both completely stuffed and the bells were silent except for an occasional "Tunk." With darkness the noise of the waterfall became closer and louder. I sat by the fire listening to it for a while. Then I put things ready for breakfast, looked to the horses and went to bed. I had no tent with me but I slept warm and dry and soft under the spreading branches of a thick old spruce; no dew could reach me there.

The frost still sparkled on the grass when I rode away from that camp. I was riding Rex; Mollie followed, running loose. From now on, through the days, she wore a sheep bell. With that, one didn't have to listen all day to the row that the larger bells made; yet the bright metallic tinkle of this small bell was enough to warn any cantankerous grizzly or fighting moose of our coming. The one thing I didn't want to do, being now minus a rifle, was to ride round some rocky point or clump of firs, catch one of these beasts unawares and scare him into attacking.

We came to the forks of the Upper Kananaskis—the place where the mountains close in on the traveller, where the strata stand straight on end and the glaciers seem to overhang. I find myself saying "we": it is because, from the bunch-grass meadow onwards, the horses and I became a unit. We were far from home and from any habitation. They depended on me and I on them, and they also on each other. Camp became home to them and they liked to see me around and about it. I carried along a small block of salt for them; where I dropped that, there they knew they would camp and rest. I could catch them easily in the open—a thing I couldn't do at the ranch except with a pan of oats. Always close friends, in the mountains they were inseparable. When one drank the other had to drink, too; if I led one into camp to saddle up, the other followed closely. If one was picketed and the other grazed away out of sight for a moment, even behind a single tree, a frantic whinnying would go up from the abandoned one (it was usually Rex), and would continue until his mate came back to him.

From the forks the trail followed the gravel bars of the Upper Kananaskis for a little way. Then we climbed—1,400 feet, up an avalanche track of grass and tall asters and dwarfed firs, to an alpine plateau of small blue lakes and ancient larches. Northward lay the glaciers and the snow mountains that I had seen from Mount Head. To the west, and less than a mile away, a vertical wall of rock held up the glaciers of the Divide. All around, in the brilliant sunlight of the timberline country, flamed the larches in their autumn glory. They flared out in their tracery of living gold against the lakes, the dark thickets of fir, and the meadows with their shining seed heads of dead flowers. There may be in the world more beautiful sights than the larch country under the low October sun—I have not seen them. Nor, for me, is there anything that can give the same lift to the heart as that wild colouring of the high mountains in the fall. Over this plateau I rode for four miles and then I made camp—not because it was time to camp but just for the sheer beauty of the place.

Always in the mountains there is some sound. Here it was a muffled roar that came from somewhere close by. It was the stream that slid so easily past camp over the limestone slabs: in a few hundred yards it plunged into a chasm so deep that one could not see to the bottom of it, bridged in places by the living rock, narrow enough to step over. Down there in the darkness the water bellowed and thundered, burrowing its way down to the Upper Kananaskis River a thousand feet below.

The colours of dawn flushed in the eastern sky. Small clouds like rose petals floated high above the unseen sunrise. I lit the fire, changed Rex's picket, stirred the porridge and cut the bacon, noting with pleasure that the eggs were travelling without casualties. The sun cleared the Spray Mountains. It fell on camp and warmed the horses' backs. I saddled up and rode away westward towards the North Kananaskis Pass.

We climbed, and the trees thinned out and vanished. Topping a rocky rise we came to a lake at the foot of a high mountain. Here the moss campion grows in summertime with its great cushions of purple flowers, but now there was only drab, frozen herbage in a wilderness of broken stone. Beyond the lake was a rounded, stony rise: that was the Divide and beyond that ridge the water flowed to the Kootenay. Rocks clattered suddenly as I rode forward, and a band of sheep raced away up the mountain to the northward. The sound roused Mollie who

Marigold holding the horses on Summit Ridge
of North Kananaskis Pass

had stayed behind on a patch of sweet grass. She came galloping after us, grunting and whinnying to Rex and with her sheep bell tinkling furiously. Together we topped the rise. New mountains hove in sight and far down below lay the valley of the Palliser. We had turned one more page of Paul's book of the mountains.

There was no horse sign anywhere. No one had come to the plateau or crossed this pass for a couple of years or more. I halted on the summit to cinch up and adjust Mollie's pack; then, walking and leading Rex, I started on the descent. The valley lay two thousand feet below; the trail zigzagged down the mountainside. Rex walked easily behind me but Mollie stayed behind to sample every patch of grass she saw. Then she would catch up by squatting and sliding straight down the mountain, short-cutting across the zigzags in a cascade of loose stones. There was nothing I could do to stop her except to tail her behind Rex, and this was no safe place for tailing. This performance of Mollie's was dangerous and one had to keep an eye open because, every now and then, she would dislodge a large boulder. One of these came bounding down the mountain straight at Rex and me. He pulled back, I jumped forward and the thing hummed past between us, crashing down another thousand feet before it came to rest. The sane thing to do on that descent was to keep one eye on Mollie and the other on your own feet and let the scenery take care of itself.

Somehow we got down the steepest part—and then came a new hazard. The old Stoney trail ran down the floor of the valley, well worn and obvious. But a forest fire had swept the Palliser in the nineties and this trail was no longer passable: it led one into a terrible tangle of huge fallen trees. No one knew that better than I did: I had got right into it with Marigold and our horse wrangler and eight horses the first time I ever came this way. In thunder, lightning and torrential rain I had somehow cut a way through for the party behind me; and the axe so wet that it was forever trying to fly out of my hands. Never again—and now I turned aside up a game trail that ran across the face of a scree.

Not so Mollie. She headed down what looked like the easiest trail—straight into the down timber. Rex whinnied; I whistled and shouted—and the obstinate little horse went on. Green spruce and fir were thrusting up out of the crisscross of old fallen trees: you could see them swaying as Mollie shoved her way through them. Out of the jungle there floated up savage grunts of wrath, the thud and slam of hoofs on sound down timber, the mad tinkling of the bell. I was worried lest Mollie should break a leg or rip herself open on some iron-hard snag, trying to jump a fallen tree. But those things were mere trifles. Listen.... A few trees of the old forest were still standing, even after fifty years, sound and gaunt and grey. The humus had been burnt away from around their roots, and now the roots themselves were rotten: the old trees just balanced there waiting for the next high wind. Mollie must have shoved against one of these booby traps with her pack—and I saw the grey old giant teeter slowly out of the vertical. I watched it, appalled; knowing the frightful leverage there would be on the butt end when the tree fell, I expected to see a little black horse catapulted into the air, disemboweled. Plans for carrying on if Mollie should be killed raced through my head as the great tree swept through its arc with gathering speed ...

The old spar hit the ground with a shuddering slam, smashing young green trees and sending lengths of broken dead ones spinning into the air. They fell back to earth—and there was a moment's deathly silence. Crushed, I thought. Poor little devil ... Then suddenly: Grunt, grunt, grunt! Tinkle! Thud, slam! Green trees bent and swayed once more—the invisible horse was at it again. Slowly she fought her way out of the deadfall and clawed up the scree to the narrow track above where Rex was screaming encouragement. She fell into place behind me with a grunt of annoyance, shook herself vigorously—and we went on.

We came to the forks, to the main Palliser River, and the Palliser Pass trail came in from the northwest. No man or horse had travelled it for at least a couple of years; we had the great empty valley to ourselves; with the high mountains to right and left it felt like the vast emptiness of a silent cathedral.

I made tea and rested the horses at a creek crossing. I saw a moose on the far side of the Palliser and some elk high up on the mountain slopes, but it was not until the water had boiled that I noticed a grizzly about five hundred yards up the creek, grubbing away at something. I made my arrangements for a hurried departure, just in case—but the bear never bothered and the horses didn't seem to worry, so I had my tea in peace. A thousand feet and more above the trail at this point there is a lake, a turquoise lake set in a forested basin. Marigold climbed up there alone one blazing July day of 1937. The lake looked most inviting and it was not long before she was swimming in it. Almost immediately a family of black bears arrived on the shore and took charge of her clothes for her.

This might have been rather awkward if these had not been remarkably well-mannered bears. The swimmer emerged lower down the shore and says that she looked at the bears appealingly. They, realizing that they were not wanted, ambled shyly off into the bush— which, I think, was very decent of them, even if they did, occasionally, look back over their shoulders. On that same day I was climbing up on the far side of the Palliser to the South Kananaskis Pass and Three Isle Lake. Several times I looked across the deep valley with the glass to the blue jewel of Tipperary Lake in its emerald setting. But not, apparently, at the right moment for I had no faintest inkling of this Arcadian scene until I met my wife again in camp at suppertime.

I gathered up Rex and Mollie and went on, leaving the grizzly to his grubbing. It was getting late and the evening shadow was reaching out towards the Palliser from the high peaks to the westward. Far down the valley a little group of cottonwoods in full golden leaf glowed like a beacon light against the dark wall of the mountain. Slowly we came to it, and, as we passed by, the last rays of the sun lifted off it and the beacon was extinguished. Dusk filled the valley. Soon the small noises of the night came out from their hiding places in the shadows. Camp was made and supper was cooked by the light of the fire at the mouth of Joffre Creek.

The Pass in the Clouds (2)

After breakfast I had a look at the canyon of Joffre Creek where that stream breaks through the mountain wall into the valley of the Palliser. The old trail had fallen into disuse and nobody had passed that way for a long time. Cleverly sited by the Indians, the trail wound between huge blocks of limestone and fallen trees; it was narrow and overgrown and I cut it out in the worst places, just wide enough for Mollie to scrape through with her pack. Then I went back to camp, packed up and got the horses.

I moved camp a couple of miles—to a meadow that lay above

the canyon barrier. I cut trees and blocked the narrow passage in the canyon trail so that the horses would be secure; then I rode around the meadow looking for the perfect camp. I found it in a park-like glade of beautifully spaced trees and tall asters still in bloom. There I unpacked and made my camp under the thick canopy of an old spruce. As things turned out, that was to be my home for several days.

The meadow was about a thousand feet above the Palliser. It lay open to the south; on the other three sides the mountains walled it in. To the east towered the full sweep of Waka Nambé, less than two miles away. A strange mountain, whichever way you looked at it; from this side also there was an overhang in the last two thousand feet; no wonder the Stoneys called it the Hand of God.

The soft blue shadow moved slowly across its tremendous cliffs while I baked bannock and explored the flats of Joffre Creek. A little distance away I came on some curious boiling springs—circular holes, two and three feet across, in which a black mud with particles of mica flashing in it heaved and swirled. To these springs game trails, deeply worn, came in from every direction. Vaguely I remembered Pocaterra telling me of these wonderful licks. Joffre Creek, he had said, was like a zoo. Goat especially ... Well, they were still here: I had seen some earlier, five head up on the slopes of Waka Nambé. No doubt there were many more unseen. And elk were calling up the valley. And I had gone and camped practically on top of the licks. Impressed by all the signs of game, I went back and caught Rex and put his bell on him. A little more noise might not be a bad thing.

This valley of Joffre Creek was the valley the Wilcox expedition had turned up, forty odd years ago, to reach the White River and Nyahé-ya-'nibi. Few had passed this way since then and the trail was obscure, even through the green timber. At intervals it had been swept by avalanches from Waka Nambé. In these places the trail was obliterated: only a waste of stones remained to show the track of the avalanche, and on each side of this there would be a tangled breastwork of smashed trees. To get the horses through this stuff to the White River, I could plainly see, was going to take more time than I could spare. So I set out next morning on foot, determined at least to see this river which had kept itself hidden from me for so long.

The trail was worse than I had expected and, what with finding it and blazing it, it was well on in the afternoon before I came to rest on a grassy knoll well above timberline. The pass lay below me, rutted with game trails. Behind me lay first the grass and then the larch country of Joffre Creek, with the high mountains beyond the Palliser in the background. Ahead lay the White River valley—grass, golden larches, green forest—falling lower, bending gently to the south, passing from view behind the spur of a mountain. On the east side of the valley the mountains rose in an unbroken wall, rising further back to sharp peaks and pinnacles. I sat there in the sun taking it all in, running the glass over this new country.

That wall on the east was not unbroken. Five or six miles south there was a gap in it—hard to see in this afternoon glare but definitely a gap. It had to be the gap that led to the Pass in the Clouds, there was no other break in the wall. I studied it for some time: it had all the lure of distance, it was difficult to get at and it led to something I had never seen ... That was quite enough: I put the glass away, ran down to the pass and hit the trail for home. My mind was made up: horses or no horses I was going to cross the Pass in the Clouds and get a sight

Marigold in camp

of Nyahé-ya-'nibi. Pondering ways and means, I went down through the larch meadows at a run; evening was coming on and it was a long way to camp.

What with the bugling of the elk that seemed to break out all around me at this sunset hour, and the small chatter of Joffre Creek and my thoughts being elsewhere, it was only pure luck that I didn't run right on top of two bulls that were fighting it out in a meadow on the trail. The grass was all torn up and the two elk were locked together, shoving and ramming at each other. One was bleeding freely from the shoulder. Not wishing to join in the fray, I looked hastily around for a good tree, found one and climbed it. Occasionally the two beasts would disengage, only to crash together again, doing more or less damage. Finally the one with the shoulder wound was driven out of the arena and out of the fight, the conqueror walking slowly after him, proclaiming his victory with the most blood-curdling screams. I came quietly down from my perch and ran on down Joffre Creek in the evening light ...

Bright and early I reinforced the barricade in the canyon gap. Then I turned the horses loose and cached my little outfit away in the branches of the big spruce, hanging the packsaddle, a gaudy Navajo blanket and a spare horse bell in strategic places where they might just possibly disconcert any inquisitive bear. And then I hit the trail with a three-day load in my pack, regretfully discarding the Rolleiflex at the last moment on account of its weight. The weather, as usual, was perfect.

In some firs by a spring at the very head of the White River I cached a small sack of grub to make a meal on the return trip. Then I went down through the meadows and the larches into green timber—down and down till the stream had become a river and the trail levelled off on the valley floor. I passed through scenes of amazing beauty, virgin forest alternating with meadows that were almost small prairies, the grass rippling in the wind and coming right down to the banks of the river. And towards evening I came to an old Indian camping place and the forking of the trail to the pass. There I made tea and ate some hardtack, cheese and raisins, and there blessed contentment urged me to spend the night.

On the other hand tomorrow was going to be quite a day. I would need all the daylight hours if I went on into Nyahé-ya-'nibi. Probably I had better try to make Wilcox' alpine lake[13] for tonight's camp. From what he said it was only about 1,500 feet above the main valley and it couldn't be more than three miles away. Regretfully I packed up and turned towards the gap in the mountains.

There was a savage magnificence to that night's camp by the shore of the lake. At suppertime a half-moon was shedding its light high up on the rocky walls of the basin; the lake itself lay in the shadow of Mount Abruzzi. Only to the southwest did the basin lie open and there, if you climbed a little way above camp, were to be seen the mountains beyond the White River, their peaks serene and silent under the moonlight and the glittering frost. Down below, the friendly flicker of the fire, burning safely on its patch of gravel, was reflected in the black, gleaming water. Even with that the place seemed lonely—perhaps because one was missing, for the first time on this trip, the snorts and cropping of the horses and the companionable sound of the bells.

In the night some heavy animal came almost into camp. It must have got wind of things quite suddenly and jumped as it did so, for I found myself suddenly awake to the sound of a breaking branch and the thud and scramble of something padding away down the valley. The moon was in the southwest now and the lake basin was bright as day. I lay awake, listening for a minute or two, but nothing else was stirring. That would probably be the end of the zoo for the day, I thought. There had been the usual elk-goat collection—and one small black bear, met head-on at a bend in the trail. And now this, whatever it was. But no moose. Why no moose? I wondered sleepily ... and the next thing I knew, the moon was gone and I was cold and the grey light of dawn was outlining the dark cliffs of Mount Abruzzi.

I climbed fast in the frost and in the shadow of the mountain. A good breakfast turned swiftly into heat and energy, and the sky was a cloudless blue—all was well. No man or horse had used this trail for many years but the goats had kept some vestige of a track visible across the stony, sliding scree. The trail had obviously deteriorated since Wilcox crossed it, forty years earlier—in many places it was no longer safe for horses and only with care and accuracy could it be travelled by a man. One slip in a bad place and that would be the end of the story; and who, finding my outfit in the meadow under Waka Nambé, would ever guess where I had gone?

Nearly 2,000 feet above camp I ran out of the shadow and into sunshine. And then the summit of the pass at 8,500 feet—a short level space of broken stone. Then came the dip over into Nyahé-ya-'nibi and the valley of Abruzzi Creek—after all those years!

Anxiously I looked down. Below me, in the head of Abruzzi Creek, was green forest. And the summit of The Warship was green. And that was all, except for scattered patches of trees at timberline. Everywhere else rose the grey skeletons of the burnt forest. I had never been able to get a sight of this valley in the intervening years since the fire—but somehow I had always thought of it as a green valley, protected. It was a place where, like Pocaterra, I had been happy when I was young, and now my vision of it had been destroyed. And when that happens you lose something of yourself. "Never again," you say, "will I give my heart to a valley in the mountains. Never again will I be that young."

I went on down the trail. A shoulder of Mount Abruzzi hid from me the nameless lake that was to have been Lake Marigold, and now I was going to get a sight of it if it took me till nightfall. I came to the rock outcrop where Pocaterra and I had turned back that stormy October day. There were twists of goat wool caught on the rock point, just as there had been then; I climbed carefully down and round the outcrop and shook hands with my own youth on the far side of it; then I went on.

I came to the old larch where we had tied the horses. It had not changed: storms had not harmed it and fire could not come near. Against it I sat for a few minutes, picking a route out with the glass. Away to the left and high up, a grizzly was digging for marmots. He was completely absorbed—and the way the rocks and the clods were flying was a sight to see. But his way was not my way, and I swung the glass over to the long spur and the cliffs from which I thought I might see the lake. There, on ledges facing the sun, a band of goats was resting—the descendants of those we had seen in that same place; even, perhaps, some of those that we had seen being taught to climb. Soon I would be disturbing them ...

Three scrambling miles went by and I reached the point of the spur. There I made tea by a small spring. Time went by. The afternoon wore on and still I sat there, above the cliffs where the goats had been, looking down on this country I would not be seeing again. I could see the meadow of Nyahé-ya-'nibi and the valley of the Elk. I could see the Elk Mountains and the Pyramid. In front of me was The Warship with its crown of green timber. And, if I swung a little to the right, there was the nameless lake, blue and wave-rippled, bordered with golden willows, giving life to its fire-blasted valley of dead sticks. A clean sweep, that must have been—just blackened trees and ashes except for two clumps of green timber up against the foot of the moraine. That old fallen giant of the forest that had been a young tree when Columbus sailed for the Americas: "In all the years since then," we had said, "no forest fire has come this way." Well—now a fire had come and the tree had gone and the green valley was no more. And something precious had gone with it—though, God knows, if you asked me to tell you just what that something was I would be hard put to find the words for it.

I turned my back on the dead valley and started on the long climb back to the Pass in the Clouds. I topped the rise at the close of day, coming suddenly out of the shadow into a golden glory of shining mountains and saffron-coloured sky. Without pausing to look back I walked straight on, westwards, into the sunset—dazzled a little but looking down into unscarred valleys that were softly cloaked with living green.

A couple of weeks later, coming in late from some job or other, I found Paul sitting in the kitchen at the Buffalo Head. He had brought us a present of sheep meat; his inner man had just been seen to and now he was waiting for me.

Riding down the Highwood on my way home from the White River I had seen a large encampment of Stoneys on the flats near Cat Creek. These were the first human beings I had set eyes on in fourteen days, for the Kananaskis ranger station had been deserted when I called there to pick up my rifle. From there I had come a different way home—by way of the Elbow River and Sheep Creek, crossing a high pass into Misty Basin to camp and hunt sheep there for a couple of days.

Leaving the Basin with its virgin bunch-grass and coming, in one day's ride, to the overgrazed range land of the upper Highwood had spoilt the pleasure of my return. If this was civilization, then give me the untouched wilderness of the mountains where a man's horses could graze and wax fat. And I had passed quickly by their camp without visiting the Indians.

Paul had seen me and it had puzzled him. No one had seen me leave home. Where had I been? he was wondering—but he was too polite to ask directly.

I told him. I described Joffre Creek to him very carefully, knowing that the name would mean nothing to him. "What do you call that creek in Stoney, Paul?"

"That's Oki-nyahé-changó," he said. "Two-Mountain Trail." He asked me if I had seen the licks, and he told me of a raid on Joffre Creek made by moccasined Stoneys passing over the glaciers of the Aster Lakes and down the cliffs of Waka Nambé—a traverse that well-equipped mountaineers would speak of with pardonable pride.

I told Paul of the White River and Nyahé-ya-'nibi and his eyes opened wide. "You go that country all alone?" he asked.

"Yes, Paul."

He began to laugh. "I think never stay one place too long," he said. "All the time travel—just like old bull moose, alone in mountains!" And a gust of laughter shook him as he sat there by the sunny window. Quite certainly he understood.

Travellers in the Snow

Things were changing on the Highwood in those last years. A road, wiping out the old wagon trail, came wriggling up the valley like a dusty, ill-omened snake. One could see that it was only the forerunner of other roads to come—for men were already talking (and not before it was time) of measures necessary to conserve the forests of the eastern slope of the Rockies, the source of the prairie rivers.

The price of beef had risen, with the war, to heights undreamed of ten years previously—but with it had risen the price of everything we had to buy, together with wages and taxes. In general, it seemed that the ranches, hitherto remote from development, were going to be taxed to provide improvements the benefits of which would not be felt in the hills, and which ranchers, anyway, did not need.

Also at the back of many minds was the fear of a post-war slump similar to the one that had followed the 1914–1918 war. A very few may have had a vision of the boom that was actually to come; they were not amongst the many with whom I discussed this point.

Family problems entered into the picture, also, and the necessity for building a new and larger ranch house at a time when materials were simply not obtainable. One way and another we began to think once more of selling while the going was good and moving to British Columbia. An offer for the place was made and considered. It would be accepted or refused purely on grounds of expediency. Instinct and sentiment alike were against leaving this place where we had spent so many happy years.

Then, one hot afternoon when I was stacking hay in the home meadow, a car appeared. A townee sort of a man got out and walked over to the stack, from the top of which I spoke with him as opportunity offered, in between incoming loads of hay. I had no time to get down and quack with him: I stayed up there and got on with the job, and finally, after the man had rambled on about the weather and the hay and everything else he could think of, I asked him point blank what he wanted.

We-ell, it was to do with the springs on the place. As we both knew, land that had springs on it was more valuable than land that hadn't, and this visit was just a little routine check-up on the part of the Something-or-Other Department with a view to arriving at a more accurate estimate of values—nothing more than that. He wondered if I could just let somebody else do the stacking for a bit while I ran around the place with him and showed him all the springs, marking their positions for him on the township plan. We could use his car.

So somebody in a government armchair had had the bright idea of taxing the springs—that was it. No matter how they wrapped it up, as a land tax or as an increased lease rental, it would be a tax on the springs. And only forty years ago this hay meadow had been part of the Northwest Territories and neither the Province of Alberta nor the Buffalo Head Ranch had been in existence. It had taken only that short space of time for the vision to be lost and men's minds to become niggling and small. And I thought of all the springs on the Buffalo Head—bubbling out of the hillsides, welling up in deep valleys, strong springs, weak springs, springs that froze in wintertime and springs that flowed clear and free of ice even at fifty below zero. Be damned if I was going to pilot the way to them. Why, it would take three full days, at least, to show this man the lot. Probably more. Let him find them for himself—if he could. And I said just about that.

"You're not very co-operative, Mr. Patterson."

"Situated as I am, I don't have to be. And now, if you'll excuse me, I'll get ahead with this hay. Good day to you."

Within twenty-four hours we accepted the offer on the ranch, retaining right of residence for ourselves and grazing for our horses until the end of the following year, or longer by arrangement.

On the eighth day of October, fourteen months later, Marigold and I saddled and packed our horses at the Buffalo Head for the last time. We had given away some of the horses and sold others with the ranch. Rather than let them fall into strange hands I had shot half a dozen of the old-timers—an afternoon that I should like to forget. And we had kept five head: Rex and Mollie, the inseparables; Bozo because he was a good packhorse and such a comical old devil; a grey mare, Bluebird, a good mountain horse; and a young bay packhorse, Turk. Keeping Turk proved to be an error. Keeping Rex and Mollie and Bozo was inevitable—they had been a part of our lives for so long.

The plan was that the two of us would take these five horses and traverse the full width of the Rocky Mountains, coming out on the other side at Spillimachene on the Columbia River. We would follow the old trail by the North Kananaskis Pass and the Palliser River—but this time there would be no returning: we would push on westwards, farther than we had ever been, to the Kootenay River and beyond, over the Brisco Range to the Columbia. The only trouble was that we were a month late: we had originally planned to start in September. One thing after another had got in the way and now several snowfalls had come and gone. We rather wondered how much snow we would find on the high passes—but we were determined to go and the solemn head-shaking of our friends had no effect. To be quite truthful, it acted as a spur ...

I considered a snow shovel for a full minute. Then I put it back in the storehouse and shut the door, giving the key to the man in charge of the place. I took the final pull on Bozo's diamond and that finished it—there was nothing more for us to do here and we rode away, past the house that was no longer ours, past the corrals and out of the home meadow by the Flat Creek gate. A mile and a half went by and then the horses thundered over Flat Creek bridge: the Buffalo Head, with its memories of sixteen years, lay behind us and we rode on in silence towards the Highwood Gap.

The silence, on my part, was one of deepest gloom. As the familiar miles passed by I wondered more and more why I had been mad enough to exchange these friendly hills and meadows for a few acres of mountainside in the East Kootenay and an orchard by the sea. I looked on the bright hillsides around me and then I thought of the scrofulous, so-called grass down on Vancouver Island, burnt to a cinder by the summer drought, made sodden as blotting-paper by the winter rains—and I cursed myself for a fool.

The worst part of leaving a well-loved home—leaving it, too, at the pace of the horse—is the memories that rise up to reproach you on every side. Here was the place where darkness caught us with the cattle that November of the deep snow—and a hell of a mess that was, with everybody cold and fed up and the cattle all set to bed down for the night. And there, across the river, was the trail old Art Baldwin and I travelled on the evening of that bachelor Christmas Day when Adolf told us about the Cossacks and the pigs. The moon on that night was full—and so was Art, who was swaying a little in his saddle as he tried to convince me that he was well able to ride on alone to the T L Ranch. "I'll be all right," he assured me solemnly. "Don't worry—I'll be all right. I left everything all fixed. I filled the manger with hay before I left the old shebang this morning, and I laid a fire in the stove. Now all I got to do when I get home is, touch a match to the manger and then take the saddle off the old crowbait here and let him stick his head in the stove. I'll be all right, don't you worry ... "

Well, there'd be no more of that sort of thing—no more moonlight rides down the Highwood with the Chinook drifting the snow off the ridges of Mount Head in a glittering cascade of frozen spray; no old cowpunchers, seasonably addled, talking solemn nonsense by your side, to the friendly creaking of saddle leather and the soft rustling of the horses' feet in the powdery snow ...

In fact, as I saw it just then, there'd never be anything ever any more that was worth a tinker's curse. Had I known, on that morning of gloom, that my trail would lead me back to the South Nahanni River and the wild uplands of the white sheep, then I might have felt better about leaving the Buffalo Head. But I did not know, and the gloom deepened. Only travel and far distance would dispel it.

We made our first camp about five miles above the ranger station. The upper valley was badly skinned off and there was very little grass for the horses. However, knowing what we would be up against, I had packed along two fair-sized sacks of oats. I gave the horses a good feed, promising them grass on the Highwood Pass for the next camp—grass and no cattle. That night an iron frost beat down upon the tent.

We ran into the first lying snow at the forks of Storm and Misty Creeks. We plugged on up Storm Creek without stopping, making poor time over frozen ground, old snowdrifts, patches of ice and fallen timber. A glittering sun that gave no heat hung in a pale blue sky that promised nothing better. The Misty Range on our right and the Elk Mountains on our left were snow-covered and hostile. I thought fondly of other Octobers in these hills—blue and gold and with the west wind blowing softly. When I was alone that was my weather, perfect, day after day. But just try taking somebody else along and look what happened.

The snow was getting deeper; we would not make it over the Highwood Pass tonight. We made an early camp on a little patch of grass that was blown bare by the wind. Things had changed, indeed, in the sixteen years since Pocaterra and Adolf and I rode up this valley towards Nyahé-ya-'nibi through bunch-grass tall and golden—cattle had been here, too, in the summertime and the little flat was grazed-off and poor. I fed the horses oats again and that night it fell below zero.

The alarm clock split through the frozen darkness and I lit the candles and rolled across the tent floor in my eiderdown to light the stove before getting up. That was the way to handle the situation in comfort. Then the teapail—which was frozen—and then the horses. Then porridge and bacon and eggs. And then a glittering winter sunrise and the trail again.

The Highwood Pass rather shook our gay confidence. All morning we plugged slowly up towards it in deepening snow. We made tea and lunched at the very head of Storm Creek, holding a council of war on a sunny bank in the lee of a clump of firs. "If it's like this here," we said, "what's it going to be like on the larch plateau and the North Kananaskis Pass? Quite a bit higher, too, and in a deeper snow country. And then the Palliser—d'you think we're absolutely crazy?" A unanimous "Yes!" was the answer to that question.

We crossed the pass and slid down into the deep valley of Pocaterra Creek, camping that night at Pocaterra's camp close under the sheep range between Mount George and Mount Paul. Planted in the middle of the little meadow there was a dead jackpine pole with a hawk's feather suspended from it, twisting and fluttering in the rising wind. That meant that Paul had been here—and, judging by the grass, with many horses. Still, there was some grass left, and one good feed of oats. And it was warmer: the northwest wind was roaring up the valley, driving wild-looking rags of cloud over the face of the moon. At suppertime a heavy tree came crashing down close to camp; the ground shuddered with the violence of its fall.

Waka Nambé and the mountains of the Divide were hidden by a swirling smother of snow and cloud as we rode towards the Lakes next morning. From the meadow by the Kananaskis ranger station we could see deep into the V of the mountains towards Three Isle Lake and it looked as if all hell had broken loose up there. "It's senseless to take the horses up into that," I said. "Let's camp here overnight and see whether it storms or clears. One more good snowfall will probably block that north pass for the winter, and if that happens we'll have to make other plans."

Marigold looked at the ranger cabin. "A pity this place is deserted," she remarked. "It would have been nice to have a roof over us on a day like this."

"You watch," I said—and I produced the key from its hiding place in the wall much as a conjurer might produce a rabbit from a hat. Very soon the horses were grazing in a swampy meadow and the two humans were sitting down to afternoon tea at a real table complete with chairs. Outside a fine snow whirled and eddied on a roaring wind. Inside all was warm and snug.

Dawn broke clear and still and cold. We saddled up and forded the Kananaskis River. Beyond the upper lake, at the bunch-grass meadow,

Marigold at Kananaskis Forks

we made tea and let the horses eat their fill; then we went on. We passed the Forks of the Upper Kananaskis, the place deep in the heart of the Rockies where the strata stand on end, and we came to the climb up the avalanche slide that led to the larch plateau. We climbed without incident in ever deepening snow for a thousand feet—until Bozo fell.

Instead of following the horse ahead of him the old crowbait thought he saw a better way. He took off along a steep grassy slope that was below the trail and separated from it by a sloping wall of smooth rock. Realizing his mistake he tried to climb this wall, slipped and went tumbling down the mountainside, rolling over and over in the snow. About a hundred feet below the wall the slope ended, dropping off in a sheer cliff for three or four hundred feet down into the valley of the Upper Kananaskis. On the edge of the cliff grew one small clump of alpine firs—the only one. Bozo crashed into it and it held him. The vast horse lay there on his back motionless, within six feet of the drop, his four legs pointing straight to heaven.

"By God's truth, that was a near one!"

"Do you think he's killed?"

"I don't know—I'm going down to see. Help me to tie these horses to something."

We got them all hitched to stunted bits of trees. I took my chaps and parka off and slid down through the snow to Bozo. He was alive and, as far as I could see, undamaged. His pack was still neatly in place—underneath him, of course—and that was my main trouble: the fall had knocked the spirit out of him and he was not going to try to get up till I had got his load off him. He probably couldn't move much, anyway.

Unpacking a horse that is upside down is a devil of a job anywhere—and worse than ever with no good footing and on the edge of a precipice. Somehow I got Bozo free and then I got hold of his halter shank and reached up with my free hand to Marigold who was hanging on to a bush of some sort and reaching down towards me with her right hand. We both pulled and the horse came up just as I had expected—with a heave and a plunge, nearly braining me and sending a pannier right to the edge of the drop. Then he stood stock still, shaking all over like an aspen leaf. I led him up to the trail and tied him there. I carried his load, piece by piece, back up the mountain slope, handing the stuff up the rock wall to Marigold. Somehow we repacked Bozo on that narrow trail and shoved and dragged him around the other horses, through the tangled dwarf fir, up to where Rex was tied. Then we got going again, myself leading Bozo from Rex. Marigold brought up the rear; she had found Bluebird quivering and shaking with fright. It seemed that the horses knew that we were getting into a country where, under these dangerous conditions, we had no business to be.

We rode through a dark wood of old firs and past the wash of a glacier on to the plateau of the larches and the small blue lakes. But this October the larch needles had already fallen, the horses plugged through snow up to their knees and the lakes were frozen and snow-covered. The yellow light of late afternoon shone upon a winter scene and the trail, where it showed at all, showed only as a wrinkle on the surface of the snow into which the wind had drifted the golden needles of the larches.

Bozo's performance had lost us precious time. There was now no earthly hope of making it over to the Palliser before dark so we made camp in the approaches to the pass, in the lee of a belt of firs. There was nothing there for the horses but the seed heads of a few tall flowers— that and water and shelter from the wind. It was the best we could do.

We flung the tent down on the wind-packed snow and spread our eiderdowns on top of it. I unlimbered the Swede saw and got to work on some dead larches. I built a winter fire of eight-foot logs; soon the flames were leaping high, writhing in the wind like crimson snakes. We cooked our supper on a few coals raked out from the blaze; then we sat there on the eiderdowns, warm and comfortable, idly talking, watching the shining mountains under the pale light of the moon ...

We slept—and a beastly dream held me in its grip. There was a low growling noise and I knew that a great grey bear was in camp, sniffing at this and that, coming closer and closer and I couldn't move ... I woke with a frightful start and looked around. There was no bear to be seen but the growling noise was real enough. It was coming, gently and steadily, from a humped-up eiderdown and a pile of saddle blankets on my left. Then I knew that at least one member of the party was sleeping serenely, unperturbed by thoughts of yesterday or of the day that lay ahead.

The fire had died down and the northwest wind was rising again— the snowy wind. It was driving its clouds across the sky, blotting out the stars and the moon. Actually, I thought, we're in one hell of a mess. Here we are, camped right on the hump of the continent, and if it puts down a heavy snow we'll have just as much difficulty getting back down the avalanche slide to Alberta as we will going on over the pass to British Columbia. That is, if we can get down at all, either way. For a man alone on snowshoes there would be nothing to it. With a woman and five horses to look after, not so good. I lay awake and thought for a bit and cursed myself for not bringing that snow shovel. But nothing was ever gained by worrying—soon I was fast asleep again, to be wakened only by the cold light of dawn over the Spray Mountains.

From that camp to the summit can't have been much over a mile, but it was one of the longest, slowest miles I have ever known. The day was grey and threatening and a thin, keen wind came snuffling through the pass, right in our faces. There was a light crust on the snow and, as the horses plunged through the drifts, fragments of this crust went hissing and tinkling away down the slope like frozen spray. My tapaderos were dragging on the snow—yet I couldn't get off and lead Rex because I had to stay in the saddle and lead Bozo who was now, after his fall, in a sort of shell-shocked condition. In the same way, Marigold couldn't get off because she had to lead Turk who was showing signs of quitting. To complete the picture, I knew that, underneath the snow, there were crevasses in the limestone. My brain was working overtime, trying to figure out where they came and how best to avoid them. We had to rest the horses every two or three hundred yards, anyway, and that gave us a chance to look around and plan the next move ...

We had passed beyond the last trees and they were now hidden from us by the lay of the country. Looking back, there was nothing to be seen but the tops of the mountains, the line of plunging horses and the winding snake of a trail that we had broken through the snow.

The outfit topped a rise and there, half a mile away, lay the rounded summit of the pass. But seemingly unattainable, for between us and it lay the partly frozen waters of a small lake and huge drifts of wind-packed snow—drifts that completely blocked the trail on the south side of the lake and made even more impassable the mountain slope on the north. About that time a fine, cold snow began to fall.

"It looks as though we've had it," I said. "And things won't stand still for us, either. We've got to move, either on or back—and quickly. You stay here and hold these horses; I'm going to try and see if we can get through in the lake—it looks pretty shrunken from its summer level. And if we *can* get through there's still one small gap between the drifts on the pass and the mountain ... "

Rex crashed through the shore ice and into the lake. There was a good gravel bottom but it was shelving and ice that had built out from the rock wall of the southern shore was forcing me into deeper water than I liked. From under my left saddle flap I unslung a 2 lb. Hudson's Bay axe and took off the cover. I rode slowly forward, slamming away at the ice with the back of the axe as I went, breaking off large cakes of it. I had to be very careful: Rex was being pretty good under trying conditions, but the axe was razor-sharp and the flying water was freezing on my mitts and chaps—it would have been easy for the axe to turn and, perhaps, cut the horse, especially as I had to use my left hand.

Somehow I got through, leaving a trail of floating ice behind me. Then I rode up the gentle slope and through the little gap between the drift and the mountain, dreading what I should see next—the Palliser Valley buried under heavy snow, I rather thought. I turned in the saddle and brandished the axe in salute to Marigold who waved back. She and her four horses looked very small and far away. Then the drifts came between us and she disappeared.

I rode easily across the summit ridge of bare, windswept gravel. A drift appeared on the western slope, made by the east wind. My spirits fell—only to rise again with a soaring rush when I saw below the drift, far, far below, bare ground, yellow grass and the golden leaves of willows. There, waiting for us, lay the snow-free valley of the Palliser. True, there was a shocking great drift in our immediate path, but that could be dealt with somehow when the moment came. And in the meantime—Hail Kootenay! Hallelujah!

The Kootenay

Once again Marigold was holding the horses—all five of them this time and up on the hump—while I prospected around for a safe way down through the western drift. I found a place that would do; then I went back and got Rex and together we floundered through the deep snow, breaking a waist-deep trail. Bozo, being the larger horse, would have made a better job of it but, in his half-witted state of that morning, there was no saying what he wouldn't have done—fallen on top of me, probably, as we wallowed down the steep slope of the drift. As it was, I had to check Rex by flicking my quirt at his nose.

I left Rex below the drift and climbed up again, going in this time over the elbows. A creaking of saddle leather and grampus-like snorts coming from below indicated that Rex was following me of his own accord—so that made two men and two horses over the trail, which was now ready for the next move. I took Bozo and stuffed him into the trench that Rex and I had made; then I hit him a crack with my quirt and followed, leading Rex. Marigold performed the same office for Turk and then followed, leading Bluebird. Mollie stayed behind, raced up and down, said all she thought about the unseemly performance, and then came through on her own, grunting as usual. We came out on the lower side of the drift with our saddles full of snow, but with no packs shifted and lucky that no horse had lost his footing and gone down. All that remained was the descent and that was easy—the snow only reached down for a thousand feet or so. After that there was bare ground.

At the foot of the mountain slope we let the horses graze for a while in a little meadow set amongst the rocks; they had had practically nothing for over twenty-four hours. We ate, too—hardtack-and-bacon sandwiches, raisins and cheese—sitting on a log with firm ground beneath us instead of snow, and with a gleam of wintry sunshine struggling feebly through copper-coloured cloud.

The horses needed rest and feed, so we decided to camp in the first good spot, no matter how early we came to it. And we hit the trail again, winding through a grassy, hummocky bit of country littered with great blocks of stone.

Over a sharp rise, just a hundred yards in front, came a grizzly. I checked Rex and every horse stopped dead in its tracks. The grizzly reared up on his hind legs to his full height and stared. We all stared—bear, humans, horses—and nobody uttered a sound. It was so still and silent that one could hear the distant roar of the wind up on the pass where a storm was now in full blast. The odd flake of snow came drifting down.

Somebody had to make a move so I made one. I eased myself off Rex on the off-side and started to slide my rifle out of its scabbard, wishing it was the old Mannlicher and not a light .256 Mauser. This slight movement was too much for the grizzly who dropped on all fours again and fled, and there was no sound to his going. I shoved the rifle back into place and swung up on to Rex. We loped up to the crest of the rise—but the bear was nowhere to be seen. And that was that.

"The welcome committee, do you suppose?"

"Might have been. The first British Columbian, anyway. Very considerate of him—but what I liked best was his tactful withdrawal."

"Same here—and I don't really care if we don't see him again."

We made camp early in a little meadow by a feeder of Le Roy Creek. We picketed Rex and Bozo and turned the other horses loose. All hands spent a comfortable, lazy afternoon and evening—in fact there was nothing wrong with that camp except that the only level place for the tent was right on the bank of the stream, at this point a roaring torrent. We couldn't even hear the horse bells—but we hoped for the best and stayed awake late, wrapped warmly in our eiderdowns, reading by candlelight, occasionally feeding more wood into the stove. I went the rounds about midnight and all was well. But dawn showed the three loose horses missing and there were no tracks visible in the light powdering of snow that had fallen: the missing horses had already been some hours on their way.

"Mollie has all the brains of that lot," I said as we ate breakfast. "I never thought she would leave Rex, but she may have got a homing fit on her. It's just possible she may have gone back over the pass—if our trail's still open. Turk and Bluebird would follow Mollie. I'll have to take Rex and ride after them. The trouble is, that pass. One more storm'll block the trail for good and it's storming up there now. I might have to follow the horses over the top and then be unable to get back to you."

"How nice that would be! And what do you want me to do?"

"There may be nothing to it; I may be back in an hour or two. But if I'm not back in two days, take Bozo and a light outfit, go down to the forks of the Palliser and turn north up the trail to the Palliser Pass. You remember that trail—we went over it nine years ago? Then follow the Spray River all the way down till it meets the Bow. You can't miss the trail—just stay with the river. And be sure and take an axe."

"How far will it be?"

"Fifty miles or so. But probably good trails most of the way." And (with the grizzly in mind, though I wouldn't have mentioned him for worlds) I showed Marigold how to use the Mauser, and also how to use the Swede saw without snapping the blade. "I'd saw and split some wood from this dead spruce, if I were you," I said. "And get it under cover in case it snows."

With that I saddled Rex and packed the things I needed. We wished each other luck in a casual sort of way, each one feeling that it would be tempting fate to make a song and dance about our parting, and then I hit the trail. From the last viewpoint, I looked back. A grey plume of wood smoke was coming from the stovepipe. Nearby, a large horse was watching a small figure that was sawing furiously.

As luck would have it I found the horses at the foot of the climb to the pass. I got around them and drove them down the valley; in less than two hours they jangled into camp and Marigold said the sound of their bells on that occasion was one of the best things she had ever heard. She had a wonderful woodpile all cut and split and camp was looking extremely neat and all fixed up for a long stay. How fortunate it was, we both felt but did not say, that we had not overplayed our leave-taking. What fools we should now have been feeling!

The weather had changed. Not a breath of wind was stirring and the sun blazed down out of a cloudless sky. We lunched and then loafed on down the valley to the forks. On the way Turk lost his footing through sheer stupidity and cussedness and fell into the creek gulch, lodging upside down, jammed between a big log and the stony cutbank, his feet pointing to the sky as Bozo's had done. I couldn't get at his pack—indeed, it was all I could do to climb down to him and keep my footing. So I got out the Swede saw, climbed up from below and sawed the log in two. With a wild leap I dodged the free half of the log as it snapped off, and then down we went—log, man and horse—into the creek bed in a cascade of sliding stones. Nobody was hurt: Turk landed on his feet and so did I—and I led the fool of a horse up on to the trail again.

At the forks we dealt ourselves a holiday. We breakfasted late with the sun lighting up the tent. Then we sorted the outfit, bathed and civilized ourselves a bit after our journey through the snow, did some fancy cooking and lazed in the sun, watching the horses eat and roll and sleep. My weather had returned to me, and the splendid mountains of the Royal Group and the Divide thrust up, covered with freshly fallen snow, into a sky of the deepest blue. Looking back up the narrow valley of Le Roy Creek we could just see, high up and far away, a level line of snow: that was the summit of the North Kananaskis Pass over which we had come. Obviously, we both agreed, it took more than just a little snow and ice to stop the Buffalo Head, once it had got its travelling boots on.

The Royal Group soars 6,500 feet above the Palliser River

After lunch I wandered off on foot up the Palliser, taking the Mauser. I stayed on the west side of the river, climbing higher and higher as I went north until I had a good view of the valley towards the Palliser Pass; then I sat down and took a look around. There was a moose browsing in the willows down below me in the valley bottom— and another moose a mile or so to the north, heading for the pass. But I was not interested in these animals; what I wanted was a good set of elk horns. I needed them for a certain purpose and they would also be a souvenir of this last ride from the Buffalo Head.

Near the spur of the mountain that separated the Palliser and Le Roy Creek two or three elk were feeding slowly northward. I looked them over with the glass but there was nothing worth taking in that lot ... One or two more elk came into sight, coming out of Le Roy Creek Valley—and then more and more. They streamed steadily round the point of the mountain, coming from God knows where—Three Isle Lake it might have been—and they kept on coming. I counted up to about seventy and then I gave it up. I just sat there entranced, watching them, cows, young bulls, old bulls with their glorious antlers, as they moved slowly and quietly across the tawny mountainside, feeding as they went, headed for the pass. The recent snowfalls must have brought them down from a hundred lonely alpine meadows and now they were on their way to some favoured winter range—in the valley of the Bow, perhaps.

A bull with an enormous spread of horn came into sight. I watched him for a bit—he had a head on him like a hat-rack. That would be the one, I thought, and I started to slide on my back down the open, grassy slope on which I had been sitting. There was no cover, but, from the little stream that was the Palliser, a long tongue of trees ran up a draw towards me; if I could get down into that I would be able to move unseen.

It was a slow process. I could pick my time and move without the big bull seeing me, but it was impossible to make even the smallest move without being spotted by half a dozen or more of this mob of migrating elk. They would stop and I would freeze, and the alarm would spread through the herd—and then, after minutes of waiting, I would be able to slide or roll downhill again.

Finally I got into the trees. They were scrub poplar, mostly; they still carried enough of their autumn leaves so that I could move without being seen, and yet there was not so much of a screen that I could not keep an eye on the bull. I swung down through the trees and the bull moved into a patch of willows on the hillside opposite me. I hurried on down; I would get him as soon as he came once more into the open ...

But I could see now that, if I went on down towards the stream, the bull would be in dead ground as far as I was concerned. So I climbed a big spruce, shoving my way through the prickly branches right to the top. I cut myself out a comfortable perch and from there I could see the vast horns moving about in the willows—and sometimes a glimpse of the head as he raised it for a moment. Then even the horns vanished, though no elk emerged from the willows: the bull had lain down to rest.

The sun moved round. The elk herd still streamed up the valley, past the willows and the resting bull. I sat there in my tree top, which was swaying gently in a warm breeze from down the valley, waiting. It was going to be awkward, shooting from here, as the Mauser was only sighted up to 250 yards and the bull was further away than that.

An hour went by ... Suddenly the willows swayed, the antlers appeared and then the head. I fired, aiming above the neck. I never knew where that bullet went but, at the crack of the rifle, every animal on that mountainside froze. It was a weird sight: there they stood, an army of elk that might have been carved from wood, listening ...

I aimed lower and fired again. A large spray of willow that arched a foot or more above the bull's neck fell with a fluttering of dead leaves. The shot might have been a signal: every animal on the mountainside stampeded up the valley. Out into full view galloped the big bull, sandwiched in between a couple of cows. Up the stony bed of the Palliser crashed the bull moose that I had seen earlier in the afternoon; he passed directly below me. Everything snorted and ran and I sat in my tree top, regarding my handiwork, amazed. I never saw so many elk in one place—and what brought them together like that I cannot think, unless it was the early snows.

I walked back to camp thinking of what I had seen. I found Marigold warm and comfortable in the last rays of the evening sun, luxuriously reclining on our two eiderdowns spread against the saddle pile. She was absorbed in Harcourt-Smith's *Cardinal of Spain*.

We left that pleasant camp very late the next morning. We passed Tipperary Creek with its memories of the naiad and the bears and, soon after that, the trail ran out on to the wide gravel bars of the Palliser. Actually we rode down the riverbed, following the finest gravel and the softest sand for the sake of the horses' feet.

It was about here that the wild animals began to act queerly. There was plenty of game in sight—numerous elk on the Royal Group side, a couple of very big bull moose on the other bank, and one black bear high up on that side of the river. The sight of our little cavalcade moving down that grey waste of river stones, fording the many channels of the shrunken Palliser, seemed to excite these beasts, and the whole variegated zoo drew level with us and accompanied us down the river. A madness seemed to have got into them: as the afternoon wore on the elk struck up their bugling, screaming noise. They would stop and fight and then come at the run along the semi-open slopes below the precipices of the Royal Group, catching up with us and coming always lower and closer to the shingle bars. The moose were worse. They would run past us close to the opposite bank and then, in turn, would stick their great Roman-nosed heads and massive,

The view west into British Columbia

palmated horns through some screen of willow or small spruce, and stare—just stare silently with a thick-skulled, imbecile curiosity. Or was it menace?

This sort of thing was entirely new to me. As for the horses, they were completely on edge: flick your chaps with your quirt and all five would shy as if the devil had popped up in front of them—horns, tail and brimstone all complete. I decided to put an end to it. There was a bull elk there with a beautifully symmetrical head of horns; I would get him and see what happened. I told Marigold and we got off our horses.

Spang! went the Mauser with a metallic ring off the shingle—and down went the elk, only to rise again. Spang! a second time—and that was the end of him. Seated on the shingle, I turned to Marigold who was holding the horses. She and they were still as statues and regarding me intently. "They're standing well," I said. "I thought they'd jump when I fired."

"They did," she replied. "About six feet each shot, pulling me with them."

The noise of the shooting settled the problem of our escort: moose, elk and our one bear were putting the miles behind them as fast as they could. And Joffre Creek lay only a few hundred yards ahead. Quickly we moved down there, to the flat below the creek mouth. Off flew the packs, three horses were belled and turned loose, and then we set up the tent and the stove. "There," I said, "that's all the heavy work done. You get a fire going and make tea and get things into their places and I'll take Rex and Mollie and get the elk horns and the best of the meat. I won't be too long." And I rode off up the flats, straight into the eye of the sun, towards the deep shadow of the Royal Group where the elk was lying.

As I worked I looked once or twice towards camp: I could see no smoke going up, nor any sign of life around the tent, but, except to think that Marigold must have made a very clear fire, I paid no more attention. Before the sunlight had lifted off the lower slopes of Waka Nambé I was riding back down the bars with a set of beautiful horns and a heavy load of meat. I was extremely happy and pleased with myself—so much so that I was singing, which is with me, happily for those present, a rare thing.

To my surprise I found camp pretty much as I had left it. No fire had been lit in the stove and hardly anything had been done. Bozo and Turk were grazing nearby. They were still a bit jittery and they showed it, every now and then, by raising their heads with a sudden clash of bells and then staring like graven images down the river. This staring business was evidently catching: Marigold had got it too. She was standing by the tent staring as if fascinated at Bluebird who had left the other horses and was standing motionless, about five hundred yards away, herself staring like an idiot straight at the mountain wall just below the Joffre Creek canyon.

Marigold came to life as I was unloading Mollie. She turned towards me with a wild look on her face. "Take me out of this place," she said. "Now. At once."

"Good heavens, what's wrong with the place? You know perfectly well, we can't travel at night on trails like these. Here's camp half made and we'll soon have supper and it's a very nice place, anyway. I had a wonderful time when I was here alone, three years ago, and—"

"I don't care *what* sort of a time you had here three years ago—I *hate* this great empty valley with its black shadows and all those frightful faces peering at us out of the bush—and now that horse has gone mad, too, like everything else around here. Did *you* ever see a horse walk straight out of camp like that—*away* from home, not *towards* home— and stand like a statue staring into a canyon? What is there in there that she's seeing? And you vanishing from sight like that—"

"Oh, come—have a heart! I was in plain view of camp all the time."

"You were not. You rode straight into the sun and disappeared into the shadow of that mountain. I couldn't see a sign of you against that dazzle, not even if I shaded my eyes. And all those insane things probably still watching us—and that mad horse. Get me out of here … "

The needle had obviously got into a groove and there was only one remedy for that—supper. I carried the grub-box into the tent, found some candles and lit them, put a fire in the stove.

Late that evening I made my usual round of the horses. The moon was rising. Already it was touching the mountain tops but the valley still lay in the shadow of Waka Nambé and his fellows of the Divide. For me it was a friendly place; there was nothing dreadful here. That weird performance of the animals, though—there *had* been something uncanny about that. And I tried to imagine how Marigold had felt, but I know I failed for I saw things differently.

If—I thought—this valley had been in the mountains of Europe, it would have seen so much: ambushes and raids, the journeyings of princes and of merchant caravans, the passage of armies. These things would have been a part of the history of our own people and we should have known of them. And so, upon this camp, with its horse bells and its crackling stove and the candlelight that glowed so warmly through the tent walls, the past would have come crowding in and we would have felt, all around us, the quiet pressure of the vanished centuries … But here nothing had ever happened. Or, at least, if it had, it belonged to another race and we knew nothing of it; so for us there could be no ghostly wayfarers marching silently along the valley trail, whispering

together out there in the darkness, watching the two alien travellers
who had invaded their mountain solitudes.

Only a lot of mad animals lived here, and even they had gone ...

"Aren't you in bed *yet*?"

"Yes, I am now—all tucked up, warm and snug. Come back in."

☆ ☆ ☆ ☆

Evening, two days later, found us riding north up the wide valley of the
Kootenay. Since leaving the Palliser that morning we had travelled all
day through a magnificent open forest of pine and western larch. There
was no undergrowth and the trail wound between the tall straight
trunks of the splendid trees; the horses padded softly along on the deep
carpet of the needles. Even on this dull day the green and gold of the
lovely forest was a thing that we would always remember.

But the grass was poor and sparse and there was no water; the flats
were wide and dry; all day we never saw the Kootenay and there were
no creeks or springs. The map showed one creek that was useless to
us, and then Yearling Creek. So we put our money on that for a night
camp—and now dusk was falling and the creek should be somewhere
near, and if we ever got out of this bit of deadfall into which I had
led the outfit we would come to it. I hewed the last tree through and
we rode out on to the main trail again. It dipped down into a stony
hollow and I saw ahead the flash and sparkle of water. The horses
drank and we looked around from our saddles. There wasn't a spear
of horse feed—just the stony ground and the water and unlimited dry
wood for a fire.

"Let's ride on for ten minutes," we said. "Then, if we find nothing
for the horses, we'll have to come back here and camp. At least there's
wood and water."

We did that, and we came out of the pines into a clearing that
seemed to be man-made. But the grass was eaten down to the ground
and we rode on ... We both saw the light through the trees but nobody
said anything, each one being convinced that it was an hallucination.
Then the light shone clearly and steadily and we knew that at last we
had fallen in with men.

An hour later the horses were in a corral, contentedly munching away at hay, the outfit was under cover, and Marigold and I, in the light and the warmth of the cabin, were sat down to a table that looked to us like the promised land. It was the old Richter place that we had dropped on to—the only house in all that stretch of the Kootenay below McLeod Meadows and inside the Rockies. It was now a hunting lodge of the Elkhorn Ranch, and their two men there, Ernie Bryan, the cook, and Dix Anderson, one of the guides, were plying us with questions about the mountain trails and, at the same time, urging us to further onslaughts on the food. We hardly needed any urging, and we did our best to oblige in both directions—a difficult feat, since these two occupations rather tend to cancel each other out.

They gave one end of the cabin to us that night, and in the warm darkness, before we fell asleep, I heard Marigold's voice from somewhere near: "From an open, stony camp by that barren creek to this!" she said drowsily. "Never in all my life ... " The voice trailed off into silence and the sentence was never completed, but I knew exactly what she had meant to say.

Early in the morning we departed from that friendly place. We forded Cross River and then the wide, swift-flowing Kootenay. Our mountain trails were behind us now: with Turk and Bozo "acting up" and requiring leading in any difficult or dangerous place, we felt unable to tackle the steep Luxor Pass to Spillimachene. Instead we would follow the abandoned, grass-grown Settlers' Road up the Kootenay and then cross the last range by the Sinclair Pass road. That would bring us down Sinclair Creek into the great valley that bounds the Rockies on the west, and so to Spillimachene. It was not what we had planned but, with two doubtful horses, it would have to do.

The Sinclair Pass road was deserted—the summer motorist had long since fled. All went well, and about four o'clock Marigold, leaving me to mind the horses, walked into the hotel at Radium Hot Springs and ordered afternoon tea for two. A trim maid took one look at Marigold's sunburnt face, leather chaps and riding boots and fled to do her bidding in record time. A noble tea was produced and, in due course, Marigold took over the horses and I went in to clean up the fragments and drain the teapot.

A thought occurred to me as I sat there by the fire—and I went and put in a telephone call to a friend in Calgary. The operator got it through just as I finished tea.

"Hullo, Frances!"

"Raymond! Where are you? Radium? Good heavens! Do you know, we held a sort of a wake for you and Marigold yesterday evening at this house. Mr. Pocaterra came and he told us what sort of a country you'd gone into. He said you should never have started so late in the season, and we got more and more gloomy and Harry said how sad it was and what fun it had been knowing you ... "

Pocaterra was quite right, of course—but otherwise, how very satisfactory. Marigold must hear this ... And I went and took over the horses from her so that she and Frances could get together and quack.

Time went by, and I thought of their voices travelling to and fro across the Rockies—down the Columbia River, up the Kicking Horse and down the Bow—backwards and forwards all that way. Magic that's what it was—straight magic.

Good heavens, were they *never* going to stop?

Surprisingly, they did.

We rode on down the steep hill into the narrow gorge of Sinclair Creek. The rock walls closed in. They overlapped and shut out the sky.

But ahead of us the warm glow of the sunset streamed into the western gateway of this arching canyon. In the shadow of the rocks we rode on towards it, leaving behind the Buffalo Head and the mountains that had been home to us—wondering if it had been wise to leave Alberta for this strange new province where they met you on the frontier with a grizzly and with a bunch of moose and elk that ran around like mad things and stared insanely at you from the cover of the trees.

ENDNOTES

[1] Paul Kruger, president in 1883 of the South African Republic.

[2] A director is an instrument that resembles a surveyor's transit.

[3] *Zimmer* means "room." We partially adopted the German words.

[4] E. Viollet-Le-Duc, *Annals of a Fortress: Twenty-two Centuries of Siege Warfare* (London: Sampson Low, Marston, Low, and Searle, 1875).

[5] Rudyard Kipling, *Life's Handicap: Being Stories of Mine Own People* (London: Macmillan, 1891).

[6] Frederick Russell Burnham, *Scouting on Two Continents* (London: Willliam Heinemann, 1926).

[7] 320 acres — that is, 160 acres homestead and 160 acres soldier grant.

[8] A democrat is a light, uncovered wagon with two or more seats.

[9] His Cree nickname.

[10] R. M. Patterson, *The Dangerous River* (New York: William Sloane Associates, 1954; London: Allen & Unwin, 1955).

[11] Bryan Williams, *Game Trails in British Columbia: Big Game and Other Sport in the Wilds of British Columbia* (New York: Charles Scribner's Sons, 1925), p. 92 et seq.

[12] With protection, they have greatly increased in numbers since then.

GLOSSARY

Chinook: warm southwest wind from the mountains

Elk: the wapiti (*Cervus canadensis*); no relation of the moose, which in Europe would be called elk

E P: the brand of the Prince of Wales ranch

Fool hen: Franklin's Grouse (*Canachites franklini*), a bird with an overconfiding nature

Kini-kinik: bear-berry, a low creeping plant

Northwesters: the men of the North West Company, the Hudson's Bay Company's great rivals prior to the union of the two companies in 1821

Pekisko: headquarters of the old Bar U Ranch on Pekisko Creek

Shooting star: *Dodecatheon meadia*, a perennial flower

"Sheep" and **"goat"** refer in this book to the Bighorn sheep and the wild goats of the Rockies; only in one place in the text do they refer to the domesticated breeds.

Stoney Indian words

changó: trail
nyahé: mountain
o: yes
óki: two
teáno: far
umpábin: stone or rocks
waptán: creek
Yetzkábi: the Stoneys' name for their tribe

Index

The Author

Raymond Murray Patterson began life in England in 1898. He attended Oxford and fought in the First World War, but in 1924 he left a predictable life behind for the unknown in the Canadian West. First he homesteaded in the Peace River country of northern Alberta. Then the lure of the fabled Nahanni gold led him on a quest into the Northwest Territories in the late 1920s.

Although he found no gold, Patterson found a way of life that suited him: pursuing adventure. After marrying Marigold Portman in 1929, he raised cattle on a dude ranch called the Buffalo Head, in the foothills of the Canadian Rockies. From this base, he spent the next 16 years exploring the high country of the Continental Divide with George Pocaterra and Adolf Baumgart.

In the late 1940s the Patterson family moved to Vancouver Island, where, over the next two decades, RMP published five books as well as numerous articles in *Blackwood's Magazine* and *The Beaver*. His vivid portrayal of the Canadian wilderness has never been surpassed.

Patterson is best known for his international best-seller *The Dangerous River*, about his adventures on the South Nahanni River. His other classics include *Far Pastures*, a collection of stories about homesteading in northern Alberta and his river escapades; *Trail to the Interior*, about the Stikine region; and *Finlay's River*, about the Peace River and its tributaries.